Shakespeare on the Global Stage

RELATED TITLES

A Year of Shakespeare: Re-living the World Shakespeare Festival
Edited by Paul Edmondson, Paul Prescott and Erin Sullivan

Emotional Excess on the Shakespearean Stage
Bridget Escolme

Shakespeare's Theatres and the Effects of Performance
Edited by Farah Karim-Cooper and Tiffany Stern

Acting Companies and their Plays in Shakespeare's London
Siobhan Keenan

Shakespeare on the Global Stage

Performance and Festivity in the Olympic Year

Edited by Paul Prescott and Erin Sullivan

Bloomsbury Arden Shakespeare
An imprint of Bloomsbury Publishing Plc

B L O O M S B U R Y
LONDON • NEW DELHI • NEW YORK • SYDNEY

Bloomsbury Arden Shakespeare

An imprint of Bloomsbury Publishing Plc

50 Bedford Square
London
WC1B 3DP
UK

1385 Broadway
New York
NY 10018
USA

www.bloomsbury.com

BLOOMSBURY, ARDEN SHAKESPEARE and the Diana logo are trademarks of Bloomsbury Publishing Plc

Editorial matter and selection © 2015 Erin Sullivan and Paul Prescott

All other matter © Bloomsbury Publishing Plc

The Editors and contributors have asserted their right under the Copyright, Designs and Patents Act, 1988, to be identified as Authors of this work.

All rights reserved. No part of this publication may be reproduced or transmitted in any form or by any means, electronic or mechanical, including photocopying, recording, or any information storage or retrieval system, without prior permission in writing from the publishers.

No responsibility for loss caused to any individual or organization acting on or refraining from action as a result of the material in this publication can be accepted by Bloomsbury or the author.

British Library Cataloguing-in-Publication Data
A catalogue record for this book is available from the British Library.

ISBN: HB: 978-1-4725-2033-3
PB: 978-1-4725-2032-6
ePDF: 978-1-4725-2035-7
ePub: 978-1-4725-2034-0

Library of Congress Cataloging-in-Publication Data
A catalog record for this book is available from the Library of Congress

Typeset by Fakenham Prepress Solutions, Fakenham, Norfolk NR21 8NN
Printed and bound in India

CONTENTS

List of Figures vii
List of Contributors ix
Preface xiv

1   Shakespeare and the Dream of Olympism 1
    Paul Prescott

2   Two Poems from the Olympic Year 39
    Kapka Kassabova

3   Performing Shakespeare in the Olympic Year:
    Interviews with Three Practitioners 43
    Frank Cottrell Boyce, Tom Bird and Tracy Irish

4   States of the Nations: *Henry VI*, the London
    Olympics and the Spectacular City 79
    Stuart Hampton-Reeves

5   Shakespeare in the North: Regionalism, Culture
    and Power 101
    Adam Hansen and Monika Smialkowska

6 Shakespeare, Spectatorship and the 'Olympic Spirit' 133
Stephen Purcell

7 Expert Spectatorship and Intra-Audience Relationships at Globe to Globe 2012 163
Rose Elfman

8 'Mind the gap': Globalism, Postcolonialism and Making up Africa in the Cultural Olympiad 191
Colette Gordon

9 A Tale of Two Londons: Locating Shakespeare and Dickens in 2012 227
Peter Kirwan and Charlotte Mathieson

10 1948/2012: Building Nations 253
Tony Howard

11 Olympic Shakespeare and the Idea of Legacy: Culture, Capital and the Global Future 283
Erin Sullivan

Afterword 323
Kathleen McLuskie

Index 339

LIST OF FIGURES

FIGURE 1 Globe Theatre coin in the Royal Mint's 'Celebration of Britain Silver Proof Collection', 2009. Reproduced courtesy of the Royal Mint. 17

FIGURE 2 'Tolerance' coin in the Royal Mint's 'Celebration of Britain Silver Proof Collection', 2010. Reproduced courtesy of the Royal Mint. 18

FIGURE 3 The Olympic Torch passes Shakespeare's Birthplace on Henley Street, Stratford-upon-Avon, July 2012. Reproduced courtesy of The Shakespeare Birthplace Trust. 40

FIGURE 4 *An Iron Forge* (1772) by Joseph Wright of Derby. Reproduced courtesy of Tate Images. 45

FIGURE 5 *All's Well That Ends Well* performed in Gujarati by Arpana theatre company (based in Mumbai) for the Globe to Globe Festival, 23–4 May 2012. Photograph by Ellie Kurttz and reproduced courtesy of Shakespeare's Globe. 56

FIGURE 6 *Cymbeline* performed in Juba Arabic by the South Sudan Theatre Company for the Globe to Globe Festival, 2–3 May 2012. Photograph by Ellie Kurttz and reproduced courtesy of Shakespeare's Globe. 62

FIGURE 7 Filming *I, Cinna*. Photograph by Rebecca Carter and reproduced courtesy of the RSC. 71

FIGURE 8 The International Youth Ensemble in rehearsal. Photograph by Lucy Hearn and reproduced courtesy of the RSC. 74

FIGURE 9 Publicity image for *West Side Story* at The Sage Gateshead. Designed by Andy Lovatt and reproduced courtesy of The Sage Gateshead. 117

FIGURE 10 Correlations between spectators' language fluency and their modes of understanding a production. Table by Rose Elfman. 170

FIGURE 11 Fluent vs non-fluent spectators' ability to follow the plot of a performance. Table by Rose Elfman. 175

FIGURE 12 A building-sized display of the Royal Family at the Queen's Silver Jubilee in 1977 along the River Thames during the 2012 Diamond Jubilee. Photograph by Charlotte Mathieson. 230

FIGURE 13 'Dickens Festival Pageant' poster from the Festival of Britain (1951). Reproduced with the permission of the National Archives, London, ref. WORK 25/243. 233

FIGURE 14 The London 2012 Olympic, Paralympic and Festival logos. Reproduced courtesy of the International Olympic Committee, the International Paralympic Committee and the Arts Council England. 294

FIGURE 15 Harry Venning's cover image for *The Stage*'s special issue on the London 2012 Festival, published 7 June 2012. Reproduced with the permission of Harry Venning. 296

FIGURE 16 'Nigel Farage's Caliban Moment' by Steve Bell, published in the *Guardian* on 30 January 2013. Reproduced with the permission of Steve Bell and Belltoons. 309

FIGURE 17 The UK Home Office's 'Go Home' van driving through the streets of London. Photograph by Alain Tolhurst and reproduced with his permission. 311

LIST OF CONTRIBUTORS

Tom Bird is an Executive Producer at Shakespeare's Globe and was Director of its Globe to Globe Festival in 2012. Previous employment includes work for the physical theatre festival Aurora Nova in Edinburgh and for a number of music groups, most notably the Northern Sinfonia. His roots are in the north-east, and as a playwright he is a regular contributor to Live Theatre's *Short Cuts* events in Newcastle. His short play *Kaz and the Coots* was recorded for the BBC Radio 3 Free Thinking Festival in 2009.

Frank Cottrell Boyce is a British screenwriter and novelist. His film credits include *Welcome to Sarajevo* (1997), *Hilary and Jackie* (1998), *24 Hour Party People* (2002), *Revenger's Tragedy* (2002) and *The Railway Man* (2013), and he is a frequent collaborator with Michael Winterbottom and Danny Boyle. He was the writer of the London 2012 Olympics Opening Ceremony.

Rose Elfman earned a PhD in Theatre Studies from the University of California, Santa Barbara with her dissertation titled 'Global Shakespeare at the Globe: Challenging the Tourist-Spectator' (2013). In addition to her ongoing investigations into the processes and politics of theatre spectatorship, she works as the managing editor for the *Journal of Haitian Studies* and *Kalfou: A Journal of Comparative and Relational Ethnic Studies*.

Colette Gordon is Lecturer at the University of Witwatersrand. Her research interests include early modern economics, economic criticism, performance studies and contemporary theatre practice. Her work has appeared in journals such as *Cahiers Élisabéthains*, *African Theatre*, *Shakespeare in Southern Africa*, *Borrowers and Lenders* and *Shakespeare*.

Stuart Hampton-Reeves is Professor of Research-informed Teaching and Head of Graduate Research at the University of Central Lancashire. He is also Head of the British Shakespeare Association and author of a number of books and articles on Shakespeare in performance. He is also one of the General Editors of the Palgrave book series *Shakespeare in Practice*.

Adam Hansen is Senior Lecturer in English at Northumbria University. He has published widely on early modern culture, in its own time and in ours, including, most recently, *Shakespeare and Popular Music* (Continuum, 2010), 'Shakespeare v The BNP', in *Literary Politics: The Politics of Literature and the Literature of Politics* (Palgrave, 2013), and 'Cities in Late Shakespeare', in *Late Shakespeare: Texts and Contexts* (Cambridge, 2012).

Tony Howard is Professor of English at Warwick University. Publications include *Women as Hamlet: Performance and Interpretation in Theatre, Film and Fiction* (Cambridge, 2007) and many translations of Polish drama and poetry with Barbara Bogoczek. He has worked with Shakespeare's Globe, the Royal Court Theatre, Theatre Royal Stratford East, the Young Vic, Riverside Studios, and groups in Britain, the USA and Poland.

Tracy Irish has worked with the education department of the Royal Shakespeare Company since 2007 as a project manager, researcher and practitioner, and as Education Programme Developer for the World Shakespeare Festival. She is currently working on a PhD on the value of Shakespeare in education at the University of Warwick, where she is also the Warwick Business School Shakespeare Scholar. She was a teacher of English and drama for 16 years in the UK and abroad and is the author of a series of books called *The Shorter Shakespeare* (Carel Press).

Kapka Kassabova is an award-winning poet and the author of *Reconnaissance* (1999), *Geography for the Lost* (2007), *Street Without a Name* (2008), *Villa Pacifica* (2010) and *Twelve Minutes of Love* (2011). Her writing has appeared in the *Guardian*, *The Times Literary Supplement*, *Vogue* and *Granta*, and in 2012 she was the Shakespeare Birthplace Trust's first Writer in Residence. Born and raised in Bulgaria, Kassabova lived with her family in New Zealand for many years before emigrating to Scotland.

Peter Kirwan is Assistant Professor of Shakespeare and Early Modern Drama at the University of Nottingham. He is Associate Editor of *William Shakespeare and Others: Collaborative Plays* (Palgrave, 2013) and co-editor of *Shakespeare and the Digital World* (Cambridge, 2014), and has written extensively on early modern dramatic authorship, book history and contemporary Shakespearean performance. He has covered the World Shakespeare Festival in contributions to *Shakespeare Beyond English* (Cambridge, 2013) and *A Year of Shakespeare* (Arden, 2013) as well as on his review blog, *The Bardathon* (http://blogs.nottingham.ac.uk/bardathon).

Charlotte Mathieson is a Research Fellow at the University of Warwick's Institute of Advanced Study. She researches Victorian literature, with an interest in the intersections of gender, space and mobility in novels by authors including Charles Dickens, Charlotte Brontë, George Eliot and Elizabeth Gaskell. Her publications include *Gender and Space in Rural Britain, 1840–1920* (ed. with Gemma Goodman; Pickering and Chatto, 2014).

Kathleen McLuskie is the author of *Renaissance Dramatists* (Harvester, 1989), *Dekker and Heywood: Professional Dramatists* (Macmillan, 1993), *Macbeth* (Northcote, 2009) and *Cultural Value in Twenty-first-century England: The Case of Shakespeare* (Manchester, 2014). She is Professor Emeritus at the Shakespeare Institute, where she served as Director until 2011. She is currently making a garden in the Cotswolds and writing now and then about cultural value and time.

Paul Prescott is Reader in English at the University of Warwick. He is the author of *Reviewing Shakespeare: Journalism and Performance from the Eighteenth Century to the Present* (Cambridge, 2013), a critical biography of Sam Wanamaker for the *Great Shakespeareans* series (Bloomsbury, 2013), and, as co-editor and contributor, *A Year of Shakespeare: Re-living the World Shakespeare Festival* (Arden, 2013). He is currently working on a book on Shakespeare festivals, and is General Editor of www.ReviewingShakespeare.com and www.ShakespeareontheRoad.com

Stephen Purcell is Assistant Professor of English at the University of Warwick. His research focuses on Shakespeare in contemporary performance and popular culture. His publications include *Popular Shakespeare* (Palgrave, 2009) and *Shakespeare and Audience in Practice* (Palgrave, 2013). His writing on the World Shakespeare Festival also appears in *A Year of Shakespeare* (Arden, 2013), *Shakespeare Beyond English* (Cambridge, 2013) and *Shakespeare Survey 66* (2013). He directs for the theatre company The Pantaloons.

Monika Smialkowska is Senior Lecturer in English at Northumbria University. Her research interests fall into two categories: the early modern genre of court masque, and post-renaissance adaptations and appropriations of early modern authors and genres. She has published articles in journals such as *Shakespeare*, *Critical Survey* and *English Literary Renaissance*. Currently, she is working towards a monograph exploring the ways in which the three-hundredth anniversary of Shakespeare's death in 1916 was celebrated across the world.

Erin Sullivan is Lecturer and Fellow at the Shakespeare Institute, University of Birmingham. She led the Arts & Humanities Research Council-funded 'Shakespeare's Global Communities' project, which resulted in the online archive www.yearofshakespeare.com and its companion book, *A Year of Shakespeare: Re-living the World Shakespeare Festival* (Arden, 2013). She also works on the history of psychology and emotion in early modern England and is the co-editor of *The Renaissance of Emotion: Understanding Affect in Shakespeare and His Contemporaries* (Manchester, 2015).

PREFACE

In the autumn of 2011, the Royal Shakespeare Company announced its plans for 'the greatest celebration of Shakespeare the world has ever seen'. The RSC's World Shakespeare Festival (as it came to be known) would form a major part of the London 2012 Cultural Olympiad, and would feature such highlights as the Globe to Globe Festival at Shakespeare's Globe. Together these projects would bring dozens of Shakespearean productions from overseas to British stages, as well as inspire a range of new interpretations by UK companies. Anticipating what was an unprecedented and possibly unrepeatable moment, a group of UK-based scholars created an informal collective with the expressed aim of documenting and debating the performances of Shakespeare in the Olympic year. Reviewers were dispatched to the nearly seventy productions, and their responses were promptly posted on the project's website, www.yearofshakespeare.com. A few months later, these pieces would be published together as *A Year of Shakespeare: Re-living the World Shakespeare Festival* (Arden, 2013).

If that book reflected the 'documentation' of the Festival, offering short, eye-witness accounts of what it was like to be caught up in the celebrations in 'real time', this book makes space for the longer view, inviting authors from the UK but also abroad to pursue the range of complex issues raised by the collocation of the Olympics and what we call 'Shakespeare'. One of the paradoxes of mega-events like the Olympics is that while the event is intensively concentrated in the host city and nation, it is nevertheless designed for the enjoyment and consumption of a truly global audience. In calling this book *Shakespeare on the Global Stage*, we try to capture the sheer reach of the internationally visible outcomes of the 2012 Olympics, but this book is also profoundly interested in the build-up and backstage histories that lie behind that final spectacle. Paul Prescott begins by exploring the overlaps between the philosophy of Olympism and the various forms of dream work performed by Shakespeare in 2012. The juxtaposition of two previously unpublished poems by Kapka Kassabova – a writer in residence in Stratford-on-Avon in the Olympic year – invites the reader to consider the relationship between a captured moment of parochial festivity and the weight and responsibilities of global citizenship. Interviews with Frank Cottrell Boyce, Tom Bird and Tracy Irish offer reflective and personal accounts about the process of scripting, producing and teaching Shakespeare for and on the global stage.

The next two chapters consider the politics of culture from the perspective of nation and region, analysing the relations between space, identity and representation. Stuart Hampton-Reeves focuses on the interrogation of nationhood offered by three Globe to Globe productions; he uses this so-called Balkan trilogy to reflect on boundaries and faultlines within London in the lead-up to the Olympics. Adam Hansen and Monika Smialkowska question the boundaries between local, national and global, and tease out the ways in which the north-east of England was and was not represented in the 2012 festivities.

The Globe to Globe Festival shifted our understanding of the nature of cross-cultural exchange between performer and audience. Stephen Purcell's and Rose Elfman's chapters draw on both quantitative and subjective accounts of spectatorship to explore the ways in which audiences collaborated in the creation of meaning and value throughout the Olympiad. The networks of global production behind the World Shakespeare Festival are interrogated by Colette Gordon in her analysis of the sometimes problematic ways in which one continent – Africa – signified and was represented across Olympiad programming.

The following two chapters offer telling comparisons, one synchronic, the other diachronic. Peter Kirwan and Charlotte Mathieson's chapter analyses the ways in which London (and other spaces, real and virtual) celebrated and remembered two canonical writers, Shakespeare and Dickens (2012 was the two-hundredth anniversary of the novelist's birth). Tony Howard finds echoes in 2012 of the last London Olympics of 1948, in which international cultural exchange benefited the British understanding of Shakespeare in another age of austerity. The promise of far-reaching legacy underwrites every Olympics, and Erin Sullivan's concluding chapter considers how investment in Shakespeare in 2012 connected with an optimistic, if unrealized, vision of Britain's global future. Finally, in her afterword Kathleen McLuskie weighs the virtues of that optimism against the almost intractable complexity of capital and culture, reflecting on the irreconcilable pressures and pleasures that Shakespeare celebration in the Olympic year exerted on the individual.

Finally, we should like to acknowledge and celebrate the contribution of a number of individuals and institutions to this volume. First thanks to the writers, practitioners and students who participated in the *Year of Shakespeare* project and especially to our co-editor, Paul Edmondson. Thanks, too, to the AHRC who made that project possible. We are very grateful to Tom Bird, Frank Cottrell Boyce and Tracy Irish for so generously agreeing to be interviewed; we are also indebted to the Shakespeare Institute Library and its staff for transcribing those interviews. For permission to include images, we offer grateful thanks to the following institutions and individuals: Arts Council England, the International Olympic Committee, the International Paralympic Committee, the National Archives, the Royal Shakespeare Company, the Royal Mint, The Sage Gateshead, the Shakespeare Birthplace Trust, Shakespeare's Globe, Tate Images; Steve Bell, Alain Tolhurst, Harry Venning.

Many friends and colleagues have lent their expertise to parts of the manuscript; thanks in particular to Will Sharpe,

Peter J. Smith, Penelope Woods and our anonymous readers at Bloomsbury, as well as all of our colleagues at the Shakespeare Institute, University of Birmingham, and in the Department of English and Comparative Literary Studies, University of Warwick. Profound thanks to our editors at Bloomsbury and Fakenham Prepress – Margaret Bartley, Emily Hockley, Kim Storry and Robert Bullard – who have offered unstinting support throughout the happy process of collaboration.

Paul Prescott and
Erin Sullivan

1

Shakespeare and the Dream of Olympism

Paul Prescott

Manly sports are good for everyone and under all circumstances. Sports will not make angels of brutes, but there is a great possibility that they will temper that brutality, giving the individual a bit of self-control. That, at least, is something!

PIERRE DE COUBERTIN, ('SPORT IS A PEACEMAKER', 1935)[1]

The scam of scams was always the Olympics: Berlin in 1936 to Beijing in 2008. Engines of regeneration. Orgies of lachrymose nationalism. War by other means.

IAIN SINCLAIR ('THE OLYMPICS SCAM', 2008)[2]

CALIBAN: You, my fellow dreamers in the dark. Lo, now our world is wracked, night rolleth towards us, yet we will drive the night back with our dreams...

PERCY MACKAYE (*CALIBAN BY THE YELLOW SANDS*, 1916)[3]

Where's Willy?

Picture this urban scene from the early twenty-first century: a darkened room in London; politicians, bureaucrats, creatives; coffee, iPads, glowing plasma screens. The occasion: a digital storyboard ('animatic') preview of the 2012 Olympic Opening Ceremony some weeks before the real thing plays out in front of a global audience. The Ceremony would define the London Olympics and this was the first time its contents had been shared in any detail with Jeremy Hunt, Secretary of State for the Department of Media, Sports and Culture and therefore the minister with oversight for the Cultural Olympiad. The animatic offers a succession of images: village green cricket, the Industrial Revolution, balletic National Health Service (NHS) nurses, descending Mary Poppins, marching Sergeant Peppers. It comes to an end. A nonplussed Secretary of State pauses. Then (as we learn from the interview with Frank Cottrell Boyce in this volume) Jeremy Hunt asks the simple question: 'Um, where's Shakespeare?'. The spectacle's chief architect and string-pulling Prospero, Danny Boyle, responds: 'the whole thing is based on *The Tempest*'.

In Jeremy Hunt's defence, it can be hard to decipher what is happening in an animatic. But perhaps Hunt had missed seeing or hearing Shakespeare because the playwright's presence in the Opening Ceremony was almost entirely disguised. If you did not recognize Caliban's words – spoken by Kenneth Branagh dressed as Isambard Kingdom Brunel – about the isle being full of noises as deriving from *The Tempest*, there was little or nothing in the Opening Ceremony that obviously said 'Shakespeare' to an unsuspecting multinational audience (or even to a Culture Secretary). No 'To be or not to be', no 'sceptred isle', no skull, no quills, no ruffs. This was a preview of a dream sequence destined for the global stage, and the meanings of that dream were not at all manifest or obvious. I will return to that Opening Ceremony and its Shakespearean echoes and allusions later in this chapter. First, to revisit and expand the scope of Hunt's question: where *was* Shakespeare in 2012?

Shakespeare was – to an unprecedented extent – everywhere in 2012. Of the Cultural Olympiad's seven major strands, only one featured a proper noun: The World Shakespeare Festival (WSF).[4] The WSF was produced by the Royal Shakespeare Company (RSC) and consisted of almost 70 stage productions, over half of them featuring in the six-week Globe to Globe season at Shakespeare's Globe, but with others scattered across the UK, most densely in Stratford-upon-Avon. The WSF was notable for the number and range of performances in languages other than English from companies that had often travelled as many thousands of miles to perform as had the athletes who attempted to go 'swifter, higher, stronger' in the Games themselves. Many of these productions were filmed and made freely available to online audiences via an Arts Council digital platform, www.TheSpace.org. Also online, the RSC's MyShakespeare project invited 'people from around the world to share their thoughts and experiences of Shakespeare and his work and ask[ed] the question "How do we interpret Shakespeare today?"'[5] The RSC claims that the WSF as a whole 'reached more than 1.8 million people'.[6]

The BBC joined the party with gusto: its 'Shakespeare Unlocked' season presented Shakespeare as an international figure (*Shakespeare in Italy*, *Shakespeare from Kabul*), as an odd hybrid of the familiar and the exotic (*Felicity Kendal's Indian Shakespeare*), and as one whose secrets could only really be unlocked by acts of homeland historical contextualization (*Simon Schama's Shakespeare*, *The King and The Playwright: A Jacobean History* and even a bespoke episode of *Antiques Roadshow*). Most prominently perhaps, the BBC commissioned Sam Mendes to produce film versions of the second tetralogy. 2012 also witnessed a rich array of educational projects: *I, Cinna (The Poet)*, Tim Crouch's decentred adaptation of *Julius Caesar*, was beamed live into schools across the UK (see Irish and Purcell in this volume), and the 'Worlds Together' conference at Tate Modern gathered students and educators from across the planet. And – although it wasn't immediately clear to Jeremy Hunt – Shakespeare was threaded throughout the Olympic Opening Ceremony (estimated global TV audience: 900 million), as well as the Olympic Closing and Paralympic Opening Ceremonies. All three ceremonies freely and creatively drew on *The Tempest* in particular. Shakespeare, then, was a ubiquitous presence throughout the Cultural Olympiad and especially during the long summer of celebrations that surrounded the Games themselves. This book is dedicated to analysing, debating, celebrating and critiquing that unprecedented presence.

Olympic Shakespeare 1612–15

Now picture this rural scene from the early seventeenth century: grass, unenclosed fields, larks overhead, warmth of late spring on skin, and a congregation of men, women and children making merry at Robert Dover's Cotswold Olimpick games, the first sporting event to employ that exalted title since the demise of the ancient Olympian ceremonies 1,200 years before. The bucolic site – a hill overlooking Chipping Campden – is barely half a day's walk from Stratford-upon-Avon, probably a couple of hours on horseback, and there were plenty of inns on Campden's handsome high street in which the weary Olimpick sportsman or spectator could sleep off the revels. These Olimpicks were an annual event and Shakespeare was certainly alive and very likely resident in Stratford for each of its first four iterations in the Whitsuntides of 1612–15. Shakespeare's awareness of the local event might have been piqued by a wider renaissance revival of interest in the classical games. His plays twice feature the adjective 'Olympian', in *3 Henry VI* (at 2.3.53) and *Troilus and Cressida* (at 4.7.78).[7] The first usage, in *3 Henry VI*, is cited by the *Oxford English Dictionary* as the earliest in the English language, though the word can be found in a pedagogic treatise by Richard Mulcaster published in 1581, a decade before Shakespeare's play (the *OED* is not alone, as we shall see, in wanting to forge a deep bond between Shakespeare and the Games).[8]

Dover's Olimpicks have been interpreted as a local intervention in a national crisis, namely the growing schism between increasingly vocal Puritans and a relatively permissive populace and establishment whose more relaxed attitudes to recreation were expressed in King James's 'Declaration of Lawful Sports', commonly called *The Book of Sports* (1618). Martin Colley writes that Dover used the games to 'bring peace and harmony to a community in danger of being torn apart by conflicting ideologies'[9] – but sport is generally powerless to alter the course of history and half a century later the Midlands would nevertheless be riven by Civil War. Shortly before that rupture, in 1636, a number of poets contributed verses to a collection *Annalia Dubrensia* ('Annals of Dover') celebrating the Olimpicks in a rather ripe, self-consciously classicist vein: the games, according to William Durham, brought '*Arcadia* to our *Cotswold-hills*'. In an otherwise perfunctory effort, Ben Jonson praised Dover for advancing 'true Love, and neighbourhood' that did 'both Church, and Common-wealth the good', an early, on-message description of what would come to be known as the Olympic Spirit.[10] After the Interregnum, the Dover Games continued until 1852, annually evoking a version of 'Merrie England' even as that England – if it ever existed – was rendered more and more quaint and dream-like by the processes of colossal industrialization so spectacularly staged by Boyle et al. in the 2012 Opening Ceremony.

Where was Shakespeare? Was he also there in the 'Arcadia' of the Cotswold Olimpick Games? Some have wanted him to be. In the late eighteenth century, editors such as George Steevens cited the reference to greyhound racing 'on Cotswold' in *The Merry Wives of Windsor* (1.1.83) as evidence that Shakespeare attended the games or at least wished to refer to them (although the play predates Dover's arrival in Chipping Campden, it might conceivably refer to the previous, less organized incarnation of the Whitsun games). As Jean Williams writes, many since Steevens have succumbed to the belief 'that [Shakespeare] somehow *ought* to have contributed to or at least that he went along to watch, moreover to support, the Cotswold Games'.[11] A mid-twentieth-century editor of the *Annalia* rhapsodized: 'how Shakespeare must have delighted in those Games in the last few years of his life with their elegance and vigour, [and the] men and women of his own native countryside who assembled for their celebration'.[12] In accounts such as these, if Shakespeare is not an actual Olimpick spectator or participant, he is at the very least an Olympian manqué.

Muscles and minds: The festive spirit of cultural Olympism

What explains this desire for Shakespeare to have made the short trip to those Cotswold games in the twilight years of his life? First, the conjunction places the national poet in a reassuringly rural, pre-industrial landscape: old Will in deep England, the native returned to his soil. Second, Shakespeare's imagined presence at the early modern inception of the Olympic movement mutually reinforces the value of two major global forces: Shakespeare is infused with the spirit of Olympism, but Olympism also benefits from association with the capacious, life-enhancing and self-improving qualities of the 'world's playwright' (as the WSF publicity routinely called him). Two peerless brands – the world's greatest sporting event and the world's greatest writer – marry in an instant; both can be traced back to the same historical moment and to the symbolic heart of England. The torch first lit in Olympia reignited by the spark of Shakespeare's genius in a green and pleasantly undulating landscape.

International Olympic Committee (IOC) literature makes nothing of the Shakespeare-Cotswold Olimpicks (pseudo-)

connection, but is elsewhere at pains to invoke Shakespearean associations. In explaining the central Olympian concept of 'fair play', for example, one of its educational handouts claims that the phrase appears 'for the first time in Shakespeare's King John [sic]', where it is employed 'in a sense similar to that which we still use today: referring to the courteous rapport between opponents in confrontation: "Shall we, upon the footing of our land, / Send fair play orders and make compromise?"' (5.1.66–7).[13] While Shakespeare is not exactly credited with inventing the concept of 'fair play', he is somehow responsible for its originating articulation. The citation encourages the feeling of an easy congruence between Shakespeareanism and Olympism, but the educational pamphlet omits to mention that the speaker, the Bastard, is invoking 'fair play orders and [...] compromise [...] and base truce' merely to discredit them and argue instead for renewed, escalated warfare.

The formation of modern Olympism was the life's work of Baron Pierre de Coubertin (1863–1937), incurable Anglomaniac, and a publishing phenomenon whose collected works – as the Sochi 2014 Winter Olympics website reminded us – would run to almost one and a half times the length of that of 'classical author of British literature, William Shakespeare'.[14] Ian McDonald summarizes the spirit of modern Olympism thus:

[It] reflects a synthesis of de Coubertin's interpretation of classical Greek and English public school conceptions of sport: its basis is a belief in the progressive educational value of sport, generalised from the individual to the sphere of international politics. [...] Thus, Olympism places sport at the centre of a universal campaign for peace and international understanding, drawing on the mythology of the truce and the symbol of peace associated with the Games in Antiquity.[15]

According to the IOC, the purpose of the Olympic Movement is to: 'link sport with culture and education; promote the practice of sport and the joy found in effort; help to build a better world through sport practiced in a spirit of peace, excellence, friendship and respect'.[16]

In reinventing and modernizing the Olympics, de Coubertin was heavily inspired by key developments in mid-nineteenth-century British culture. Viewed from this perspective, the Victorianism of the first section (entitled 'Pandemonium') of the 2012 Opening Ceremony seems peculiarly apt. To one decade alone – the 1850s – can be traced a number of prototypes for the modern Olympic Games and indeed for Shakespeare's presence in the 2012 Cultural Olympiad. In 1850, the first athletic club was established at Exeter College, while across the country's public schools, educationalists such as Thomas Arnold stressed the connection between sport and enlightened self-discipline. (Arnold is fictionalized as the Doctor in Thomas Hughes's *Tom Brown's Schooldays* [1857], the work that would inspire de Coubertin to visit Rugby School.) It is no coincidence that the 1850s witnessed the demise of the folksy, nostalgic Dover games and the emergence of the more disciplined and genteel games at Much Wenlock in Shropshire. An Act of Parliament stopped the former in 1852 following local objections to the sustained rowdyism the games apparently engendered.[17] These included disruptions caused by 'navvies' working on the Chipping Campden Tunnel of Brunel's Great Western Railway. (We might contrast these anarchic real-life shin-kickers with the compliant, choreographed labourers who worked under Branagh/Brunel's paternalistic gaze in the 2012 Opening Ceremony.) Across the UK – but especially in the education of its ruling classes – certain sports were codified into the curriculum with the aim of producing generations of muscular Christians equipped mentally and physically with the wherewithal to administer their homeland and the farthest reaches of the British Empire.[18]

That Empire's confidence can be gauged by a major shift in the spectacular dimension of international capitalism. In 1851, the year before the Dover games' demise, London held its Great Exhibition of the Industry of all Nations. Prince

Albert's insistence that the Exhibition 'must embrace foreign productions' and the subsequent invitation to other nations to exhibit created the template for the World's Fairs of the later nineteenth and early twentieth centuries (three of which 'hosted' or coincided with the early modern Olympic Games in Paris, St Louis and London, and one of which – Chicago 1934–5 – introduced a teenage Sam Wanamaker to his first experience of an ersatz Globe in the 'Merrie England' section of the International Village).[19] The Prince's invitation stemmed from his confidence that British industry would bear favourable comparison with the 34 nations that ultimately agreed to exhibit. Four years later, the 1855 *Exposition Universelle* in Paris made fine arts central to the Exposition in an effort to prove French cultural pre-eminence to a global audience. With their urge toward total display and spirit of (ostensibly friendly) international competition, these mega-events of the 1850s created the template not only for the modern Olympic Games, but also for its artistic component, the Cultural Olympiad (as it has come to be known). It is not an enormous leap from Albert's insistence that the Great Exhibition must 'embrace foreign productions', via the World's Fair logic of concentrated display of exotic wares and bodies, to the structure if not the spirit of the 2012 Globe to Globe Festival.

For de Coubertin, the World's Fair model was instructive but debased in its focus on commerce and industry. Each Fair was, in Umberto Eco's words, a 'Missa Solemnis of capitalist culture', and de Coubertin yearned for more authentically spiritual grounds for international exchange.[20] The link between sport and culture/education was central to de Coubertin's sense of the missionary calling of the modern Olympics: 'Olympism did not reappear within the context of modern civilization in order to play a local or temporary role. The mission entrusted to it is universal and timeless. It is ambitious. It requires all space and time.'[21] The ambition was to broker a match, arrange a marriage. In a speech at the Comédie-Française in 1906, de Coubertin addressed the delegates:

> Gentlemen, we have gathered in this unique place to hold a unique ceremony. Our purpose is this: to reunite the Muscles and the Mind, once divorced, in the bonds of a legitimate marriage. I would verge on being untruthful if I said that ardent desire compels them to renew their conjugal life today.[22]

Why did this rapprochement need to be forced? Because sport without culture might dwindle into mere displays of brute strength and raw speed, and international competitions – even between amateurs – might risk 'outbursts of [the] crude nationalism that give our era a semi-barbaric stench'[23] without an enlightened and deodorizing creative-intellectual component. De Coubertin wrote: 'because I felt it would give my country and mankind as a whole the educational stimulus they needed, I had to try and restore the powerful buttresses that had supported it [the Games] in the past: the intellectual buttress, the moral buttress and, to a certain extent, the religious buttress'.[24]

In London 2012 it was perhaps inevitable that responsibility for providing the intellectual and moral (if not explicitly religious) buttresses would fall to Shakespeare. As Erin Sullivan has noted, 'it should have been Dickens's year' (see also Kirwan and Mathieson in this collection), but Dickens does not have the same global, Olympian credentials.[25] Shakespeare and the Olympics are 'nonpareil[s]' (*Tempest* 3.2.98) and their marriage – like that of Ferdinand and Miranda – promises 'fair play' (5.1.75) and the possibility of redeeming the sins of past generations and catalyzing the world into goodness.

Claims about the Olympian-global reach of Shakespeare were rife during the Cultural Olympiad. In 2012, an RSC/British Council survey reported that half of the world's schoolchildren at some point in their educational careers will have an encounter with Shakespeare, ranging on a very broad spectrum from passing acquaintance with some biographical facts to the more detailed textual study mandated by, for example, the UK National Curriculum. Politicians and other interested parties immediately simplified the report into an arresting soundbite, encouraged by the RSC's headline assertion that 'we know that 50 per cent of the world's children study Shakespeare in the classroom – that's over 64 million children worldwide'.[26] But even if one introduces the basic but fundamental clarification that the RSC *meant* to say 'half of the world's *school*children', the 64m/50 per cent 'statistic' looks very vulnerable. In 2012 UNESCO reported that 'approximately 131 million children of primary and lower secondary school age are currently out of school'. At least half of these would probably never enter school, and a further quarter (*c*.33m) had left before secondary level and would be unlikely to have 'studied' Shakespeare in any meaningful sense, especially in countries with such high rates of educational attrition.[27]

As Tracy Irish comments in her interview in this book, it is surprising how few people queried these claims. Furthermore, there was little or no question as to why the global study of Shakespeare might be a good thing or not. If, in de Coubertin's words, 'Manly sports are good for everyone and under all circumstances', so, it would seem, is Shakespeare; we are implicitly invited to pity the benighted other '50 per cent', to see the lack of Shakespeare in their national curricula as a symptom of 'under-development'. The 'progressive educational value' and moral benefits of the mental exercise of studying Shakespeare are as evident as those of physical exertion. Shakespeare, just like manly sports, might not make angels of brutes – even Prospero cannot do that – but it might equip global citizens with a level of self-knowledge and self-discipline, qualities that their own culture's literature doesn't quite foster to the same extent as that of the 'world's playwright'. A similar assumption underwrites cultural programming: that Shakespeare's works – and the festivals that produce them – are powerful catalysts for international exchange and understanding and therefore help to produce a more peaceful and civilized world. (This logic is clearly demonstrated in Tony Howard's analysis of the cultural internationalism of the last London Olympics in 1948.)

In 'Ode to Sport', the prose poem with which de Coubertin (under the Franco-German pseudonyms Georges Hohrod and M. Eschbach) won the gold medal for Literature at the 1912 Cultural Olympiad, de Coubertin apostrophized:

> O Sport, you are Peace!
> You forge happy bonds between the peoples by drawing them together in reverence for strength which is controlled, organised and selfdisciplined [sic]. Through you the young of all the world learn to respect one another, and thus the diversity of national traits becomes a source of generous and peaceful emulation.[28]

Perhaps alone of any cultural icon, Shakespeare's name might here (and throughout de Coubertin's 'Ode') be substituted for 'Sport'. (Indeed, two years later, American Charles William Wallace, addressing the Peace Centenary celebrations of the Poetry Society, described Shakespeare as 'a universal civilizing force, a world-power that needs no armaments to enforce peace nor the panoply of armies to prevent war'.[29]) As Dominic Dromgoole and Tom Bird wrote about the Globe to Globe Festival: 'Shakespeare is the language which brings us together better than any other, and which reminds of our almost infinite difference, and of our strange and humbling commonality'.[30] Such claims are not new, of course, but they were precisely calibrated to resonate in the 2012 Olympic moment and are entirely consistent with de Coubertin's internationalist outlook. As John MacAloon notes, de Coubertin 'discriminated between "cosmopolitanism" and "true internationalism"'; the latter, in MacAloon's words, 'understands cultural differences as an enduring and marvellous feature of the human landscape and argues that world peace depends upon the celebration of human diversity and not the eradication of it'.[31] It is easy to see how Globe to Globe and the hosting of foreign companies elsewhere in Newcastle and Stratford were congruent with de Coubertin's vision: 'To ask the peoples of the world to love one another is merely a form of childishness. To ask them to respect one another is not in the least utopian, but in order to respect one another it is necessary to know one another.'[32] In this prominent strand of the Cultural Olympiad (CO), the ground for knowledge of self and other was Shakespeare. As prompt and platform for cross-cultural exchange, Shakespeare is a lingua franca, or – in more Olympian terms – his works offer a level playing field for all. As Dromgoole wrote elsewhere:

> Companies from all around the world wanted to come and play with us, and wanted to play raw, human and dirty as the simplicity of the Globe demands. No concepts, no mediation, no filter, just the plays, those remarkable and eternal human documents, told straight from the lit eyes of the actors to the lit eyes of the audience.[33]

In this account, the Globe stage is a *tabula rasa* on which, without mediation, humans 'play [...] human' while transmitting 'eternal human documents' to each other. Playing 'dirty' somehow produces fair play and a courteous rapport between performers and audiences. The encounter is primarily ocular and non-linguistic – 'No tongue! All eyes!' (4.1.59) as Prospero instructs the lovers before the masque. Shakespeare is therefore pre-verbal ('raw', 'dirty'), non-national and available to all. Or, put another way, 'here's sport indeed' (*Antony*, 4.16.33).

In the lead-up to 2012, this post-national, sporting Shakespeare offered a predictable solution to a systemic dilemma. Cultural Olympiads always face what de Coubertin defined – in a suitably neo-Grecian fashion – as the problem of 'eurythmy'. Forging some alliance between athletes, artists and spectators was, he wrote, 'a monumental task, because we have lost all sense of eurythmy. Today, the masses are incapable of linking the pleasures of various sorts of art together.' The masses should, he averred, be disgusted by 'the whole apparatus' of the tasteless 'public festivals' of his day.[34] How to create a harmonious or beautiful rhythm between the range of Olympic sports and the arts? More prosaically put, how do you design and market a Cultural Olympiad?

The early planning stages for the 2008–12 Cultural Olympiad were predictably upbeat about the challenge. Chair of the CO Board, Tony Hall, claimed that the programming offered 'a chance to change the way this country looks at art and culture by making a statement that this [the Cultural Olympiad] is as important as sport'.[35] (Perhaps he could not have known that the relative importance of sport and culture would be confirmed by the appropriation of £100m of Arts Council of England funding to help towards the spiralling costs of the Olympic and Paralympic Games.)[36] By 2010, however, the Board appeared to be struggling to communicate its vision; Hall told journalists, 'I think people find the two words ['Cultural' and 'Olympiad'] really difficult to understand. People say to me: "What is it?" We want to bring clarity to it.' Raymond Williams notoriously described 'culture' as 'one of the two or three most complicated words in the English language', so it is hardly surprising that the adjectival form coupled with the unfamiliar 'Olympiad' might have befuddled the Great British Public.[37] The Board's solution was to rebrand the CO as a 'festival of festivals'.[38] As Shane Collins and Catherine Palmer noted shortly before the Games:

> Without conceptual clarity as to how the term culture is to be used and interpreted in the context of the Cultural Olympiad, it is already proving difficult for organisers to schedule a programme of activities that will have a definitional coherence throughout, and that will appease public disquiet as to the 'value' of the event.[39]

One way of manufacturing 'definitional coherence' is through the Author-function, or Bard Branding. Another is to manufacture the predominant sentiments of festival time – joy and celebration – and try to prevent anything breaking through those affective frames. The job of the Cultural Olympiad, in short, is to make Mirandas of us all, to have us exclaim regularly and in good faith, 'How beauteous mankind is!' (5.1.186).

Being true to the Olympic Self

The rebranding of the 2012 Cultural Olympiad as a 'festival of festivals' sent an unambiguous message to potential spectators and participants, a message neatly captured in de Coubertin's pronouncement in 1918: 'If anyone were to ask me the formula for "Olympizing" oneself, I should say to him, "the first condition is to be joyful"'.[40] In his 'Ode to Sport', de Coubertin devoted a stanza to joyousness:

> VI: O Sport, you are Joy!
> At your call flesh makes holiday and the eyes smile; the blood flows free and strong in the arteries. Thought's horizon grows lighter and more clear.[41]

Thomas F. Carter has argued that the Olympics constitute an 'apparatus that captures individuals and makes them into specific kinds of subjects: Olympians'. This identity supposedly 'transcend[s] other group affiliations. To be an Olympian is some quasi-utopian state of being that brings those individuals together in "brotherhood", a kind of utopian collective on a world scale.'[42] Carter sees this manufactured band of brotherhood most saliently among the athletes in the Olympic Village, but it is surely also the case that the Cultural Olympiad attempts to forge certain kinds of subjects who will 'Olympize' themselves into a state of optimistic joyfulness. Indeed, many written and anecdotal responses to the Globe to Globe Festival capture exactly this festive spirit and a sense that the normal rules of cultural/political engagement might be suspended for the duration of the Festival. Elizabeth Schafer's thoughtful account of watching an uncomplicated production of *The Taming of the Shrew* is representative of many responses to 'foreign' offerings in the WSF, forced as she was to conclude that the production 'produced a great deal of laughter even in a grumpy feminist like myself'.[43]

De Coubertin offered his formula for 'Olympizing' the self in 1918 when that act of self-fashioning must have felt especially counter-intuitive. But that challenge remained stiff throughout the twentieth century in the face of the repeated convulsions of world history and, on a more micro level, the periodic scandals that have plagued the Games. 'If', as MacAloon writes, 'joyfulness cannot be reliably anticipated, either because of chronic disputes and interruptions or because of the moral ambiguities of the events themselves', the injunctions that frame the Olympics – 'this is a festival' and 'be joyful!' – shift from the indicative and imperative to the interrogative moods: 'Is this a festival?' – or as the opening of *Julius Caesar* has it: 'Is this a holiday?' – and 'Am I joyful?'. These questions are produced by and in turn create what MacAloon, following Erving Goffman, calls frame-breaking events or out-of-frame behaviour.[44]

Two Shakespearean citations from the years leading up to 2012 reveal how Shakespearean Olympism is supposed to function and how – in the 'wrong', unofficial mouth – it can be exposed as a fragile fantasy and the frame of joyful celebration easily shattered.

In 2009–10, the Royal Mint issued its 'Celebration of Britain Silver Proof Collection', designed to 'capture the Mind, Body and Spirit of the nation' in the (long) run-up to the Olympics. These £5 coins were intended to help purchasers 'Keep the feeling' of the 2012 Olympics, even though those feelings had yet to be felt – a reminder that, as pointed out by David Whitson, 'staging (sports mega-) events is as much about engineering the emotions of the local populations as welcoming foreign visitors'.[45] Two of these commemorative coins were branded with Shakespeare's words. One coin featured an aerial/Ariel view of the Globe, the 2012 Olympic logo in green, and the words 'We are such stuff as dreams are made on' (Figure 1). Fair enough. A few months later, the Mint issued a coin devoted to 'Tolerance' (presumably an official Olympic 'feeling'). It featured a well-dressed black man in late Georgian/early Victorian clothes, an unidentifiable book in his right hand, and to his left the words 'Abolition of SLAVERY' and 'BRITISH DOMINION, January the 24th 1825' (Figure 2). That was not all. Between the man's head and the mandatory 2012 logo were the words 'To thine own self be true'. The quotation is unattributed; the man's name is also absent, a kind of blank. In designer Shane Greeves's words:

FIGURE 1 *Globe Theatre coin in the Royal Mint's 'Celebration of Britain Silver Proof Collection', 2009. Reproduced courtesy of the Royal Mint.*

Featured on this coin is Olaudah Equiano, a former slave who managed to earn enough money to buy his own freedom and campaigned arduously against slavery. The quote 'To thine own self be true' comes from Shakespeare's 'Hamlet' and encapsulates the Olympian spirit of always doing your best and realising that the taking part is as important as the winning.[46]

The 'abhorrèd slave' (1.2.353) Caliban would be central to the Opening Ceremony, but here was a 'real life' slave.

FIGURE 2 *'Tolerance' coin in the Royal Mint's 'Celebration of Britain Silver Proof Collection', 2010. Reproduced courtesy of the Royal Mint.*

Equiano's story is remarkable for a number of reasons, not the least of which is that his 'enlightened' Quaker master Robert King guaranteed that Equiano would be freed if he worked sufficiently hard (shades here of Prospero and Ariel). Equiano did so, purchased his freedom and proceeded to write *The Interesting Narrative of the Life of Olaudah Equiano, or Gustavus Vassa, the African* (1789), perhaps the first influential memoir by a former slave and one that helped galvanize the anti-slavery movement in Britain. And yet, on the Royal Mint coin, it was not Equiano's but rather Shakespeare's words that were minted and circulated as an encapsulation of the Olympic spirit and guarantor of the individual's humanity. To paraphrase *Pericles*, the big cultural fish eats the smaller.[47] Furthermore, the Royal Mint clearly felt the need to explain how the abolition of slavery exemplified British/Olympian/ Shakespearean 'tolerance' and integrity, when the British had themselves forged and maintained an Empire on its proceeds:

> Although it is indisputable that Britain profited from the trade that cast such a shadow on the 18th and early 19th centuries, the role the nation played in bringing the transatlantic trading of human souls to an end is also without question. British merchants transported almost three million African people across the Atlantic, building a slave-trading empire. But millions of British people played their part in bringing the practice to an end.[48]

On numerical balance, then – 'almost three million' vs 'millions' – the 'British people' are to be congratulated for the abolition of slavery. The riches rained down on the 'isles of wonder' during the nightmare of slavery, but here the British are cast as a fundamentally benign nation of Prosperos – yes, we had slaves, but, look, we also freed them! We acknowledged, finally, that the things of darkness were not ours to own. (No mention must be made of the fact that the continent from which those slaves were trafficked remains the only inhabited continent never to have held the Olympic Games.) Nothing must be allowed to interfere with the celebratory message. This is, after all, a commercial transaction in which the buyer is investing in a 'feeling' and that feeling cannot be shame. When it went on sale in 2010, this £5 coin could have been yours for only £54.95.

Elsewhere, on another part of the global stage, in September 2011 – almost a decade after the occupation of Afghanistan – a Royal Marine sergeant murdered a severely wounded Afghan insurgent whose life, according to the Geneva Convention, he should have done everything in his power to save. The incident was captured on a head camera worn by the soldier referred to as 'Marine B' in the transcript. The most pertinent section – recorded just after the Marine had shot the Afghan – reads:

> Marine A: There you are, shuffle off this mortal coil you cunt. It's nothing you wouldn't do to us.
> Marine B: I know.
> [...]
> Marine A: Obviously, this doesn't go anywhere, fellas.
> Marine B: Yeah, roger, mate.
> Marine A: I've just broke the Geneva Convention.[49]

Hamlet's words are incongruous in this context, but it is possible that the Marine was quoting Monty Python quoting Shakespeare – in the 'Dead Parrot' sketch, the eponymous bird is described as having 'shuffled off 'is mortal coil'.[50] Whether it was Shakespeare or Python that had taught the Marine this language, his profit on it was to know how to couple it with a curse. The crime shocked many – both inside and outside the Army – because it cut deep into a cherished national self-image, namely the reputation for 'fair play' (glossed by the IOC in the document cited above as 'the courteous rapport between opponents in confrontation'). The moral superiority to insurgents should be demonstrated by acting differently than that insurgent would if the roles were reversed. Army training is designed to have the effect de Coubertin claimed for manly sports: it should temper brutality and endow the individual with 'a bit of self-control'. Sense of humour, no less than 'fair play', is commonly cited as a positive characteristic of British national identity and featured strongly in the 2012 Opening Ceremony. A Royal Marine (quoting Python) quoting Shakespeare having just broken the Geneva Convention damages multiple treasured self-conceptions at once.

The use of Shakespeare's words on the Equiano coin was consistent with a wider trend in which, as Colette Gordon notes, Shakespeare is often 'invoked as a comrade in struggles for political liberation, distinguishing the freedom fighter, with his high humanist ideals, from the guerrilla soldier or terrorist' (see p. 209). But the problem with this strategy of associative citation is, bluntly, that anyone can quote Shakespeare. If the branding and marketing of the Equiano coin co-opted Shakespeare's words in order to align both playwright and the spirit of Olympism with the abolition of slavery and the redemption of a brutal past, the snatch of Shakespeare spoken in Helmand Province offered a painful reminder that the nightmare of history was very far from over.[51]

Sweet dreams are made of this: Shakespeare in the Opening Ceremony

The Mint coins and the Marine's crime offer more or less marginal parables of the role of Shakespearism in frame affirmation and frame-breaking in the Olympic years. There were also, to be sure, significant examples of complicated or compromised festivity within the theatrical arenas of the Cultural Olympiad itself.[52] But in the stadial-televisual Opening Ceremony, the relationship between British identity, Shakespearism and the spirit of Olympism was played out on an altogether different scale. The Opening Ceremony is the observed of all observers, the cynosure of the global gaze. MacAloon puts it powerfully:

> No other sports festival, no other cultural event, no arts performance, no church, no political movement, no other international organisation, including the United Nations, indeed no other anything has ever managed to generate regularly scheduled and predictable performances which command anywhere near the same focused global attention as do the Olympic ceremonies.[53]

Such a monstrosity – no less than the man-fish Trinculo-Caliban under the gabardine – offers a hybrid spectacle. The Opening Ceremony is edutainment and infomercial, religious rite and military parade, paean to mankind financed by Mammon. As mega-event it can 'provide host nations with a universally legitimate way to present and promote their national identities and culture on a global scale'.[54] In every Ceremony there will be a collision – more or less violent – between the imperatives of Olympism on the one hand and, on the other, the image and values the host country wishes to project to the watching world. In London 2012, three major brands – Olympism, Shakespearism and what we might call brand Britannia – featured strongly. The latter was arguably the least prestigious and therefore had most to gain – or lose: some research has sought to demonstrate that the Beijing Olympics 'were not successful in reputation and image enhancement of either the Olympics brand or of China'.[55] According to this marketing logic, the host nation needs 'to know what it wants "to say" by hosting the appropriately chosen events that align or fit with the message to enhance desired reputational image transfers'.[56]

Boyle and Boyce and their team were inevitably aware of the pressure to transmit and transfer images of Britain and Britishness that might be easily read and approvingly consumed by the national and global audience. As Boyce wrote:

> I could sense that there was some expectation that [the Opening Ceremony] would put a pin in the national

identity, that we would have to decide – is Britain rural or urban, ancient or modern, riot or clean-up, roundhead or cavalier, multi-cultural or divided?[57]

To avoid these binary pitfalls, the creative team adopted a collage approach, filling their office with scraps of text and images that captured something that each of them found essential and valuable about British national identity. In employing this method, they followed the example offered by Humphrey Jennings's remarkable book *Pandæmonium 1660–1886: The Coming of the Machine as Seen by Contemporary Observers* (1985). As Boyce wrote in the introduction to the 2012 reissue of the book, Jennings 'puts highly charged images alongside each other and lets sparks fly between them. I think we subliminally used that lesson in the Opening Ceremony.'[58] These 'images' are mostly textual in *Pandæmonium* and, according to Jennings, are 'symbols for the whole inexpressible uncapturable process. They are what later poets have called "Illuminations".'[59] In the fifth section of Arthur Rimbaud's visionary *Les Illuminations* (1886), the speaker appears to encounter a parade of metamorphic jesters before concluding: '*j'ai seul la clef de cette parade sauvage*' ('I alone have the key to this savage parade'). Boyle's Opening Ceremony – no less than the book from which it drew inspiration – offered the spectator an illuminatory puzzle. But very few emerged from the Opening Ceremony completely sure of what they had seen, fewer still pretending to have alone grasped the interpretative key to the parade. A number of critics have written incisively about the Branagh–Brunel–Caliban conundrum of the opening 'Pandemonium' sequence;[60] here I will focus on a later episode in the dream.

'This is for Everyone': The dream of Jerusalem

'Frankie and June say "Thanks Tim"' was a fifteen-minute sequence placed after the London Symphony Orchestra (featuring Mr Bean) and Simon Rattle's rendition of 'Chariots of Fire' and before the lighting of the Olympic Torch. Glossed by the BBC's Huw Edwards as 'a typical Saturday night' and 'a story of the digital age', 'Frankie and June' followed the progress of a chance encounter between a boy and a girl (apparently in their late teens or early twenties) on the London Underground. At first sight they 'change eyes' (*Tempest* 1.2.443–4). When leaving the 'train', she accidentally drops her phone; he picks it up and, smitten, determines to return it to her. June is mixed race (we've seen her earlier with her white mum and black dad in what is presented as an irreproachably 'average' British house). Frankie is black. At their first meeting, an image of Leonardo DiCaprio's Romeo flashes up on June's 'house'; later in the Ceremony, the Arctic Monkeys sing 'Oh there ain't no love, / No Montagues or Capulets / Just banging tunes in DJ sets and / Dirty dance floors and dreams of naughtiness'. Frankie and June's dream of naughtiness played out to a mash-up of popular tracks of the last four decades and so celebrated 'music, one of the great British exports' (in TV commentator Trevor Nelson's words). At its climax, the couple was reunited through the technology of their smartphones. Having navigated this digital foreplay – textual intercourse? – they sealed their new love with an actual kiss. At which point, the 'house' at the centre of the stadium morphed into a glowing white cube; as the cell appeared to take off vertically, it revealed beneath the man who had been pulling these digital strings, the magus of mass communication, Sir Tim Berners-Lee. We had been led to believe Frankie and June were Romeo and Juliet, but this revelation rewrote the script: instead of a bungling Friar Laurence, the pair had been blessed with a benign Prospero, deploying his Techno-Utopianism at the service of a brave new multiracial world. Berners-Lee then live-Tweeted of his invention, the World Wide Web, 'THIS IS FOR EVERYONE', before rising from his computer to take the applause of the crowd, the 'help of [our] good hands' setting him free (*Tempest*, Epilogue 10, 20).

This touching, Shakespeare-inspired ode to technology, racial harmony and youth was seductive but also demanded to be read in the context of London's original bid to host the Games, of see-sawing government attitudes to multiculturalism and immigration, and of the London Riots of summer 2011. Multiculturalist rhetoric had been central to the bid. On the day that London was awarded the Games, Prime Minister Tony Blair told reporters: 'London is an open, multi-racial, multi-religious, multicultural city and rather proud of it. People of all races and nationalities mix in with each other and mix in with each other well.'[61] On the day after – 7 July 2005 – four British Islamists exploded four bombs in London, killing 52 civilians; the attack was in part intended as a 'blowback' reaction to the British role in the occupations of Iraq and Afghanistan. As a partial consequence of the 7/7 bombings, perhaps, the word 'multiculturalism' began to fall out of favour and was often replaced by 'diversity' 'as the preferred language of politicians and associated agencies': in the London Organizing Committee of the Olympic and Paralympic Games's 2008 diversity and inclusion strategy, for example, 'multiculturalism' was used just once, 'diverse' or 'diversity' nearly 200 times.[62]

In February 2011, a few months into the Conservative–Liberal Democrat Coalition Government, Prime Minister David Cameron made a widely hyped speech on the 'failure' of multiculturalism. Addressing 'the weakening of our collective identity [...] under the doctrine of state multiculturalism', he argued that many immigrants were refusing to assimilate into British society because:

> We have failed to provide a vision of society to which they feel they want to belong. [...] we must build stronger

societies and identities at home. Frankly, we need a lot less of the passive tolerance of recent years and much more active, muscular liberalism.

It is impossible here not to catch a strong echo of the 'muscular Christianity' of the British Imperial nineteenth century; it may also be pertinent that Cameron's opponents in Parliament nickname him 'Flashman' after the public school arch bully in *Tom Brown's Schooldays* (a core text in the history of the Olympics given its influence on de Coubertin). Cameron drew a distinction between passively and actively tolerant societies – the latter take practical steps such as 'making sure immigrants speak the language of their new home [...] and ensuring that people are educated in elements of a common culture and curriculum'.[63] Training the immigrant Caliban to become a muscular liberal meant, therefore, the acquisition of the English language and a sense of the nation's history, combining to form a rigorous induction into the ways of British 'tolerance'. The question of what exactly that 'common culture' might be is always a matter of live debate in democratic societies, but it would be put under severe strain in August 2011, a few months after Cameron's speech, when the shooting by police of Mark Duggan, a young, mixed race man, triggered riots, first in Duggan's neighbourhood of Tottenham, then rapidly elsewhere in London and across a number of English towns and cities. At the time of the riots, pre-Olympic preparations were well underway for a new, semi-militarized infrastructure of defence systems and anti-terrorist surveillance. (This in a city that was already the most surveilled in the world, a fact that inspired the Horse Hospital's 2006 production of *The Tempest*, the poster for which simply and strikingly consisted of the play's title beneath the block silhouette of a CCTV camera.) But this infrastructure seemed largely unprepared for these less apocalyptic but no less disruptive civil insurrections in which (for a very complex set of reasons) young Britons, white, black and Asian, chose to speak in 'the language of the unheard'.[64] Mayor of London Boris Johnson wrote during the

Riots: 'Yes, the UK has been going through the worst recession for 50 years, and yes, times have been tough. But you don't boost London's job-generating prospects by smashing London's shops'. By the time the Olympics came to London in the following summer, he added, 'we must all hope that we will look back on these events as a bad dream'.[65]

Within these contexts, the 'Frankie and June say "Thanks Tim"' segment – as with much else in the Opening Ceremony – offered a 'most majestic vision, and / Harmonious charmingly' (4.1.118–9). To paraphrase The Beatles' 'Hey Jude' (with which the Ceremony concluded), it took a bad dream and a sad song and made them better. Graeme Hayes and John Karamichas argue that while the arrival of the Olympic Games does not 'invent' systemic contradictions in the host nation, the 'event staging *emphasizes* contradictions and dynamics that are already manifest'.[66] The mashed-up soundtrack to Frankie and June's postmodern courtship featured a snatch of the Eurythmics' 'Sweet Dreams (Are Made of This)' and indeed the trope of the 'Dream' acted as a harmonizing leitmotif – a eurythmic agent, if you like – in pulling the spectacle together.[67] But such a self-conscious and insistent confession that the Ceremony was performing dream work could only alert its viewers to the vexed relationship between what we were seeing and what we might crudely and un-joyously think of as 'reality'. For MacAloon, theorizing the nature of what he calls the 'metagenre' of spectacle, such a cognitive dissonance is entirely predictable:

> the spectacle invites what it simultaneously cautions against: delight in its content. Its contents are images – grand, alluring, unusual, epic images – but 'mere images'. The metacommunication of the spectacle frame says 'admire but do not be deceived'.[68]

Which is exactly how Prospero retrospectively frames the betrothal masque he stages for Ferdinand and the most admired and admiring Miranda. Like Prospero's Masque,

Olympics and Cultural Olympiads are 'spectacular gestures which briefly held the universal attention before disappearing, often into an abrupt oblivion, victims of their planned temporality'.[69] Like the debate between Gonzalo and Antonio/Sebastian in Act 2, scene 1 of *The Tempest*, these events will inevitably produce clashes of perspective about the 'real' nature of the island – is it of a 'subtle, tender, and delicate temperance [...] with everything advantageous to life' (44–5; 53–4) or the inhospitable, fen-stenched, ungreen and unpleasant land described by Antonio and Sebastian? Whatever the official messages of Olympism, for many the Games represent a 'freefall into a neoliberal paradise'.[70] 'There be some sports are painful' (3.1.1) and, from one perspective, the truth behind the Olympic movement is that, for all its egalitarian and progressive posturing, it represents 'the precise negation of socialist rationality, solidarity, and the improvement of ordinary life for the greatest number'.[71] By way of demonstration, we might note that Jeremy Hunt, the Secretary of State for Culture, Media and Sport who could not identify Shakespeare's presence in the Opening Ceremony, would go on, rising without trace, to be promoted to Secretary of State for Health, in which capacity he is, at the time of writing, overseeing what many see as the privatization of the NHS so joyously celebrated in the Opening Ceremony.

None of this would have surprised Humphrey Jennings. While *Pandæmonium* does indeed put 'highly charged images alongside each other and lets sparks fly between them', it nevertheless has a clear thesis: that 'when the "bourgeoisie" took over in 1660, they began the final subjugation and exploitation of this island'.[72] This island might once have been 'ours' – just as the island of *The Tempest* was once Caliban's – but the enemy from within has slowly defeated us. By the time Coleridge wrote 'Kubla Khan', Jennings argued, Xanadu ('the opposite of Pandæmonium') was

> Now only a dream possibility, now only to be found in dreams or opium – only fragmentarily written down. It is the

same place as Blake's Jerusalem once builded [*sic*] on Pancras and Kentish-town, but now no more. Paradise Lost again.[73]

Such a message has no place within the Olympic frame and the festival imperative to be joyful. Olympism self-consciously manufactures dream possibilities and creates a time/space in which, however much the 'outside' world is wracked, 'a fragile, temporary Utopia' might be experienced.[74] As Frank Cottrell Boyce wrote in the Olympic programme:

> flickering in the smoke and noise and excitement, you can sometimes glimpse a single golden thread of purpose – the idea of Jerusalem – of the better world, the world of real freedom and true equality, a world that can be built through the prosperity of industry, through the caring nation that built the welfare state, through the joyous energy of popular culture, through the dream of universal communication. A belief that we can build Jerusalem. And that it will be for everyone.[75]

Whether in the IOC's educational materials, the claims made based on the RSC/British Council survey of global education, the commemorative coins issued by the Royal Mint, the programming logic of the organizers of the Cultural Olympiad, or the redemptive imaginations of the authors of Opening Ceremony, the bard of this brave new Jerusalem and the magus charged with making angels of brutes was Shakespeare.

Notes

1. Pierre de Coubertin, *Olympism: Selected Writing 1863–1937*, ed. Norbert Müller (Lausanne: International Olympic Committee, 2000), p. 241.
2. Iain Sinclair, 'The Olympics Scam: The Razing of East London', *London Review of Books*, 19 June 2008, pp. 17–23,

http://www.lrb.co.uk/v30/n12/iain-sinclair/the-olympics-scam [accessed 10 February 2014].

3   Percy MacKaye, extract from *Caliban by the Yellow Sands*, reprinted in Mel Gordon, 'Percy MacKaye's Masque of "Caliban" (1916)', *The Drama Review: TDR*, 20:2 (1976), pp. 93–107 (p. 107).

4   The other eight strands in the Cultural Olympiad were entitled: Disability Art and Culture; A Collection of World Stories; Film; Discovering Places; Somewhereto; Outdoor Arts; Sounds; Artists Taking the Lead.

5   'myShakespeare', http://myshakespeare.rsc.org.uk/ [accessed 10 February 2014].

6   'World Shakespeare Festival 2012', http://www.rsc.org.uk/about-us/history/world-shakespeare-festival-2012/ [accessed 5 May 2014].

7   All reference to Shakespeare are to *The Oxford Shakespeare*, 2nd edn Stanley Wells, Gary Taylor, John Jowett and William Montgomery (eds) (Oxford: Oxford University Press, 2005).

8   Richard Mulcaster, 'Positions vvherin those primitiue circumstances be examined, which are necessarie for the training vp of children, either for skill in their booke, or health in their bodie' (London, 1581). The link between the 'training up of children' and Olympism is suggestive and anticipates de Coubertin by some three centuries.

9   Martin Colley, *The British Olympics: Britain's Olympic Heritage 1612–2012* (Swindon: English Heritage, 2011), p. 22.

10 William Durham, 'To my Noble Friend Mr Robert Dover, on his Dauncing Assembly upon Cotswold', B3, and Ben Jonson, 'An Epigram to my Jovial Good Friedd [*sic*] Mr Robert Dover', D2, both in *Annalia Dubrensia* (London, 1636).

11 Jean Williams, 'The Curious Mystery of the Cotswold "Olimpick" Games: Did Shakespeare Know Dover… and Does it Matter?', *Sport in History*, 29:2 (2009), pp. 150–70 (p. 162).

12 Quoted in ibid., p. 160.

13 'Fair Play: Where does it come from? What is it?', International Olympic Committee, http://www.olympic.org/Documents/Reports/EN/en_report_1065.pdf [accessed 4 March 2014].

14 'Pierre de Coubertin', http://www.sochi2014.com/en/pierre-de-coubertin [accessed 4 March 2014].

15 Ian McDonald, 'The Olympic documentary and the "spirit of Olympism"', in *Watching the Olympics: Politics, power and representation*, John Sugden and Alan Tomlinson (eds) (Abingdon: Routledge, 2012), pp. 108–21 (pp. 110–11).

16 'The Modern Olympic Games', International Olympic Committee, 2007, http://www.olympic.org/Documents/Reports/EN/en_report_668.pdf [accessed 23 November 2013].

17 F. D. A. Burns, 'Dover, Robert (1581/2–1652)', *Oxford Dictionary of National Biography* (Oxford: Oxford University Press, 2004), online edition, http://www.oxforddnb.com/view/article/7954 [accessed 6 March 2014].

18 To take but one pertinent example: at Shakespeare's old school, King Edward VI's in Stratford-upon-Avon, in the 1880s a young headmaster Robert Laffan introduced compulsory physical training as a means of inculcating discipline, courtesy and moral rectitude. Laffan would subsequently work closely with de Coubertin on the International Olympic Committee for the first three decades of the twentieth century. See Steve Bailey, 'The Reverend Robert S. de Courcy Laffan: Baron Pierre de Coubertin and the Olympic Movement', in *Coubertin et l'Olympisme: Questions pour l'avenir: Le Havre 1897–1997*, ed. Norbert Müller (Lausanne: CIPC, 1998), pp. 64–71, http://www.coubertin.ch/pdf/PDF-Dateien/113-Baily.pdf [accessed 5 May 2014].

19 Henry Cole's account of Prince Albert's intervention is quoted in Paul Greenhalgh, *Fair World: A History of World's Fairs and Expositions from London to Shanghai 1851–2010* (Winterbourne: Papadakis, 2011), p. 25. For Wanamaker and the World's Fair, see Paul Prescott, 'Sam Wanamaker', in *Great Shakespeareans Vol. 15*, ed. Cary Mazer (London: Arden, 2013), pp. 151–210 (pp. 156–62).

20 Robert W. Rydall, *World of Fairs: The Century-of-Progress Exhibitions* (Chicago: University of Chicago Press, 1993), p. 15.

21 Coubertin, *Olympism*, p. 595.

22 Ibid., p. 611.

23 Ibid., p. 562.
24 Ibid., p. 620.
25 Erin Sullivan, 'Olympic Performance in the Year of Shakespeare', in *A Year of Shakespeare: Re-living the World Shakespeare Festival*, Paul Edmondson, Paul Prescott and Erin Sullivan (eds) (London: Arden, 2013), pp. 3–11 (p. 8).
26 See: http://www.worldshakespearefestival.org.uk/about.html [accessed 10 January 2014].
27 'Opportunities lost: The impact of grade repetition and early school leaving', UNESCO Institute for Statistics Global Education Digest, 2012, http://www.uis.unesco.org/Education/GED%20Documents%20C/GED-2012-Complete-Web3.pdf [accessed 12 September 2013].
28 Coubertin, *Olympism*, p. 630.
29 Charles William Wallace, 'Shakespeare and America: The Perpetual Ambassador of the English-Speaking World', in *Americans on Shakespeare, 1776–1914*, ed. Peter Rawlings (Aldershot: Ashgate, 1999), pp. 501–7 (p. 503). Wallace's address was delivered on 10 June 1914, 18 days before the assassination of Archduke Franz Ferdinand.
30 Globe to Globe website, http://globetoglobe.shakespearesglobe.com/archive/2012/ [accessed 15 October 2014].
31 John J. MacAloon, 'Olympic Games and the Theory of Spectacle in Modern Societies', in *Rite, Drama, Festival, Spectacle: Rehearsals Toward a Theory of Cultural Performance*, ed. John J. MacAloon (Philadelphia: Institute for the Study of Human Issues, 1984), pp. 241–80 (p. 257).
32 Pierre de Coubertin, *The Olympic Idea: Discourses and Essays* (Stuttgart: Olympischer Sportverlag, 1966), p. 118.
33 Dominic Dromgoole, 'Foreword', *Shakespeare Beyond English: A Global Experiment*, Susan Bennett and Christie Carson (eds) (Cambridge: Cambridge University Press, 2013), pp. xxiii–xxiv (p. xxiv).
34 Coubertin, *Olympism*, p. 612.
35 Quoted in Shane Collins and Catherine Palmer, 'Taste, ambiguity and the Cultural Olympiad', in *Watching the Olympic* Sugden and Tomlinson (eds), pp. 138–50 (p. 146).

36 Ibid., p. 148.
37 Raymond Williams, *Keywords: A vocabulary of culture and society* (London: Fontana, 1976), p. 87.
38 Nick Collins, '2012 Cultural Olympiad "too hard to understand"', *Daily Telegraph*, 30 January 2010, http://www.telegraph.co.uk/sport/olympics/london-2012/7105123/2012-Cultural-Olympiad-too-hard-to-understand.html [accessed 10 October 2013].
39 Collins and Palmer, 'Taste', p. 147.
40 Coubertin, *The Olympic Idea*, p. 57.
41 Coubertin, *Olympism*, p. 629.
42 Thomas F. Carter, 'The Olympics as sovereign subject maker', in *Watching the Olympics*, Sugden and Tomlinson (eds), pp. 55–68 (p. 62).
43 Elizabeth Schafer, 'A *Shrew* full of laughter', in *Shakespeare Beyond English*, Bennett and Carson (eds) , pp. 251–60 (p. 258).
44 MacAloon, 'Olympic Games', p. 262
45 Quoted in John Horne, 'The Four 'Cs' of Sports Mega-Events: Capitalism, Connections, Citizenship and Contradictions', in *Olympic Games, Mega-Events and Civil Societies: Globalization, Environment, Resistance*, Graeme Hayes and John Karamichas (eds) (Basingstoke: Palgrave, 2012), pp. 31–45 (p. 41).
46 Royal Mint, 'Explore your coin', http://www.royalmint.com/en/olympic-games/explore-your-coin/tolerance [accessed 12 September 2013].
47 A similar manoeuvre of traditional heavyweights muscling out and silencing the cultural underdog could be observed in a 2012–13 controversy over the National Curriculum. Equiano's story was included in the National Curriculum in 2007, but weeks after the end of the 2012 Olympics, it was reported that Secretary of State for Education Michael Gove was considering removing the achievements of Equiano and comparably significant human rights figures such as Mary Seacole in order to refocus the curriculum around more traditionally key individuals such as Cromwell and Churchill. It is through

such adjustments to the curriculum – and the systematic downgrading of 'soft' subjects such as drama, music and dance – that Gove promised to make Britain more competitive in the zero-sum capitalistic athletics he called 'the global race'. After widespread complaint and a petition from Operation Black Vote, Seacole and Equiano were retained on the curriculum. See Kevin Rawlinson, 'Another Gove U-turn: Mary Seacole will remain on the Curriculum', *Independent*, 7 February 2013, http://www.independent.co.uk/news/uk/politics/another-gove-uturn-mary-seacole-will-remain-on-the-curriculum-8485472.html [accessed 5 May 2014].

48 Royal Mint, 'Explore your coin'.

49 See Steven Morris, 'Royal Marines court martial: video transcripts', *Guardian*, 25 October 2013, http://www.theguardian.com/uk-news/2013/oct/25/royal-marines-court-martial-video-transcript [accessed 28 October 2013], and Steven Morris, 'Military court releases audio of moment marine sergeant shot Afghan', *Guardian*, 7 November 2013, http://www.theguardian.com/uk-news/2013/nov/07/military-court-audio-marine-shot-afghan [accessed 10 November 2013].

50 My thanks to Bill Brewer for reminding me that this Shakespearean quotation might be indirect.

51 The marine's court martial occurred in 2013, some months after the London Olympics, so news of his conviction could not break the Olympic frame. Nor could it draw attention to cuts to military funding and the consequent intensification of pressure on individual soldiers that the marine's defence team cited as mitigating circumstances for the crime and which will no doubt feature in his (currently pending) appeal. Partly because of the lamentable shortcomings of the Government's preferred private security company, G4S, something like 14,000 British troops were mobilized to provide the massive security apparatus the Olympics demands, a number greater than that playing out the end game of the Afghanistan occupation. See Dave Zirin, *Game Over: How Politics has Turned the Sports World Upside Down* (New York: The New Press, 2013), p. 57.

52 Other potential or actual frame-breaking events within the WSF included the controversial presence of companies from

Israel, Palestine and China in the Globe to Globe Festival, and the corporate sponsorship of some productions in the WSF by British Petroleum, which led to creative protests in Stratford-upon-Avon; see the website of the protest group 'BP or not BP?', http://bp-or-not-bp.org/news/protesters-take-to-the-stage-at-rsc-over-bp-sponsorship/ [accessed 12 March 2014].

53 MacAloon, 'Olympic ceremonies as a setting for intercultural exchange', in *Olympic Ceremonies, Historical Continuity and Cultural Exchange*, M. de Moragas Spa, John MacAloon and Montserrat Llinnés (eds) (Lausanne: IOC, 1996), pp. 29–43 (p. 33).

54 Harald Dolles and Sten Söderman, 'Mega-sporting events in Asia – Impacts on society, business and management: An introduction', *Asian Business and Management* 7:2 (2008), pp. 147–62 (p. 147).

55 Louise A. Heslop, John Nadeau, Norm O'Reilly, Anahit Armenakyan, 'Mega-event and country co-branding: image shifts, transfers and reputational impacts', *Corporate Reputation Review* 16 (2013), pp. 7–33 (p. 7).

56 Ibid., p. 28.

57 Frank Cottrell Boyce, 'Foreword', in Humphrey Jennings, *Pandæmonium: The Coming of the Machine As Seen by Contemporary Observers*, Marie-Louise Jennings and Charles Madge (eds) (London: Icon, 2012), pp. vii–xii (p. xi).

58 Ibid., p. xi.

59 'Introduction', *Pandæmonium*, pp. xiii–xix (p. xiv).

60 For very good descriptions of the cultural dynamics of the 2012 Opening Ceremony, see: Erin Sullivan, 'Olympic Performance'; Stephen Purcell, '"What country, friends, is this?": Cultural Identity in the World Shakespeare Festival', *Shakespeare Survey* 66, pp. 155–65; Richard Wilson, 'Like an Olympian Wrestling: Shakespeare's Olympic Game', *Shakespeare Survey* 66, pp. 82–95 (esp. pp. 82–4).

61 Mark Tran, 'London celebrates Olympics decision', *Guardian*, 6 July 2005, http://www.theguardian.com/uk/2005/jul/06/olympics2012.olympicgames3 [accessed 22 November 2013].

62 Daniel Burdsey, 'The Technicolor Olympics? Race,

63 Cameron's whole speech on multiculturalism can be read here: http://www.newstatesman.com/blogs/the-staggers/2011/02/terrorism-islam-ideology [accessed 20 February 2014].

64 David Zirin quoting Martin Luther King's resonant phrase, 'The London Olympics and the London Riots', *The Nation*, 12 August 2011, http://www.thenation.com/blog/162742/london-olympics-and-london-riots# [accessed 20 February 2014].

65 Boris Johnson, 'London can – and will – come back from all this', *Evening Standard*, 9 August 2011, http://www.standard.co.uk/news/mayor/boris-johnson-london-can--and-will--come-back-from-all-this-6430974.html [accessed 3 March 2014].

66 Graeme Hayes and John Karamichas, 'Conclusion. Sports Mega-Events: Disputed Places, Systemic Contradictions and Critical Moments', in *Olympic Games, Mega-Events and Civil Societies*, Hayes and Karamichas (eds), pp. 249–61 (p. 261).

67 The dream leitmotif was threaded throughout the Opening Ceremony, from the musical performance of 'Caliban's Dream' (a version of which would reach no.5 in the charts), via the NHS sequence in which the dreams of sleeping children were populated by figures from popular literature, to IOC President Jacques Rogge's crowning injunction to the athletes at the end of the Ceremony: 'Make us dream!'

68 MacAloon, 'Olympic Games', p. 265

69 Paul Greenhalgh, *Fair World: A History of World's Fairs*, p. 11.

70 This is the suggestive phrase of Christopher Gaffney, the vice president of Brazil's National Fans' Association, about the forthcoming FIFA World Cup 2014 in Rio de Janeiro, but the 'reality' is equally true of the effect plans for the 2016 Olympics are having on his country. Quoted in Zirin, *Game Over*, p. 52.

71 John Hoberman, 'Toward a theory of Olympic internationalism', *Journal of Sports History* 22:1 (1995), pp. 1–37 (p. 19).

(The first entry, numbered 62 implicitly, begins:) representation and the 2012 London Games', in *Watching the Olympics*, Sugden and Tomlinson (eds), pp. 69–81 (p. 73).

72 Jennings, *Pandæmonium*, p. 37.
73 Ibid., p. 110.
74 Boyce, 'Foreword', in *Pandæmonium*, p. xii.
75 Ibid.

2

Two Poems from the Olympic Year

Kapka Kassabova

Kapka Kassabova was Writer in Residence at the Shakespeare Birthplace Trust in 2012. Her experiences there included the passing of the Olympic torch relay through Stratford-upon-Avon and the marking of Amnesty International's 50th anniversary.

Olympic Torch

While the Coca Cola truck passed,
and the Lloyds truck, followed by the ambulance
truck, the official tasselled girls truck,
and the Moment to Shine truck,
not to mention – but we must – the
'Great Britain, celebrate your future flames' truck

While the man dressed as Shakespeare
marched up and down, feeling ridiculous

and the mayor was furious, they said afterwards,
when none of this mattered, not even
the torch which finally arrived and was small
and unremarkable like all real things

While the rest of us enacted
the duty of ceremonies that take too long
– the children stood, undimmed yet
by disappointment or censure,
holding, as if giving flowers,
torches made from orange paper.

FIGURE 3 *The Olympic Torch passes Shakespeare's Birthplace on Henley Street, Stratford-upon-Avon, July 2012. Reproduced courtesy of The Shakespeare Birthplace Trust.*

Border Story

On the 50th anniversary of Amnesty International

Imagine a line that runs through a house.
Then imagine a girl in a half-room of books
about far away. One day, she will leave,
this will become her life. Sometimes

she returns to the house, the half-bed,
the half-table, unpacks the half-library.
Listens for voices. But the girl
on the other side is gone. The noise

of twenty years passing stops one day
when they meet on a translated page,
or pass each other in a foreign street
and look away, and miss the cue.

Anyway, borders have moved,
other things matter, this is another age.
Their memories churn in revised mouths,
houses burn elsewhere. They have lovers.

Now imagine that's you and I.
This the story of how and why
the world is getting better, the world
is getting better for some and not for others.

Reproduced by kind permission of the author.
Commissioned by The Stratford-upon-Avon Poetry Festival,
The Shakespeare Birthplace Trust, 2012.

3

Performing Shakespeare in the Olympic Year: Interviews with Three Practitioners

Frank Cottrell Boyce, writer of the 2012 Olympics Opening Ceremony

Interview with Paul Prescott and Erin Sullivan by video conference on 6 November 2013

How did you get involved with the Olympic Opening Ceremony, and what was the process like?

Well, Danny [Boyle, director of the Ceremony] and I are friends, and he just asked me! You've got to ask him why. The process was very straightforward. It must have been two years before, I just bumped into Danny, and he said come and have a cup of tea. He said he was doing the Olympic Opening Ceremony, and asked me if I would do it with him. I asked him what that meant, and he said he didn't really know! He was doing *Frankenstein* at the time, so he and Mark Tildesley, who's the big genius in the team, had rented a little room in London. Mark was designing sets there for *Frankenstein*, and it was handy for Danny because he was also editing a film. It was in that little room, for the first six, seven, eight months, that me, Mark, Danny and a woman called Suttirat Larlarb, who is by profession a costume designer, would meet up very frequently and just talk and exchange pictures and swap poems. We had a wall that we put ideas on. We also had a washing line, because there was a timeline to the Opening Ceremony, so we had these marks to hit and gaps to fill. And then six, seven months down the line we moved to Three Mills, which is a film studio right next to the stadium, and the team just kind of grew around that core. Rick Smith, who is from the band Underworld, joined at that point, I think. So the core team was just those five people, and really until rehearsals started, that's all it was. It was really, really, really straightforward. The process was just, 'Can you fill this washing line with interesting things?'.

At what point did Shakespeare become one of those interesting things?

Because the Opening Ceremony meant a lot to people and because it's often read as a kind of snapshot of where we're up to as a nation, I think people sometimes feel as though we had this list of things to get in but it never worked like that. The process of creating the Ceremony always came from a dramatic point of view. The primary thing we asked ourselves was, 'How do you make something look really thrilling?'. So, for instance, in the first few minutes you have to show the rings. Previous ceremonies have just gone bigger and bigger and bigger and spent more and more and more doing that. We didn't have the money. Danny's thing was, what can we do that other people don't do? What can we do to make the rings visceral? And we talked about creating something not just surprising, not just spectacular, but visceral, which is always Danny's watchword. One of the pictures that was up on the wall, which was one of Danny's favourites, was a little Joseph Wright of Derby picture of molten metal coming out of a furnace [Figure 4]. That image tied in with William Blake, among other things. And pretty quickly we came to the idea of *making* the rings, and that's where all that imagery of work and molten metal came from, and the Industrial Revolution came after that [for an image of this moment in the Ceremony see the cover of this book].

The Shakespeare thing came in almost by osmosis. Pretty early on I had to write up a document that would take people through the contents of the Ceremony. That was for Jeremy Hunt, the Minister of Culture at the time. Without thinking about it, I called it 'Isles of Wonder' and after that, loads of wonderful island imagery crystallized and *The Tempest* just sort of seeped in. So I guess what I would say is that Shakespeare was ambient, it was sort of there, and then it crystallized around the idea of the title. Again, it's not like

FIGURE 4   An Iron Forge *(1772) by Joseph Wright of Derby. Reproduced courtesy of Tate Images.*

we were trying to get Shakespeare in, he's just there, part of the cultural air that we breathe, and he helped us with that issue of how to make things have a governing narrative that's hidden. I do remember this – and it is probably the only worthwhile thing I'm going to say – that when we started on this cultural adventure by choosing which British paintings we like, which British poems we love, which British songs we love, Danny kept coming back to it every now and then and he would say, 'I want all of this in there but I don't want people to know it's in there until they've gone home. I want them to be thrilled and have a great time and only afterwards think, oh wow, that was William Blake, or that was Milton' – because there's as much Milton as there is Shakespeare in it. And so it would be in the Ceremony's DNA, it wouldn't be us. I would say that the difference between us and the Closing Ceremony is that they did seem to have an official list, here's Churchill, here's that, whereas we were trying to be part of the flow of British culture rather than trying to pick out certain bits of it. So the 'Isles of Wonder' was almost an accidental thing, but everyone seemed to like it, and it just stuck. If you asked the others, they wouldn't know where that phrase came from – do you know what I mean? We hadn't talked about it, it just seemed right. *The Tempest* got in that way, and once it was in there, it just fit in so beautifully.

One of the things that Danny loved was if you go to the Kop [a legendary end of the Liverpool Football club stadium at Anfield], if you go to Anfield to watch football, you have these huge, huge flags that come down over the crowd, I mean massive when they come down. Danny really loved them. He had the idea of doing them in blue, which came from wanting to get Hockney in there, and so suddenly we had the possibility of covering the audience in blue and turning that pastoral opening into an island, the shipping forecast. So all these island images just came together and crystallized around *The Tempest*. We weren't looking for Shakespeare, it's that once you've got an island, once you've got the sea, once you've got the shipping forecast – which had to be in, it's kind of a national magic spell, isn't it, the shipping forecast? Out of the shipping forecast, out of the blue sheets, *The Tempest* just spawned itself. And I guess what's good about *The Tempest* is that it's a masque, and that therefore it's about transformation, and it kept beating for us because it fit so well with that first section of the Opening Ceremony [when the entire stage changes from a grassy landscape to an industrial scene], which is the bit that everyone's most proud of, and everyone loves. It's the biggest scene-change in history, we think – no one's ever changed a set on that scale, even if you go back to the Coliseum. It's the biggest scene-change, and that's the essence of masque, isn't it, that you change the scene. So it's got that element to it. And that whole idea of 'Be not afraid, the isle is full of noises' just fitted so well with the title for that part of the Ceremony – 'Pandemonium'.

Did you talk much about the fact that the 'Isle is full of noises' speech is spoken by Caliban, a native – and enslaved – inhabitant of the island?

Do you mean the fact that it was Caliban, rather than someone else? It's weird, we knew that we were doing the *Windrush*, slavery, the Caribbean, a new world, but like I said, because the Ceremony means so much to people, they think you put the meaning in on purpose. But actually I think what you're doing is choosing things that you know work, that you know are brilliant, and part of their brilliance is that they trigger all these meanings that go into people's heads. And you're not really in charge of what those meanings are. I think a very important person in the creation of that scene was Rick, from Underworld, who's used to the power of mixing and collage – take a theme from Elgar and throw it into a drum and bass thing, and it's just like, 'Well that's it'. I do remember writing Caliban's speech out and putting it up on the wall and thinking – 'Fuck'. And I tell you something, I remember going to the dress rehearsals, because we didn't really want any spoken words at the start, and then that speech came up, and we just thought, that's so good, and it's got that storytelling feel. You wanted a moment of a human voice that turns the crowd into an audience, that just says settle down now, it's going to start. And those words were kind of unbeatable – whatever they meant, whatever their problem, they are incredible words. I remember going to the dress rehearsals, which were incredibly fraught and very, very noisy because as well as the noise of the Ceremony itself you had your earphone in, and there were people shouting and a lot of running around, and those words coming on and just absolutely tearing up and thinking, 'That's amazing'. There are all these fibre optics and pyrotechnics and choreography and everything, and these words spoken by a human voice still punch through. I was with my daughter and she burst into tears, it was just so moving hearing those words. If you analyse why, I'd say I don't really know why – it's a madly inappropriate speech in a way. Why the hell would Brunel be quoting Caliban?

Do you know how Shakespeare and The Tempest *ended up in the Olympic Closing Ceremony and then again in the Paralympics Opening Ceremony? Did the creative teams for the different ceremonies talk to each other?*

I'm sure Danny did, because I can remember rows about 'they've booked such and such a body and we wanted such and such a body' – do you know what I mean? Rows about personnel. But I don't remember any conversations about what they were doing. That doesn't mean Danny didn't know. Danny was incredibly protective of us. We had a couple of meetings and presentations with politicians, but we were completely protected from issues about budget or ideology or anything like that.

Were you surprised then, when the Closing Ceremony also used the 'Isle is full of noises' speech?

I was absolutely gobsmacked. But that doesn't mean that they didn't know. Maybe they did, because we all had the same exec, which was Stephen Daldry [Creative Director for all of the Games Ceremonies], so there obviously must have been discussions across the teams, but it wasn't like we were working together.

Are we right in thinking that you scripted not just the Opening Ceremony but some of the material around it?

Yes, I wrote more or less on my own the programme, which became a kind of anthology of poetry and pictures that had inspired us. So the other place that Shakespeare crops up in the Opening Ceremony of course is the Saturday Night sequence which has got a bit of *Romeo and Juliet* in it – 'When he shall die, take him and cut him out in little stars'. That was actually the working title of that section [for more on this section see Paul Prescott's chapter in this volume].

You also scripted Huw Edwards's commentary, which was spoken during the UK television broadcast. Can you tell us about that? Why was it important to you to do it?

It wasn't important to me, it was important to Danny! Danny's a great one with an eye for detail, and dealing with corporate things – even with me writing the brochure you still had to deal with the fact that every politician wanted a page in it. Danny wanted it not to be corporate and for it to be written by someone who had been part of the creative team, and who understood what it was all for. If you leave it to someone who's just been hired to do the job, they'll blow surprises and things like that. So he wanted someone who was in the groove of the drama of it. So I wrote that, and that was quite fun actually. Most people watched the Ceremony on television, and the commentary was part of the show, so we needed to be in control of that. And I think Danny probably had quite a few fights about it! Huw was great – he came and watched an animatic of the whole thing [a computer-animated storyboard or mock-up]. He was very cooperative. Danny's big thing was that there would be times when we wanted people just to be quiet, to let it play, and not be loud. I think the thing that he was worried about was that because it was being done by BBC Outside Broadcast, who were great, that they would treat it as a sports event rather than an arts event.

A couple of days after the Opening Ceremony you published a piece about the meaning of the Olympics in the Guardian *online.[1] Do you feel that the London Olympics lived up to some of the social and political ambitions you outlined there?*

I can put that metaphysically, but I can't really put it politically. I think it would be foolish to say anything changed, wouldn't it really? The only thing I think the Olympics really changed was people's image of what Britain is – changed it for British people, I mean. I think the Games did portray us as very inclusive, positive, competent – you know, everyone expected us to be rubbish! We took ourselves by surprise, and that is important. I'd love to think that that gave people confidence to try and change things. I don't know whether it would or not. I mean, I thought it exposed all kinds of incredibly explosive political truths accidentally, but no one seems to have fully recognized that. For instance – I'm always saying this – the people who got paid a fortune during the Olympics were shit, and the people who got paid nothing were brilliant. There's a truism that there's a market in talent, in management and entrepreneurship, and that you pay the best money to get the best people. Actually the worst people are motivated by money. And therefore if you go get the most expensive CEO, they're probably going to be shit. It's not a justice thing or a morality thing. The footballer who is motivated by money ends up on the bench at Real Madrid. The actor who is motivated by money is the same. You see it all the time, they don't do their best work, do they? I hope that the Olympics will help expose that – that footballers are rubbish and athletes are brilliant.

I kind of thought as well that because the Olympics are framed politically and sportingly around the idea of individual triumphs, that they would also result in a kind of festive individualism. Every single one of the athletes ended up saying something like, 'I'm not an individual – you know, my mom, my dad, my coach got me here'. The grace of them – I just thought that would have a bigger effect. But I don't know if it did. Those are the things I noticed, but I don't know if they had any effect, really.

Before you worked on the Opening Ceremony, what was the extent of your interaction with Shakespeare? Did the project change in any way your feelings about him and his work?

I think there are a number of really interesting things there. I was flirting at one point with doing a Shakespeare play on stage. The big difference that I came to appreciate is that if you're doing a modern play or any play, you start by thinking, 'How do I fill the stage up? What do I bring, as a director, what do I bring to the party?'. The thing about Shakespeare is that the minute you read it, it's all there. The words are so full, the special effects are in the lines. You don't need to have a big bell or a railway train. I remember realizing that and thinking, 'That's interesting'. I guess ambience is the thing. If you asked me if I loved and appreciated Shakespeare, I'd have to say that I haven't seen very many Shakespeare productions that have blown me away. It's in the lines and poetry. Do you know what I mean? It's there, it's there for you. I think that's the thing.

I'll tell you something personal about this. My family and I went to live abroad in France for a year, and when we came back one of my sons was taken to see *Henry V*. He was about 13 or 14 years old. When he got back from it he was like an eight-year-old who had seen *Star Wars* for the first time. He was like, 'I just can't believe this'. And he learned huge chunks of it off by heart. He can still do massive chunks of it off by heart. That year abroad was full of impressionable times – we could go to the pictures and think, 'This is great!', without having to understand every word. That was a revelation to me – that you can ride it, and you can just take the visual thrill. You don't need to understand every word. That was important.

Thank you so much. Is there anything else you'd like to add before we finish?

Can I tell you the Jeremy Hunt story before I go? Jeremy was the Culture Minister at the time of the Olympics, and he came in and watched an animatic of the Ceremony before the actual event. I've never told anyone this before because it seemed undiplomatic at the time. But now the day is gone so we can. He came in and watched this animatic that included pretty much everything the final Ceremony did. Nothing really changed. To be fair to him, it's quite a hard thing to watch, and you kind of have to know what you're looking at. But you start from the written press materials anyway. At the end of it, he said, 'Um, where's Shakespeare?' And Danny went, 'Well, it's actually based on *The Tempest*. The whole thing is based on *The Tempest*'. Absolutely blank look from Jeremy Hunt. Danny said, 'That's… *The Tempest*, by William Shakespeare?' And then Jeremy Hunt said, 'Oh yeah, right!' I want the world to know that.

Note

1   Frank Cottrell Boyce, 'The Dangerous Conversation: Creating an Enduring Moral Legacy for 2012 Games', *Guardian*, 29 July 2012, http://www.theguardian.com/sport/interactive/2012/jul/29/olympics-2012 [accessed 5 November 2013].

Tom Bird, Director of the Globe to Globe Festival

Interview with Paul Prescott and Erin Sullivan in person on 18 June 2013

How did you first get involved in Globe to Globe?

I'd been at the Globe for four or five years, doing all sorts of different things in the casting department and in the music department and generally helping out. And then Dominic Dromgoole got an agreement in principle to have some funding as part of the World Shakespeare Festival to do something with Shakespeare in the wider world. We are talking about really broad brushstrokes at this time, but the idea was then in Dominic's head to do all of the Shakespeare plays in different languages as part of the Festival. He pulled me over at the end of the 2010 season and said, 'I'd like to do this in 2012', and it's sort of as simple as that. And then, we were suddenly going on sale with Globe to Globe in the October of 2011. So we suddenly had to move very, very fast. Nothing here is over thought through before we do it – we tend to jump in, and have a swim around before testing the water, if you see what I mean.

I think Globe to Globe has a fair claim to be one of the most ambitious theatrical projects that anyone has ever tried, and a lot of people, right at the beginning, including some people within LOCOG were saying, 'This is mad', and 'Don't do it'. Lots of people – lots of people in this building, lots of people we talked to, lots of people in the know, lots of festival organizers. Dominic and I always had a feeling that there were particular idiosyncrasies about Shakespeare's Globe as a building that meant it could probably work in here in a way that it probably couldn't have somewhere else.

Originally there were ideas about maybe having ten productions, ten full productions, and then some workshop stuff, you know, maybe a concert of Armenian songs around *King Lear* for example. Mad things, like having all the toilet paper in the building printed with an Icelandic version of *All's Well That Ends Well*, or projecting the Cantonese characters of *Richard III* on the outside walls – making it more like a big installation in which all the plays were involved. We didn't really entertain that for very long. The prospect of 37 full productions felt like something that was just too mouth-watering not to do.

How did you decide which productions would feature in the Festival?

Quite early on in the process we had a breakfast here and we invited cultural attachés from all over London. We didn't ever want 37 of the national theatres. At all. But it just seemed like a good way of starting, to get everyone in the same room. It was a completely bizarre gathering, but what we did get were certain people coming up to us and making suggestions. In a festival like this you can find a million *Romeo and Juliet*s and a million *Hamlet*s, but finding a *Pericles* is very complicated, and at that breakfast, the Greek cultural attaché came up to me and said, 'I'd love our national theatre to be involved. It's a top, top company, and I know they're interested in dealing with the Shakespeare plays that are set in Greece or the Mediterranean.' So, suddenly, I had a meeting with the National Theatre of Greece's director, who was offering to produce either *Pericles* or *Troilus and Cressida*, which is suddenly a big win. So that was one way we started it.

Then we got the first tranche of LOCOG funding – that was really what gave us the resources to research. It would have been lovely to have done three years of research, and to have really travelled around, and talked to people, but that's pie in the sky, so we did it very quickly. We programmed the Festival in ten months. So we took off and watched stuff, watched Shakespeare plays that were happening all around the world, watched other companies whose work we'd been recommended by actors, directors, journalists, politicians, all sorts of people that we talked to. And some productions that we brought in were happening anyway – *Titus Andronicus* from Hong Kong is a good example. We saw work from other companies that were doing Shakespeare plays or Chekhov plays or whatever else; we then said, 'We love your work, but we've already got *Hamlet* in the Festival. Is there another Shakespeare play that floats your boat?'

How many countries do you think you visited on these scouting trips?

Between 20 to 25 and most of those led directly to invitations being issued. Because, you know, there wasn't that much money. I mean, there was only £500,000 from LOCOG, which sounds like a lot of money, but for a thing like this, it's not, at all. We don't get any Arts Council money here so there wasn't a huge amount of research funding or anything like that. All the capital we had was going into actually getting people here, buying people flights, putting people up, paying people fees to do their work. So we had a very small research budget in the end.

But we also wanted to cover the range of languages spoken in London and also what we called the 'Shakespeare languages', by which I mean Japanese and Georgian and other languages in which Shakespeare is being produced in huge amounts around the world but which might not be big languages in this country.

Did you consciously consult a linguistic map of London?

Yes, we got the stats – we pulled up all the stats from local authorities, and education departments, and had a real go at covering everything. We didn't cover Punjabi and that was the only major London language that was left out, and that was simply because we already had work in Bangla and Urdu, and Hindi and Gujarati.

FIGURE 5 All's Well That Ends Well *performed in Gujarati by Arpana theatre company (based in Mumbai) for the Globe to Globe Festival, 23–4 May 2012. Photograph by Ellie Kurttz and reproduced courtesy of Shakespeare's Globe.*

Once you'd explicitly identified those linguistic communities and then programmed for them, how did you set about making connections with them?

That was a big challenge, but great fun. We tried all sort of ways. We had what we called ambassadors within each community who really showed an early interest in the Festival, and who we invited over to eat with us a few times. They acted as liaisons within the community and tried to interest people. We went out, physically, onto the streets in Southall to try to invite people to the Hindi show. We found that there was a price-point that people would pay and we often dropped the prices down to a level that would attract them. We found that there were certain communities that will pay ten quid for a theatre show, full stop, and there were certain communities that will pay 180 quid for a theatre show – not that we charge that, but you know… What worked in the end was physically showing up, as a way of marketing. We found that you can put up as many posters as you want to, you can have this huge complicated digital campaign, and in the end, just a few weeks before the Festival, we went, 'Right, we're going to have a number of street teams and we're just going to show up and talk to people', and that's what we did, and that's what worked.

Are you a native Londoner? Did it change the way you saw London?

I'm not a Londoner, I'm from Newcastle, in the north, and I grew up watching the RSC in the back seats of the Newcastle Theatre Royal every year when they came. Globe to Globe completely changed the way I saw London. I mean, as a theatre-goer in London, whether you make theatre or not, it was so extraordinary to be sitting there watching *The Tempest* with three thousand people from Tower Hamlets because you realize this never happens. A lot of theatres sing out their audience development successes, and some with good reason, but I don't need to tell you, it's still a hugely white, middle-class world, and a lot of the specific linguistic and cultural communities in this city don't feel any kind of stake in the theatre as a whole. The risk is that it stops, that things like Globe to Globe happen and then it's back to square one, back to your normal audience, which would be a huge shame. 'Legacy' was the most overused word in the city last year, but it is a massive question, I think particularly about audiences. It's the one thing I feel really happy to boast about, because we were really, really overwhelmed by what happened with audiences, and yes, we dropped the price, but we didn't just say come for free, so people made a choice about how to spend their money and decided to come, which was great.

Globe to Globe, as a single entity, paid for itself in the end. It did break even, which was extraordinary considering the number of people who told us it would be a complete disaster.

So once it was happening, what was it like being here for the six weeks it was on?

Part of my job was to watch everything, so I did. The different things that went on in the theatre, not just on the stage, were absolutely fascinating. Watching the audiences took up a massive proportion of my time during the Festival. Not just those new communities, but watching how people from Tunbridge Wells were reacting to shows that were more close to the bone, like the politically charged shows such as *Richard II* or things like the Polish *Macbeth*.

On the subject of politically charged shows, how did the invitations to Ashtar Theatre (based in Ramallah, Palestine) and Habima (the National Theatre of Israel, based in Tel-Aviv) come about (an issue that generated considerable press coverage as well as some protests)?

The first thing is that theatre in that part of the world is extraordinarily good, and I really mean that part of the world; we could have invited work from Lebanon, easily, at that time we could even have invited works from Syria. We knew there were four or five theatres in Israel and four or five theatre companies in Palestine that we could work with. We knew there was going to be trouble, but the whole thing of Globe to Globe was 'let's jump in head first, let's go with it and see what kind of reaction it provokes', so we decided to have both an Israeli and a Palestinian show very early on. With the Palestinians, we talked to them about what kind of show would be interesting. *Richard II*, a show about regime change, was something we had discussed with the Afghan company early on, but they had made it clear they were just not interested and wanted to do *The Comedy of Errors* – which is fascinating in its own right. The Palestinians on the other hand said, 'Yes, let us tell our story about us through this play'.

As for *The Merchant of Venice*, we talked to the Habima, and the Gesher Theatre in Israel, and the Cameri Theatre, and a few other top theatres in Israel, but ended up with the Habima because they were in a position artistically and practically to do it at that time. In fact, they came to us with *The Merchant* as an idea. We didn't know at the time that Habima were touring into occupied territories. It is a condition of their funding from the Israeli government that they have to tour into the occupied settlements – which they shouldn't be doing, full stop – and we were then faced with a choice of whether to revoke the invitation and sort of censor them in a way, or to continue to discuss and allow that discussion to happen, and we decided to do the latter. Some people think that a cultural boycott is necessary, equally some people don't. There was a letter to the *Guardian* from a number of people who said that we should ban Habima, we should revoke the invitation, and then there was a letter from Howard Brenton saying, no, you can't really do that. So there were reactions on both sides, but we came down to that fact that people meeting and talking to each other is better than silence. It would have felt really, really odd, and not really part of what the Festival was about, to ban someone from coming, because of what their government was telling them to do. You know, there were things that were unreported at the time and there were things that were misreported at the time. The actor who played Bassanio in that show is an Arab actor, and there are people within that company who say, 'We don't want to tour to the West Bank', and they don't have to go, and their jobs are safe. So the company is slightly more enlightened than it was reported as being.

Did companies in the Festival ever query the inclusion of other companies?

Yes, a few companies asked us why we'd invited Habima. The Ashtar's Palestinian director came up to us and said, 'We don't like what the Habima do and we just want to register that'. We were terrified they would walk away but thankfully they didn't. But it's odd. On the Habima night there was a group of pro-Israeli demonstrators in an area sort of fenced off by police there and a group of pro-Palestinian/anti-Israeli demonstrators in an area down here, again sort of fenced off by police; it was the most extraordinary evening. This was towards the end of the Festival, and I realized we'd had the National Theatre of China doing *Richard III* at the beginning of the Festival and not one, not one person, queried it or protested. And if you're talking about human rights, if you're talking about companies who are funded by governments that we should disapprove of – it's extraordinary that there's that differential.

Was there much discussion about whether China should be involved or invited?

There was a bit, but again, it all emerged quite informally through individual artists rather than any great international diktat. We were introduced to a director called Wang Xiaoying, one of the directors at the National Theatre of China, which is why the National Theatre and his production of *Richard III* ended up coming. Just like the sports team of China wasn't banned from coming to the Olympics, you know, we didn't want to censor anyone out of the Festival.

Has the Festival influenced theatre practice here at the Globe? Are we right in thinking, for example, that this was the first time the Globe featured recorded music?

I think the Festival has and will have a massive influence on us, although probably not specifically in the use of recorded music – I think that it was lovely to experiment with it, but that it probably won't stay. But there are lots of other things that will. There was no single Globe to Globe aesthetic obviously, it was massively varied, but I've seen things, little bits and bobs being picked out, the way that people stand on stage, the way that people move around the stage, the way that people are made up or costumed; a certain kind of boldness that I think was shown in the Kenyan *Merry Wives of Windsor* and the Maori *Troilus and Cressida* and a few others, which was just about walking onto the stage and going, 'Here we are, like it or not, here we are', bof! I think we've become even bolder after seeing shows like that which come from a tradition of playing where you have to get people's attention first. It's a certain type of initial announcement of presence.

When was the decision made that Henry V *would be the Globe's offering, and that it would close the Festival?*

I think we were always going to do *Henry V* because we'd done *Henry IV, parts 1* and *2* the year before, so we had Jamie Parker who played Hal and most of that company, and then we were always going to do the *Henry VI* plays this year [2013]. So it was really a decision to do with practicality rather than making it the 'English show' – that just didn't come into it at all. I can understand why people would think that, given that play's odd but definitely existing relationship with a certain type of nationalism, or a certain type of nationalist discourse, but it wasn't like that at all.

Can you say something about the basic parameters in which the companies were asked to work?

Again they were practicalities to make the Festival happen, really, rather than points of ethos. So we abandoned quite a few of our normal ways of working. For example, like you said, we invited the companies to experiment a bit with the use of recorded music. But we did have to be firm about the length of the performance – which is a rule everyone broke – but we did say, 'Try and do it in two hours fifteen minutes', which was because we were having two different shows every day for six weeks. What else did we do? We said no English. At first we said no English and then the brilliant Hindi Company Theatre from Mumbai wrote to us and said, 'Yeah, the thing is, this is the way we speak' – that is, slipping freely between

Hindi and English. So we said okay and abandoned the hard-and-fast rule. Frustratingly, one book about the Festival said that we reinforced in the middle of the Festival run that we wanted people to speak English, which was the opposite of what we did: we clamped down hard at the beginning and then eased up, I suppose.

FIGURE 6 Cymbeline *performed in Juba Arabic by the South Sudan Theatre Company for the Globe to Globe Festival, 2–3 May 2012. Photograph by Ellie Kurttz and reproduced courtesy of Shakespeare's Globe.*

English was the language of the Q Brothers' adaptation of Othello, *even if officially that language was described as 'Hip-hop'. What kind of discussion led to this invitation?*

America was so difficult, because you want a show from America and we had no idea how to play it. We looked at Latino companies. I tried to find Native American work, but couldn't find it, it's just not really happening. There were various translations and small-scale projects, but no one's actually performing Shakespeare in Native American languages, which was a shame. We were interested in finding some kind of idiom from the States that would work, and looked at all sorts of things, and ended up watching the *Much Ado about Nothing* that those guys [the Q Brothers] did and we commissioned *Othello* from them on that basis, and really we had no idea what to expect. Lots of academics told me off beforehand about that show, which was slightly disconcerting because I thought what would follow was a serious critical backlash, but what followed were five stars left, right and centre. The reaction to the *Othello* was really, really interesting, because it was sort of *a priori*, a reaction before the show happened. There was a brilliant thing in the *Daily Mail*, in which a guy reviewed the show without watching it. He says, 'This is disgusting, dumbing down, et cetera et cetera', then, 'I must confess I've not seen the show'! And that was as much fun as anything else, seeing the way that people react to the idea of a show, without seeing the show.

In terms of language, one of the big decisions was the use of scene summaries rather than surtitles for every line. There must have been pragmatic reasons for that decision, but was it also to some extent philosophical?

Yes, we did get a bit philosophical about it. There were three options. One option is to surtitle every single line, translate every single line, into either Shakespearean English or modern English. Or you can do nothing at all. Or you can do what we did, which was a synopsis of each scene. It would have felt slightly elitist to do nothing: an assumption that people know the plot of *Pericles*, if they don't speak Greek, was a bit too much to assume. Then the idea of translating everything line-by-line had a practical consideration but also a sort of vaguely philosophical/practical consideration in that, in this theatre particularly if you've got 1,500 heads turning around every five seconds, it'd be bizarre, a bit of a disaster, like

Wimbledon centre court gone mad. We desperately wanted people to watch and listen to what was going on, even if they didn't understand the way that people were moving their bodies or what they were saying immediately. We wanted to find a way of making sure that people knew what was going on, knew the plot of *Pericles*, but also were listening to Greek, watching those actors move around on stage, and in the end, it became the only thing that we could possibly do. There are pros and cons to everything but that's how we ended up doing it.

How did you feel about the way Globe to Globe fitted into the wider landscape of the World Shakespeare Festival and Cultural Olympiad?

I think that the ambition of the project here was what people felt the extra investment was for. There was a feeling here that a lot of other artists were just sort of taking the money and doing what they would have done anyway, which I think is a valid criticism. And we did do something extraordinary, you know? It didn't end up having that much to do with the Olympics apart from the fact 500,000 quid came from the Olympics, but it wasn't a competition. It happened to be in 2012 and be funded because there was that tranche of funding, which was great, but otherwise it felt at the time and it still feels like a thing that happened on its own. It happened in that year because the money was there in that year, rather than being part of the Olympics.

Tracy Irish, RSC Education Programme Developer for the World Shakespeare Festival

Interview with Paul Prescott and Erin Sullivan in writing on 5 July 2013

How did you get involved with the Cultural Olympiad?

In September 2010 I was appointed as the Education Programme Developer for the World Shakespeare Festival, which was the Royal Shakespeare Company's contribution to the Cultural Olympiad. My remit was to explore where, how and why Shakespeare is taught around the world. I had been working at the RSC by then for four years as a project manager and practitioner, following previous experience in international education, and as I also have a particular interest in how Shakespeare's language works across different cultures, the Cultural Olympiad provided a great opportunity.

What did the RSC's education programme involve?

The first stage was initial fact-finding and for this we sent out a questionnaire to British Council Offices around the world. Officials were asked to consult with education experts in their country in order to provide responses to questions concerning where, if at all, Shakespeare appeared on their curriculum and why. Forty-three surveys were returned from a wide geographical spread of countries, which between them accounted for two-thirds of the population of under-18-year-olds. From the information on those returns, came the headline claim from the RSC that '50 per cent of the world's school children study Shakespeare'. Those initial findings indicated Shakespeare as the world's most widely prescribed author. In many English-speaking and European countries, there is compulsory study of at least one play. Other countries may look at excerpts or abridged versions and more introduce Shakespeare as a significant historical figure. Where survey responses had given useful contacts in their region, we were able to follow up and we set up a 'Wiki Shakespeare' on the WSF website to record information and find out more, encouraging teachers and students to contribute to a community database. This all helped to confirm and expand our original information. Although the wiki proved difficult to navigate, it did record information at varying levels of detail on 65 countries, and was testament to a widespread familiarity with Shakespeare across formal and informal education contexts.

The second stage was to delve deeper and create a number of case studies. In order to do this we set up a special WSF project with the support of the British Council's Connecting Classrooms programme and the RSC's Learning and Performance Network (LPN). A student, teacher and teaching artist from each of Hong Kong, Kolkata (India), Los Angeles and Limpopo (South Africa) first came together with two students and teachers from each of four LPN schools in September 2011, in Stratford-upon-Avon. After that the overseas partners visited their UK partner schools, and over the following year the partner schools exchanged films, resources and 'culture boxes' to help them understand each other's cultures better. A core group from each school also followed the WSF: Shakespeare Challenge Bronze Arts Award with a total of 103 gaining their certificate. Most schools included a performance as part of the project, digitally sharing their plans and rehearsals. During the spring of 2012, I visited the four countries involved in this project, guided by the passionate and generous teachers. In addition I worked with the British Council on separate projects in Brazil, Oman and the Czech Republic, visiting each of those countries in late 2011. On each trip, I went to schools, talked with students and educationalists and led workshops.

The final stage was the 'Worlds Together' conference at the Tate Modern in London in early September 2012. This international education conference was a project conceived between Tate and the RSC with further support from the National Theatre and the British Museum; the shared aim was to explore the place of the arts in young people's learning. The RSC led a Shakespeare strand within the broader arts education agenda, effectively placing Shakespeare as the world's best-known artist, and inviting teachers, practitioners, academics and young people into a dialogue about how and why we teach him. It included a performance of *King Lear* by our International Youth Ensemble, which was made up of the students we had worked with from around the world.

What was the RSC's educational mission at the time of the Cultural Olympiad?

The company's guiding principles were 'to connect with Shakespeare, be defined by ensemble and be engaged with the world'. Michael Boyd, our Artistic Director from 2002–12, developed his ensemble principles during his work with the 2007–8 Histories company. He drew up what he called 'a set of behaviours' to create the 'conditions for creativity and community', which include cooperation, trust, empathy, imagination and rigour. The application of those ensemble principles to education can be seen in the RSC's manifesto for schools, 'Stand up for Shakespeare', which was published in 2008. It states, 'The best classroom experience we can offer is one which allows young people to approach a Shakespeare play as actors do – as an ensemble, using active, exploratory, problem-solving methods to develop a greater understanding and enjoyment of the plays'. Our practice was about the fundamental value of Shakespeare's extraordinary language and the added value this language in the form of a play-text brings to make us think about ourselves, each other and the world around us. Michael often spoke of Shakespeare as a 'Trojan horse' for knowledge.

What opportunities did the Olympic year offer for the company's existing work?

The Cultural Olympiad helped us to see Shakespeare's value in a global literary heritage. Again and again working with young people from very different cultural contexts, I found they were drawn to the complexity of the text because in that complexity, which was always odd and foreign even for a first-language speaker of English, there was also a familiarity of experience to be discovered through working together. There were always words – but not always the same words – that expressed their own feelings and thoughts despite differences of culture and geography. Michael described theatre as less substantial than an ice sculpture, something that really only exists in a moment of trust between actors and audience – 'A collective encounter hanging in the air'. I think it's that collective encounter, those moments of trust, that drama education is about. Moments where pupils are fully engaged, sharing the physical and mental space where learning is happening and knowledge is built, which in some often intangible way adds up to more than just the skills and information each pupil individually takes forward into their exams.

How did the context of the Cultural Olympiad inform your educational work during the project?

I think what delighted people most about the whole Olympic project was the sense of coming together and celebrating who we are alongside the rest of the world. RSC educational pedagogy is based in this concept of sharing spaces and voices and the Cultural Olympiad allowed us to test our ideas on a much bigger platform. Our two education 'festival' events, *I, Cinna* and the 'Worlds Together' conference, both brought a sense of shared community in the immediacy of making, watching, doing and discussing with others, all with the added frisson of being part of the even bigger collective experience of the Olympic summer. On a very practical level, the funding from LOCOG allowed us to reach out more widely than normal. This meant I could visit other countries to talk, listen and lead workshops, to share their spaces and find out what Shakespeare means for their young people, and it meant we could invite some of those young people and their teachers to come and share our spaces. It meant we could fund students to take the Arts Award, and run a highly subsidised conference to explore what it might all add up to.

What did you learn about how Shakespeare is studied in other countries?

The predominant mode of study in schools around the world remains transmissive, desk-bound analysis of text, where teachers convey knowledge to students which is repackaged for written exams. Whatever education initiatives emerge, ultimately students are judged on their ability to pass tests and there has been a lot of discussion in this country about our place on international education score cards like PISA (Programme for International Student Assessment) and how we can improve our education systems in order to 'win the global race'. I visited Hong Kong, one of the countries that regularly achieves highly on the score cards, and was struck by their hunger for more arts education and their envy of the UK in this regard. The teachers I spoke to knew their students were good at exams and wanted to stretch them further, recognizing that a good arts education could do that. Students around the world typically encounter Shakespeare in their own first language but as competency in English is becoming increasingly important, there seems to be an accompanying aspirational value to learning Shakespeare in English, often as a performance text. Maybe a boost in drama approaches to Shakespeare in those high-achieving countries might make policymakers think twice about discouraging curriculum drama here.

You also mentioned I, Cinna *schools broadcast. Can you tell us more about that?*

I, Cinna was a very new venture. It was a production targeted at young people which ran alongside Gregory Doran's main house 'African' production of *Julius Caesar*. Written and directed by Tim Crouch and starring Jude Owusu, who also played Cinna the poet in the main house production, the format followed the series of 'I' shows created by Tim where we experience a Shakespeare play through the eyes of a relatively minor character. Although conjuring a parallel world, complementary to Greg's African-styled production, *I, Cinna* was written and designed to stand alone with a contemporary set which could be anywhere in the world. In Tim's play, Cinna the poet, like most of us, watches history unfold at a distance, not knowing what to do or think; however, this particular history is happening right outside his own front door. The fact that the footage on Cinna's TV was recognizably footage of the UK riots from the summer of 2011 brought the experience closer and many young people commented on how the production gave them a window into a different world, but one not too far away [for additional discussion of the 2011 riots see Prescott, Hampton-Reeves, Hansen and Smialkowska's chapters in this volume]. In the production, Cinna encourages the audience to write on the blank spaces in their programmes in order to understand the big issues being played out around us all, leading us towards writing a poem of our own. It was a different kind of concept to the previous Young People's Shakespeare productions, requiring (not just inviting) the audience to enter into a dialogic relationship.

This production was also broadcast digitally. What was that like?

Yes, in addition to many live performances for schools, we also undertook a pilot broadcast *I, Cinna* over the web in

July 2012, when it was watched by 15,000 young people in schools across the country. The practicalities both of making and transmitting the film as a live event were carried out mainly by students from Ravensbourne College of Design and Communication in London. There were inevitably a few technical glitches but this seemed to add to the festivity of the occasion – something too smooth may not have given the same sense of 'being there', and being part of something was what many students on both sides of the camera valued. In the Warwickshire comprehensive where I watched with a class of Year 8 students, they knew only an outline of the story of *Julius Caesar* and didn't really understand who Cinna was or why he died, but their curiosity was piqued. At their best, both theatre and education are not about explication of every detail, but about making us think and question. For thousands of young people, *I, Cinna*, live or via webcast, did exactly that. It also made us think more about the possibilities of digital resources for reaching out to a wider and global audience whilst keeping that important sense of shared spaces and voices.

FIGURE 7 *Filming* I, Cinna. *Photograph by Rebecca Carter and reproduced courtesy of the RSC.*

What, for you, were the most memorable or revelatory moments of the project?

There were some fascinating snippets of information that came up through the initial survey that really made me want to know more. One was the inclusion of the trial scene from *The Merchant of Venice* on the Chinese national curriculum. Another was the inclusion of a page on Shakespeare in the standard English textbook studied by every Sudanese child at secondary school. The British Council office sent me a scanned copy of that page. It is a traditional comprehension exercise about Shakespeare's life and work with an assertion that he is 'the world's greatest dramatist'. The most interesting thing about the passage for me was the last line which asks: 'Was he really Shakespeare or Sheikh el-Zubier?'. Like many children around the world, Sudanese children may not study a Shakespeare play in any depth, but they learn who he is, and what is more, they learn that he can be thought of as one of their own. Perhaps that will encourage them to ask questions and one day find out more.

I also found the malleability of the text to so many different cultures quite astonishing. The first overseas visit I made was to Oman to spend a week, with a colleague, training local teachers in practical approaches to Shakespeare. Few had used Shakespeare at all with their students and our pedagogical approaches were very new for them. Obvious cultural differences made the situation uncomfortable and confusing at times for all of us, and we had the added distance of working through a translator. However, that made the journey towards their enthusiastic embrace of the work all the more rewarding and certainly opened my eyes to different perspectives and interpretations of the plays we explored. From Oman, I went straight to Brazil and the cultural contrast could not have been greater; I was exchanging polite reserve, gender divides and circumspection around physical contact for tactile exuberance. But once again, Shakespeare's words, albeit in translation, provided a rich meeting ground for intercultural understanding. Working with young people and hearing what connections they made to the text was constantly revelatory. A group of Indian teenagers told me how they had once stayed up all night debating why Banquo is not seduced by the witches like Macbeth. They said they loved how Shakespeare made them 'think and think harder'. Czech students loved playing with the sounds of the language. South Africans recognized the Zulu sense of *ubuntu*, our interconnectedness as human beings, and one student told me, 'He must have come and lived here for a while, because I could relate to so many things'. An American student said he had thought Shakespeare difficult and boring but had now come to see him as like his favourite Aunty, who is old and wise and has a story to tell for every occasion.

Some of those students were part of the International Youth Ensemble you mentioned earlier. Can you tell us more about that?

Yes, that was the most revelatory experience of all. I was working with director Aileen Gonsalves in Oman when we first had that idea. The Omani teachers and students shared an instinctive ability to use the language unselfconsciously and clearly tell a story, and after being so moved by the acting of the Omani young people the idea of an International Youth Ensemble (IYE) suddenly seemed obvious – if the 'Worlds Together' conference was to explore why Shakespeare matters in the lives of young people around the world, we needed a group of young people to tell us.

From all the countries I'd visited, we brought together 19 students speaking at least ten languages between them. Their task, over two days, was to work with Aileen and movement director, Lucy Cullingford, to create a 15-minute version of *King Lear* for the conference delegates. In our discussions, Aileen and I had chosen *Lear* because of the words about what makes us human in the storm scenes. Is unaccommodated man no more than this? What do we all share once we have torn off the lendings? Aileen stripped it down to breath – how we use breath to create language and through language we create ideas, hopes, stories, culture. We asked the students to bring images of poverty and wealth from their own countries which provoked deep discussion. Aileen used the thoughts, skills and voices of the young people so that the final piece was a cultural mash-up and their authentic response, including Shakespeare's words in Arabic, Czech, Mandarin, Hindi, Spanish and Zulu. We gave an additional piece of homework to Tray, our talented student from South Central, Los Angeles, and bringing his own connotations to the text he playfully used his words mixed with Shakespeare's to write a performance poem which created the storm raging within and around a modern Lear.

For the young people who formed the IYE, it was of course a seminal moment in their lives. Their sheer joy in working together was beautiful; their joy in working with Shakespeare was palpable and they achieved as part of something bigger.

FIGURE 8 *The International Youth Ensemble in rehearsal. Photograph by Lucy Hearn and reproduced courtesy of the RSC.*

They loved the complexity of the issues they were asked to grapple with and they loved the language they were given as tools in that struggle. They all spoke of finding a common language through Shakespeare.

How was education discussed in the national and political arena during the project period?

In the UK, the Cultural Learning Alliance continues to question the exclusion of an arts subject from the English Baccalaureate (subjects deemed vital for our children's success). Shakespeare, of course, is not under threat. His position as the only compulsory author on the National Curriculum for schools in England has been assured since its introduction in 1988, and despite provocative questions occasionally raised in the media, neither teachers nor policymakers show any appetite to change that. However, while few question that all our young people should study Shakespeare at school, there is still plenty of debate over why and how they should study him – and that debate is far from exclusive to the UK. Our 'Worlds Together' conference was, I think, unique in bringing together an international audience focused on the role of the arts in education with Shakespeare at its centre, and many people commented on how this in itself shifted their perceptions – placing Shakespeare as an artist of international renown as well as an icon of English Literature.

You mentioned the '50 pers cent statistic' earlier. How did you feel about the way that was picked up by the media and in political discussion?

Of all of the work we did, newspapers and politicians were most interested in the headline statement that '50 per cent of the world's schoolchildren study Shakespeare'. I never felt entirely comfortable with it, particularly when I heard it in the mouth of the Secretary of State for Education when he missed out the word 'school'. There are of course a number of qualifications to the claim. First, there are still many areas of the world where children do not go to school beyond the age of 14, 11 or sometimes at all, and Shakespeare is less likely to be studied below secondary level. Although we tried to take account of this in the statistics, 'children who manage to get to high school' becomes invisibly implicit. Secondly, the research relied on the integrity of the official completing the form, with follow-ups and checks only taking place with those countries used for closer study. Thirdly, the word 'study' covers a wide range of engagement, from knowing a few facts about Shakespeare's life to detailed analysis of several plays. What actually intrigued me most about the 50 per cent claim was how few people questioned it. It seemed to fit with a general world view held by many that of course young people across the world are studying Shakespeare; why wouldn't they? I was surprised and delighted by the level of international engagement I found but fascinated by the cultural influences behind that engagement. [For further discussion of this statistic and its use in politics and the media, see Prescott's chapter.]

What do you think will be the legacy of the WSF education project for the RSC?

A clear legacy is greater engagement with digital resources. 'Teaching Shakespeare' (www.teachingshakespeare.ac.uk) is an online resource that we developed during 2012 and a gateway to further study that is now available to teachers anywhere in the world. And building on the pilot broadcast of *I, Cinna*, the RSC has launched a schools broadcast series, starting with *Richard II* in November 2013. Potentially this will allow a global audience of young people to share spaces and voices across the ether.

Another legacy is the connections that were made through 'Worlds Together'. 'Sharing' was an oft-used word in the conference feedback. One delegate wrote, 'In my 26 years in education, I have never attended a conference where so much knowledge and experience was shared between attendees'. Another wrote, 'There was a spirit of sharing; you never felt that your opinion didn't matter'. Another talked of the international sharing as something that 'informs, stimulates and inspires our practice by opening minds to other ways of approaching Shakespeare study'. There was a strong sense that the international dialogue was a major strength of the conference and a major part of this was the symposium, which, aside from the International Youth Ensemble, was the event at the conference closest to my own heart. The symposium was set up as a 'marketplace' environment in the newly opened main Tank at the Tate Modern. Delegates chose four 20-minute presentations to attend from a choice of 34 presentations spanning 14 countries, and had time to share and discuss what they heard with their randomly assigned home groups. An example of the value of that dialogue would be the practitioner from Kolkata who told me of her moment of clarity listening to a practitioner from Australia describe Bell Shakespeare's work with Aboriginal communities and realizing how much they shared working through Shakespeare with 'hard to reach' groups. I hope the RSC can continue to fuel that kind of dialogue and support teachers, theatre artists and other educationalists around the world in giving young people the most valuable experience of Shakespeare.

4

States of the Nations: *Henry VI*, the London Olympics and the Spectacular City

Stuart Hampton-Reeves

Pico Iyer argues that the Olympics are an uncritical throwback to redundant notions of national culture: 'they affirm affiliation to nation-states in an age that has largely left them behind', he writes, 'mass-producing images of nationalism and universalism without much troubling to distinguish between them'.[1] Iyer could also have been writing about Shakespeare, or at least a view of Shakespeare that it is readily available particularly in the history play cycles that have, for some time, been classical theatre's way of making grand statements about the nation.[2] The intersections between these two forms of representing national culture were made manifest in the Opening and Closing Ceremonies at the London Olympics in 2012. Lines from *The Tempest* connected both, and provided a theme for the Opening Ceremony, which was directed by

Danny Boyle. In the Opening Ceremony, they were spoken by Kenneth Branagh, dressed as Brunel. This connected Shakespeare with the spirit of progress, of technology and industrialization. The Closing Ceremony, directed by Kim Gavin, included the same lines, this time delivered by Timothy Spall, dressed as Churchill, emerging from a miniature Big Ben and facing a stadium that had been transformed into a giant Union Jack. Now Shakespeare was connected with a different version of national culture, one defined by defiance against foreign invaders. The two performances exemplified the main themes of the London Olympics: an assertion of Britain's role in creating the modern world combined with a chauvinistic spirit of defiance in a world in which Britain's influence has long been eclipsed by other nations.

Shakespeare's own epic representation of the nation was an absent presence. Indeed, Boyle's vision of British history began after Shakespeare's era with Shakespeare present only in his words. The history plays were staged that year as part of the Cultural Olympiad, a parallel event that inflated the Olympics from being a sporting event into a widespread cultural engagement with what it means to be British in a modern, globalized world. The plays were staged as part of Globe to Globe, which invited companies from around the world to perform two-hour versions of each play in their own language at Shakespeare's Globe. It was almost as if performing Shakespeare had become an Olympic sport, with each company representing their own country. The dramatization of English history in this context was always going to be a fascinating opportunity to explore the critical tension between different national histories. The Globe reserved *Henry V* for itself and placed it at the end of the Festival as a kind of closing ceremony. But that play ends by invoking the civil wars of the *Henry VI* plays, in which any sense of nationhood is broken apart by a progressively violent civil war. The Globe invited companies from Balkan countries to perform the *Henry VI* plays and presented them as a Balkan trilogy, although all three companies involved worked independently on their assigned play. The performance of one of England's bloodiest civil wars amid the celebrations of London 2012, by companies representing countries involved in the most recent European civil war, will be the focus of this chapter.

Iyer is right to be suspicious about the role that the Olympics play in articulating national culture. The sense of national competitiveness that the ceremonies harnessed has been a part of the Olympics since the Berlin Games of 1936, under the auspices of the Nazis.[3] Cultural performance had been an important part of the modern Olympics since their inception at the end of the nineteenth century. Indeed, in its original formation, the 'Cultural Olympiad' (as it came to be known much later on) was a competitive strand of the Olympics, with medals awarded to the best performers.[4] Pierre de Coubertin, the founder of the modern Olympics, achieved his only Olympic medal not for running, throwing or athletics, but for poetry, and artists were still receiving medals until the 1948 London Olympics.[5] Until 1936, the Opening Ceremony had been little more than a flag march for each national team.[6] Although this did occasionally cause friction between nations jostling for position in the march, it hardly figured as a spectacle with any more meaning to it than a ceremonial opening to an international sporting event. Only with the Nazis was the spectacle of the Games elevated to a level of national importance.[7]

Under Hitler, the Opening Ceremony was a spectacle that was overtly political. He had already appropriated the Olympic salute for his own party – the outstretched arm, now and forever a symbol of fascism, was until the 1930s known as the Olympic salute. Hitler received the spectacle like a general at a military parade. Each team promenaded past him and as they did so, turned and gave the Olympic salute. All the nations of the world stretched their arms out, the Olympic salute vanishing forever into the Nazi salute as they did so (footage of the event is easily available on video websites such as YouTube). The ambiguity was surely deliberate: the whole world, as represented within the stadium, saluting the

Führer like true Nazis. Hitler added other innovations to the Opening Ceremony, most notably the lighting of the cauldron, a spectacle that displaced the flag parade as the focus of the event.[8] This remains an essential part of the Olympic Opening Ceremony and was the climax of the 2012 Opening Ceremony. The idea that the Olympics could be a spectacle through which the achievements and supremacy of the host nation could be articulated began in Berlin. These Games also acknowledged an audience beyond the stadium. The Opening Ceremony was filmed and broadcast in newsreels across the world. The Olympics were televised live for the first time: not to people's homes, but to specially erected tents where the general public could go to watch the Games in over 20 viewing halls and see for themselves how other nations subordinated themselves to the Nazis.[9]

The evolution of the Opening and Closing Ceremonies of the Olympics, together with the parallel rise of the Cultural Olympiad as a side-show of cultural events, has been marked with a persistent and deepening sense that it is through such spectacle that the host nation not only celebrates itself, but out-does all previous national events.[10] Over the last 70 years, the ceremonies have become less and less about the ceremonial entrance of the teams and more about the theatrical spectacle that precedes and in many ways upstages the parade. What began as decoration for the actual ceremonies now dominates the event and each subsequent ceremony is judged against its predecessors. This has led to an exponential growth in the length, lavishness and complexity of this articulation of national culture. The 2012 Opening Ceremony eclipsed all other associated cultural events in terms of spectacle and audience, costing £27 million to stage.[11] This compared to £52 million for the London 2012 Festival, which formed the climax of the four-year Cultural Olympiad – in other words, one-third of the expenditure on cultural events related to the Olympics that summer went on one performance.[12]

Boyle's production was part of a series of performances across London that summer that collectively turned the city into an international spectacle. Although they were not artistically co-ordinated events (in the sense that a single vision informed them all), they were nevertheless part of a theatricalization of the city through which the ideals of the Olympics were married to a sense of national triumphalism. In his study of violence and performance in urban Bolivia, Daniel M. Goldstein argues that any kind of performance in a city takes 'place in relation to all other performances [...] and must be understood in terms of the "generic context" of their performance'.[13] Goldstein looks at different city acts, including spontaneous lynch mobs and street parades, and approaches both as performances which relate to and speak to each other, in different ways constituting what he calls the 'spectacular city' in which both authority and political resistance are incorporated into the overall field of performance, each reading and being read by the other. Goldstein draws on what Don Handelman (who has written one of the definitive studies of the anthropology of public events) calls the 'logic of meta-design' of civic spectacles to 'see past the graphic visual imagery' and explore instead the underlying political logic that both binds and divides them.[14] In other words, it is possible to explore the critical tension between different acts of performance. In this case, I propose to read the Globe's Balkan trilogy against the 2012 Opening Ceremony to see how the performance of civil war contributed to and undermined the representation of nation. Boyle avoided pandering to an overly simplistic representation of nationhood. His 'Isles of Wonder' included shades of darkness and light, and took a critical risk in celebrating the British people and its institutions rather than focusing on great historic figures. Yet Britain's own history of civil war was nowhere addressed: history began with a rural idyll and was then transformed into iron and coal. History was about progress, and the Ceremony included itself as the endpoint of that progress.

I will explore the 'spectacular city' of the London Olympics through three Shakespearean productions of the *Henry VI* plays staged in the run-up to the Olympics in the wider context of the Olympics as a meta-event which articulated concepts of national and global culture. My argument is that these productions can be read by these concepts, but they in turn offer the possibility of a retrospective critique of them. The *Henry VI* plays tell a very different story about England from the one eventually performed in the Olympic Stadium. They dramatize the English civil wars of the fifteenth century, starting with the crumbling of Henry V's empire. In *Part One*, the French territories are contested and held at a terrible price, only to be bargained away at the opening of *Part Two*. From then on, England itself atrophies, falling first into an anarchic popular uprising, and then into civil war, the full horror of which is explored in the extraordinary, unflinching *Part Three*. That play concludes with Richard Gloucester speaking to the audience, having killed King Henry, denying his family and snarling, 'I am myself alone' (5.6.83). Together, the plays stage a shocking collapse of the social and political fabric of national identity.[15]

Pitched within the wider narratives of historical reconciliation exemplified by Boyle's Opening Ceremony, the *Henry VI* plays would have sounded a discordant note however produced. But to add to the cultural complexity, the Globe appointed three Balkan national theatres (from Serbia, Albania and Macedonia) and staged all three over a weekend in May as the 'Balkan trilogy'. The Globe's publicity was focused on the superficial similarity between the civil wars in the plays and the conflicts that erupted across the Balkans following the collapse of Yugoslavia in the 1990s. The Globe website headed each production with an image from the Balkan wars of the 1990s. However, of the three nations represented, only Serbia was materially involved in those wars. Macedonia's secession was peaceful, its struggle for national identity more affected by its difficult relationship with Greece than with its former compatriots. Albania's own modern history has more to do with its concern for Albanian refugees from the Kosovo crisis. Bosnia, the country which in many ways was the contested centre ground of that conflict, was not represented, so the trilogy could never really lay claim to being a theatrical form of reconciliation.[16] Instead, the three productions allowed the national theatres to explore, in different ways, their countries' emergence as nation states in the last 20 years. The Serbian director Nikita Milivojevic told the magazine *Balkan Insight*, 'I like the name Balkan trilogy, because this Henry has something in common with Balkan history' but, he added, 'I see this as a good marketing move'.[17] The three productions were not planned together, nor were they rehearsed together: each pursued an independent path of artistic development. Although they were played together over a weekend, with each production being performed twice, the 'Balkan trilogy' was an illusion, an enabling fiction. Performed to a largely empty Globe theatre in the performances I experienced, they may have been among the least-watched events of the Olympics, yet the stories they brought into the compass of the meta-design of the Olympics – of England's civil wars, of the Balkans' own recent history – challenged the concept of the nation state as the guarantor of peace. I will analyse how the productions foreshadowed and called into question the representation of nation in the Opening Ceremony; I will also explore their resonance with other performance events, both intended and spontaneous, that collectively told the story of the Olympics in London and co-created the 'spectacular city'.

Ashes

The production of *Part One* was in many respects the most problematic engagement with the notion of reconciliation which the Balkan Henries invoked, if for no other reason than it was produced by the National Theatre of Serbia, the country which had been the aggressor in the Bosnian wars. The production coincided with another global spectacle, the trial of the Serbian General Ratko Mladic at the International Tribunal at The Hague, where he faced 11 charges of war crimes and crimes against humanity. The trial began on 17 May, only a few days after Milivojevic's production closed at the Globe – and reports from that trial, together with that of Radovan Karadzic, were a latent reminder all through the Olympic summer of the dark side of virulent nationalism.[18] As Bosnia was not one of the three Balkan countries taking part in the Festival, the opportunity to see this *Henry VI* as either a memory of or an opportunity to explore national guilt was elided. Bosnia was an absent presence which haunted the production. The play offers ample material for an exploration of a concept of national identity which is founded on, and founders on, acts of invasion, occupation and eventual defeat. However, Milivojevic cut virtually all of the play's battle scenes, telling reporters that he wanted to focus on the politics of the play.[19] Bringing Serbian actors to play soldiers may have been too difficult a proposition for Olympic London, but nevertheless the memory of that war haunted the production, unsettling and dislocating the triumphant nationalism of the Games' Opening Ceremony for those few who saw it. The closest the production came to invoking the wars directly was in an unusually unsympathetic portrayal of Talbot. Robbed of his main battle scenes, including his death, and with young Talbot and the Countess of Auvergne also cut, Talbot's story was reduced to that of a swaggering soldier, defeated and emasculated by Joan. He looked a relic when he faced Henry's parliament, an old soldier representing a bankrupt order.

Milivojevic also explored the idea of civil war in more subtle ways. The production revolved around a large round table which could be dismantled into several pieces and reassembled to create different divisions of stage space. It was a set: scenes were played on the table. It enabled a sense of the subterranean: scenes were played under the table. Joan was tried on the table and she disappeared beneath it for her execution. The table was a battlefield, a space to be fought over. It was repeatedly dismantled, reconfigured, contested – representing in turn unity and division, wholeness and fragmentation, with every coming together of the table leading to difference and bitter division. In this way, the space of the Globe was itself subverted – the Globe was simply the platform that the table, acting as both stage and set, occupied. But it was also a powerful metaphor for the faultlines in the very concept of national culture, a reminder of the cracks and divisions in the concept of Olympic nationalist idealism.

The table was inadvertently remembered in Boyle's Opening Ceremony with the Olympic cauldron, which was composed of 204 'petals', each one representing one of the competing nations – among them Serbia and Bosnia – and each one lit simultaneously, but separately, before they were brought together in one spectacular image of fire. It was a brilliant *coup de théâtre*, a perfect emblem of the theme of international cooperation that the Olympics set out both to perform and enact. *Part One* displaced this Olympic vision of national harmony with its own opening and closing ceremonies. It opened with most of the cast spread inert across the table, with only Beaufort on the stage itself. He walked round the table, speaking the first lines of the play in Serbian (the language of the entire performance); as he did so, the actors stirred to life, became their characters, felt their way onto the stage and took their seats. Yet this was not a rebirth but a funeral – two messengers, who became recurrent comic characters, brought on a small silver urn and placed it on a throne at the back of the stage. The urn contained Henry V's ashes and stayed onstage for much of the production as a continual reminder of a ruined history. Milivojevic added a closing ceremony too. After the nobles had exited the stage, the same two clowns tidied up after them and started to pretend to be them, anointing each other with imagined crowns. One brought Henry's urn onto a chair but, in playing with it, he accidentally knocked the urn onto the stage, sending the ashes everywhere. This surprising moment of irreverence re-read everything that had gone before: the dead body, memorialized and contained, and the image of the King which oppressed Henry VI and overshadowed the loss of empire, were revealed to be nothing more than dust. The clowns ran round the stage, trying to gather the ashes back up again, but the attempt was futile and they ended up sneezing all over the dead King. Checking no one was watching, they kicked the ashes under the table, returned the urn to its place, wiped it carefully to remove all the ashes, put their cowls back on and sneaked off stage. This closing ceremony returned us to the production's opening ceremony, but at the same time reworked it. Where that was solemn and formal, this was comic and irreverent; the restoration of authority at the end, emptied of its body, also meant that Henry V, as symbol of national history, national culture, was literally and figuratively empty – the legacy that the English will fight over in the coming plays was revealed to be nothing more than an empty box.

Walls

The representation of nation in 2012 contrasted directly with a moment of anxiety about the state of the nation the previous year, when riots and looting across the UK had dominated newspaper headlines.[20] Boyle's Opening Ceremony wowed the British media into a state of forgetfulness, replacing narratives of anxiety with hope. One of the ways in which Boyle made an impact was through the huge number of participants in the spectacle – there were 15,000 people involved in the performance, more than three times as many people as were arrested during the 2011 riots.[21] The performance continually emphasized a spirit of inclusion – but the story of the London Olympics as a physical place begins with a story of exclusion.

During the building of the Olympic stadium, the construction site was hidden by a ten-foot-high, 11-mile-long blue fence, made out of 15,000 plywood panels, which appeared in 2007 in Hackney and Stratford East and was erected by the Olympic Delivery Authority (ODA). The enclosure, which one reporter described as a 'city within a city', was achieved by removing allotments, a travellers' encampment, some long-established artists' studios and several local businesses.[22] Political blogger Philip Comerford compared the fence – and its successor, a wire and steel fence – to a modern form of enclosure, removing access by local communities to what was previously free and open land.[23] In its first incarnation, the Olympic site was an act of enclosure that literally displaced local communities and transformed a free area with its own histories and memories into a secure and secret area with a patrolled perimeter.

This inevitably attracted local graffiti artists. One piece of graffiti 'showed the rings of the traditional Olympic logo hanging from a gallows' while another 'showed pounds and euros and dollars pouring into a black hole marked "OLYMPIC DEATH PIT"'.[24] The ODA employed a team of people whose job it was regularly to patrol the fence on a quad bike. They had with them blue paint and whenever they found graffiti, they sprayed over it, restoring the fence's blank colour. The graffiti artists got their own back when the fence was decorated with official sponsor logos and artwork from local schools – the graffiti artists covered them with blue paint.[25] An arts group called the Office of Subversive Architecture, in response to aggressive security around the fence, constructed a set of blue stairs in protest against 'the secrecy surrounding preparations for the games' – it was removed by security after two days.[26]

Part Two is at least in part about the politics of enclosure – both of barriers which need to be guarded, and the disenfranchisement of ordinary people by the aggressive annexing of land. In the National Theatre of Albania's production, directed by Adonis Filipi, blue, red and gold costumes unintentionally called to mind the Olympic wall, but it was in the staging of the Cade rebellion scenes in particular that the politics of the wall and the politics of national uprising coincided. The rebels mixed with the audience, blurring the barrier between stage and spectator, and in the space of an act mocked and subverted the nobility. The scene started percussively, a drum beat marking a sudden change in pace. Cade addressed his first public speech to the audience, including them in his popular uprising. In the play, each of Cade's lines is undercut by an aside from another character exposing his fraudulent claims, but this production deleted those lines. Cade was surprisingly sincere, a maverick but still a political hero rather than the psychopath he is often depicted as in modern British productions of the play. When taking London, he bowed to the real London audience; at one point, alone on stage, he sat at the front and talked to the audience in soliloquy. As Cade led his rabble, they followed him in a strange disjointed dance, processing in a line across the back of the stage, their movements scored by eastern European folk music. One of the rebels, a young blind girl who found her way round the stage with a white stick, was introduced to add a counter-narrative to Cade's confident swagger. She tried to join in, but was frequently pushed aside, left to fend for herself, walking off in the wrong direction, looking more and more frightened and dishevelled as the rebellion unfolded.[27] This strange procession adumbrated, but also appropriated, the parade of athletes in the Opening Ceremony. This performance of disorderliness brought out the dissonance suppressed in the ideal of national and international harmony in Olympic ideology. The rabble dislocated and deformed the Olympic ideal, distorting the enclosure of the Globe through their disjointed parade. But when the blue wall in East London came down, a new wall went up, made of steel and wire, patrolled remotely through CCTV cameras that kept a constant surveillance on the Olympic perimeter.

For many artists who engaged with the Olympics in the early days of its construction, the impulse was first of all to resist the enclosure and secondly to recapture the community histories that risked being forgotten, lost. When the blue fence was dismantled (to make way for a steel wall), it was literally recycled in a number of arts projects. The fence became a form of history play with Immediate Theatre's Big Blue Fence Project, which produced an installation based on a replica of the fence containing, in boxes, local histories embedded in the form of objects, images and oral histories.[28] A student-run group Studiosuperniche has made a boat-house, a ping-pong table and a bird-watching post from them.[29]

The National Theatre of Albania enacted its own form of reclamation with its own opening ceremony. Four actors wearing paper crowns entered on scooters and encircled the stage in a bizarre parade that seemed to lay an Albanian claim to the stage of a British history play. If Cade's uprising failed, Albania's own intervention succeeded. Whereas the Serbians occupied the Globe, the Albanians possessed it, took it as their space, traversed it in a way which mocked and claimed the stage of English history for itself. Albania has its own recent history, its own story to tell – not about the Balkan wars of the 1990s, but of the persecution of ethnic Albanians in other Balkan countries, most famously Kosovo. The most powerful image of history in the production was the blind girl who followed Cade – bewildered, lost, angry, feeling her way through the darkness.

Flags

The contestation between national culture and the Olympics took a different form in the National Theatre of Bitola's *Part Three*. The production was by a Macedonian theatre company, although it was ghosted by an earlier American production directed by John Blondell, an American who was brought in to direct the Macedonian company. As 'preparation' for his work with the National Theatre of Bitola, Blondell staged the play in Santa Barbara in 2011 with his own company, Lit Moon.[30] The performances at the Globe were outstanding and forceful, and whether the national culture being traced was American or Macedonian, the company claimed it for themselves. They were the only company of the three to celebrate in Olympic style at the end of the performance, bringing onstage several Macedonian flags – a reminder that, if England is one of the oldest nation states, Macedonia is one of the most recent, only gaining its independence after the Second World War.

The flag passionately paraded by the company is the third flag Macedonia has had since the Second World War, each iteration of red and yellow reflecting different stages of its postwar identity. For much of the last 50 years the flag has shown a Soviet-style yellow star against a red backdrop. In 1992, Macedonia marked its secession from Yugoslavia the previous year by replacing the star with a sun – the Vergina Sun, sometimes known as the Macedonian Star, which is associated with the family of Alexander the Great. It has been interpreted as a symbol representing the 12 Gods of Olympus and this is one of the reasons that Greece objected to the use of the image on Macedonia's flag. After several years of diplomatic and economic pressure from Greece, Macedonia designed a new flag in 1995. Greece also disputed the choice of name when it seceded from Yugoslavia in 1991, with the consequence that the country's formal title is the Former Yugoslav Republic of Macedonia and appears on maps as FYROM.[31] The rising sun draped across the Globe stage claimed the English Globe for Macedonia – a national triumph, but also a reclamation of autonomy and an assertion of identity. For the Macedonians, the Globe performance was probably a more significant national event than the Olympics themselves, to which the country sent only four athletes and won no medals. Although the flags brought on by the crew were all the current design, one of the crew wore a t-shirt with the Vergina Sun emblazoned on it. This was a statement – a submerged and subdued statement, but a statement nevertheless – about Macedonia's still-emergent nationalism and the compromises it has been forced to make in its national symbology. It was a gesture both of defiance and comradeship – any Macedonians in the audience would have recognized at once the statement that this t-shirt made.

The invitation from the Olympics to Macedonia to stage a play in its own language did not go unremarked among Greek

Londoners. One reporter, Areti Kotseli, a British-based Greek, complained that it was 'an incident of insult to the Greeks' to allow the company to perform traditional songs in the Macedonian language. The article provoked a furious argument in the user comments section, with one Macedonian fighting back with, 'You people are so uneducated [...] Start minding your own yard before you fall apart and leave Macedonia and Macedonians alone, you've done enough damage to them. UNITED MACEDONIA!'[32] The performance was also the climax of another London festival called Days of Macedonian Culture, which deliberately dovetailed with the Globe to Globe Festival and the Olympics as a way of promoting Macedonia to Londoners. This included music events and the publication of 130 books of Macedonian literature in English translation. The Embassy of the Republic of Macedonia held an event at University College London to commemorate both events with a day of talks on 14 May on Macedonia's language and literary heritage.[33] *Part Three* was turned into a Macedonian cultural product, captured and claimed, like an explorer claiming a new territory by planting their national flag. As one Macedonian blogger put it: 'Through the play, Macedonian culture and climate was pulsing above Macedonian language, Macedonian music and Macedonian actors' performance. Theatre play performed on [*sic*] Macedonian language in London is a big point for Macedonia.'[34]

Macedonia's struggles for independence and sense of self echo the England that Shakespeare described in the 1590s. However, if Macedonian history and identity coincided with the England of *Part Three*, it was not as a memory of civil war, but as fear of civil war through a displaced memorialization of a semi-fictive past event. This was not a memory of war as such, but a memory of a war that could happen, an expression of the nightmare of national collapse that underlies the articulation of national identity in both Shakespeare's England and the National Theatre of Bitola's Macedonia.

One of the most powerful expressions of this was the 'father who has killed his son' scene (2.5), set during the

Battle of Towton. Henry was on the edge of the battlefield watching the fighting from a distance. At first horrified by the intensity of the war he is watching, he then loses himself in a pastoral fantasy as he imagines what it must be like not to be a king. The performance powerfully conveyed the devastating, horrific impact of civil war. Petar Gorko played a haunted, angry Henry, white make-up and black mascara giving him the look of a faded clown. He delivered the first part of the scene at the edge of the stage, sitting casually, his crown off, talking to the audience as a confidant. As his speech became more passionate, angry, he stood and held his crown as if it were a curse, a burden. A soldier came on stage right with his father, who stood, apparently still alive. Above stage, a woman wailed a sad Macedonian folk song, the native words of her own language interweaving with Shakespeare's to colour and texture the miseries of civil war. Listening to the son's speech, which was delivered direct to the audience, Henry clutched his crown and moaned, 'o heavy times'. As he spoke, the father slowly knelt, fell flat on the floor; the son knelt and crouched over him. In a parallel movement, two other actors came on stage left and performed a similar scene, this time the son falling while the father spoke, and the two forming in slow motion a pièta; Henry, his arm outstretched towards them, was horrified but impotent. As the scene shifted its focus from each onstage tableau, the father speaking, then the son, Henry spoke his lines through the hollow ring of the crown. Rewatching it after the Olympics (the performance was filmed and temporarily streamed at www.TheSpace.org) this image immediately called to my mind the Olympic rings forged in the Opening Ceremony – but the voice of history speaking to us through this ring is a lament, a mourning, a cry of pain, pain from the tragic realization that the symbol of power, the symbol of eternity, when turned on its side, is ultimately hollow.

A different kind of history was remembered with Martin Mirchevski's riveting performance of Gloucester's major soliloquy before the first interval. He played Gloucester as a proper bunch-backed toad, one arm limp, his leg lame so that every time he walked across stage he hobbled, but he was vicious too. As he took the audience into his confidence, shared his schemes with them, he built his speech into a Hitler-like intensity, waving his one good arm in a way which seemed to recall both the Nazi salute – and the Olympic salute. At points, his whole body arched backwards, possessed with murderous anger. He spat words, seemingly stuck on percussive syllables, a vocalization of hate, a violent language and a violation of language. Gloucester repeated his Hitler-like hand gestures in the performance's penultimate scene, when he killed Henry by splattering a jar of red blood across Henry's white smock. The Olympic-cum-Nazi gestures pointed in different directions – back to the 1940s, when the Macedonian state was born out of resistance to the Nazi occupation which saw 98 per cent of its Jewish population killed; but also to the present, to the Olympic moment at which a Macedonian nationalism was triumphantly reclaimed.[35] This was not a globalized Shakespeare, but a Shakespeare taken back to the world of the 1590s and its parallels with the present: two nation states, proud but precarious, asserting a right to exist through an exploration of the horrors of the past and energized by a fear of instability in the future.

Conclusion

There is something about the *Henry VI* plays which means that, although they are almost always staged as part of wider festivals, they call attention to the faultlines in any articulation of national identity. The plays themselves were an uncanny reminder that the ideals of the nation, even of the Olympic nation, also have their nightmares. The ground on which Danny Boyle's actors strode, into which athletes from many nations piled in to fill the arena, was a space constructed through exclusion. The presence of these harrowing stories about what happens when a nation turns in on itself, performed as both a memory of the past and an anxiety about a potential future, struck a note of discord in this celebration of global peace and harmony.

Notes

1 Pico Iyer, *The Global Soul: Jet Lag, Shopping Malls and the Search for Home* (London: Vintage, 2000), p. 176.

2 For more discussion of the role of Shakespeare's history plays in the performance of national culture, see Nicholas Grene, *Shakespeare's Serial History Plays* (Cambridge: Cambridge University Press, 2007); Stuart Hampton-Reeves, 'Theatrical Afterlives', in *The Cambridge Companion to Shakespeare's History Plays*, ed. Michael Hattaway (Cambridge: Cambridge University Press, 2002), pp. 229–46; and Robert Shaughnessy, *Representing Shakespeare: England, History and the RSC* (London: Harvester Wheatsheaf, 1994).

3 M. Payne, *Olympic Turnaround* (Westport: Praeger, 2006), p. 134.

4 The Olympic arts programme was known by various titles until the 1992 Barcelona Olympics when it became officially recognized as the Cultural Olympiad. However, the term had been used unofficially in previous Games as far back as Mexico City in 1968; Andy Miah and Beatriz García, *The Olympics* (London: Routledge, 2012), p. 53.

5 Lincoln Allison, 'The ideals of the founding father: mythologised, evolved, or betrayed?', in *Watching the Olympics: Politics, Power and Representation*, John Peter Sugden and Alan Tomlinson (eds) (London: Routledge, 2012), pp. 18–35 (p. 30).

6 Miah and García, *The Olympics*, p. 51.

7 Payne, *Olympic Turnaround*, p. 134.

8 Jackie Hogan, *Gender, Race and National Identity: Nations of Flesh and Blood* (London: Routledge, 2009), p. 101.

9 Andrew Billings, *Olympic Media: Inside the Biggest Show in Television* (London: Routledge, 2008), p. 1.

10 For more discussion of the role of the Opening Ceremony in the Olympics, see Alan Tomlinson, 'Olympic Spectacle: Opening Ceremonies and Some Paradoxes of Globalization', *Media Culture Society*, 18 (1996), pp. 583–602; and Odd Are Berkaak, '"In the Heart of the Volcano": The Olympic Games as Mega Drama', in *Olympic Games as Performance and Event: The Case of the XVII Winter Olympic Games in Norway*, ed. Arne Martin Klausen (New York: Berghahn Books, 1999), pp. 49–74.

11 Owen Gibson, 'Danny Boyle's Olympic opening ceremony: madcap, surreal and moving', *Guardian*, 27 July 2012, http://www.theguardian.com/sport/2012/jul/27/olympic-opening-ceremony [accessed 27 July 2012].

12 Mark Brown, 'Your Cultural Olympiad questions answered', *Guardian*, 20 July 2012, http://www.theguardian.com/culture/2012/jul/20/london-2012-cultural-olympiad-questions [accessed 20 July 2012].

13 Daniel M. Goldstein, *The Spectacular City: Violence and Performance in Urban Bolivia* (Durham: Duke University Press, 2004), p. 4.

14 Don Handelman, *Models and Mirrors: Towards an Anthropology of Public Events* (Cambridge: Cambridge University Press, 1990), p. 4.

15 For more on the *Henry VI* plays' performance history in relation to national culture, see Stuart Hampton-Reeves and Carol Chillington Rutter, *Shakespeare in Performance: The* Henry VI *Plays* (Manchester: Manchester University Press, 2006).

16 The literature on the civil wars in the former Yugoslavia in the 1990s is extensive. For a general academic introduction, see Steven Burg and L. Paul S. Shoup, *The War in Bosnia-Herzegovina: Ethnic Conflict and International Intervention* (New York: M. E. Sharpe, 1999).

17 Nemanja Cabric, 'Balkan Henry VI at the Globe Theatre', *Balkan Insight*, 5 May 2012, http://www.balkaninsight.com/en/article/balkan-henry-vi-at-the-globe-theatre [accessed 5 May 2012].

18 Both trials are still in progress at the time of writing.
19 Cabric, 'Balkan Henry VI'.
20 R. Ball and J. Dury, 'Represeting the Riots: the (Mis)Use of Statistics to Sustain Ideological Explanation', *Radical Statistics*, 106 (2012), pp. 4–21.
21 Over 4,000 people were arrested as a result of the riots (Ball and Dury, 'Representing the Riots', p. 9).
22 Andy Beckett, 'Cordon Blue', *Guardian*, 21 September 2007, http://www.theguardian.com/society/2007/sep/21/communities [accessed 20 February 2014].
23 Philip Comerford, 'The Olympic security fence is a modern day form of enclosure', *Open Democracy*, 26 July 2012, http://www.opendemocracy.net/ourkingdom/philip-comerford/olympic-security-fence-is-modern-day-form-of-enclosure [accessed 26 July 2012].
24 Beckett, 'Cordon Blue'.
25 John Horne and Garry Whannel, *Understanding the Olympics* (London: Routledge, 2012), p. 146.
26 Rose Etherington, 'Olympic viewing platform by Office for Subversive Architecture', *dezeen*, 12 August 2008, http://www.dezeen.com/2008/08/12/point-of-view-by-office-for-subversive-architecture/ [accessed 12 August 2008].
27 Some critics were uncertain how to respond to this figure. See for instance Peter Orford, '*Henry VI Part Two*', *Year of Shakespeare*, 15 May 2012, http://bloggingshakespeare.com/year-of-shakespeare-henry-vi-part-two [accessed 15 May 2012].
28 For more on this work see Immediate Theatre's website, http://www.immediate-theatre.com/projects/detail/big_blue_fence_project/ [accessed 20 February 2014].
29 Rose Etherington, 'The Blue Fence Project by Studio Superniche', *dezeen*, 18 September 2009, http://www.dezeen.com/2009/09/18/the-blue-fence-project-by-studiosuperniche/ [accessed 18 September 2009].
30 Randall Martin, '*Henry VI Part 3* in Santa Barbara', *Blogging Shakespeare*, 27 March 2012, http://bloggingshakespeare.com/henry-vi-part-3-in-santa-barbara [accessed 27 March 2012].

31 John Shea, *Macedonia and Greece: The Struggle to Define a New Balkan Nation* (Jefferson: MacFarland, 1997), pp. 190–1.

32 Areti Kotseli, 'London Recognizes Macedonian Language During Cultural Olympiad', *Greek Reporter*, 9 May 2012, http://eu.greekreporter.com/2012/05/09/london-recognizes-macedonian-language-during-cultural-olympiad/ [accessed 9 May 2012].

33 'London to Host Days of Macedonian Culture', *Macedonian International News Agency*, 15 November 2010, http://macedoniaonline.eu/content/view/16846/2/ [accessed 20 February 2014].

34 M. Trajkovska, 'Macedonian theatre groups performs at World Shakespeare Festival', *Presenting Macedonia* blog, http://skopje.blogs.lincoln.ac.uk/macedonian-theatre-groups-performs-at-world-shakespeare-festival/ [accessed 5 June 2012].

35 Aleksandar Matkovski, *A History of the Jews in Macedonia* (Skopje: Macedonian Review Editions, 1982), p. 205.

5

Shakespeare in the North: Regionalism, Culture and Power

Adam Hansen and Monika Smialkowska

If globalization recontextualizes and reinterprets cultural localism, it does so in ways that are equivocal and ambiguous.[1]

'The World Shakespeare Festival was part of the London Olympics – a UK-wide eight-month celebration, produced by the RSC, which reached more than 1.8 million people.'[2] This short sentence, opening the Royal Shakespeare Company's description of the 2012 World Shakespeare Festival, brings together several spatial designations: the world, London, UK, aside from the associations of Stratford-upon-Avon which the RSC itself evokes. Accordingly, the World Shakespeare Festival confirmed Shakespeare's status as an icon with international significance. His plays were staged across the globe, and companies from around the world performed in localities across Britain. These interactions of the 'global' and the 'local' produced innovative hybrids, and raised some intriguing questions. How did these interactions query, enrich or make strange our conceptions of the global and the local, and their differences? Was the World Shakespeare Festival truly a 'world' event, if it was 'produced' by the Stratford-based RSC? To what extent and in what ways were people across the UK involved in the celebrations? What was the relationship between the Festival's London/Stratford centre and the diverse regions making up the United Kingdom? This chapter attempts to address these questions by focusing on one locale: the North East of England, in particular Newcastle upon Tyne and Gateshead. What happened to Shakespeare *there* during the year-long celebration of his work that this collection reflects on, commemorates and problematizes? By restricting the focus to such a specific geographical area this chapter is not making a claim that the issues associated with 'the local' uses of Shakespeare are the same everywhere, that Newcastle and Gateshead stand for all regions, or even that they unproblematically represent the entire North of England. Instead, we hope that this case study of Shakespeare's use in one local place will encourage further studies of his uses in comparable places, and so pave the way to a fuller theoretical understanding of the dynamic interactions of global, national and local Shakespeare.

Theorizing global, national and local Shakespeare

Thinking about Shakespeare's role in, and appropriation and construction by, the various, conflicted and devolved communities of the British Isles has become a critical orthodoxy. As work has been produced that builds on and complicates his long-standing status as England's national poet, or the laureate of Empire, we have become used to correlating Shakespeare and Scotland, Wales and Ireland.[3] Similarly, much work has been done on Shakespeare's global 'travels', especially in relation to the processes of colonization and postcolonial emancipation.[4] As Martin Orkin notes in his discussion of the relations between Shakespeare and particular locales,

> Since their first performances, Shakespeare's texts have been and are, in a manner of speaking, travellers to countless and always different locations [...] Engagement with the Shakespeare text always entails in part, therefore, cultural encounter or clash.[5]

It is now a critical commonplace, thankfully, that Shakespeare is at once the property of the world, and subject to specific and local appropriations, often at the same time. This does not mean that what is understood as 'local' and what is conceived of as 'global' are simple constructs or concepts, as Orkin's gloss on his use of the term 'local' attests:

> By 'local' I mean here what characterizes each reader who comes to the text, in terms of her or his place and time, what is within that place epistemologically current, the particular institutional position or struggles within which she or he is situated or with which she or he is actively engaged or, again, the particular knowledges and ideologies she or he exemplifies or legitimates.[6]

Consequently, 'local' does not simply mean 'individual' or 'independent from social forces', but rather consists of the ways in which individuals, in their specific places, respond to and interact with larger ideological or institutional structures. Thus, it is inescapably connected with the national and the global. In other words, theorizing local uses of Shakespeare inevitably involves discussing his national and global applications.

In an introduction to a collection of essays aggregating diverse studies of Shakespeare's place in the world in the new millennium, R. S. White depicts his subject in what are now familiar terms: 'Shakespeare is a global commodity'. White goes on to note that 'his plays and words, taken in and out of context, have been shamelessly exploited, most notably in a cultural imperialism that seeks to homogenize and imprint certain values on all countries in the world'. Yet he suggests that Shakespeare and what we do with him presents more complex experiences than those of cultural hegemony:

> At the same time, however, the opposite also applies. Shakespeare has, since the early nineteenth century, been regionalized, and given a local inflection, a whole new set of specific meanings based on a unique geographical location, or ethnic group, or political affiliation. [...] His plays are both global and local[.][7]

To describe this facet of Shakespeare, White applies a neologism 'glocal'.[8] Such a coinage, however awkward, accords with descriptions of the current production and consumption of culture more generally, by geographers of globalization such as Kevin Robins:

> Whilst globalization may be the prevailing force of our times, this does not mean that localism is without significance. [...] The particularity of place and culture can never be done away with, can never be absolutely transcended. Globalization is, in fact, also associated with new dynamics of *re*-localization.[9]

Globalization, then, influences what is considered local and the ways in which localism is constructed. When it comes to Shakespeare, this can mean, as Mark Thornton Burnett has suggested, that '[t]he local is not always to be found where one might conventionally expect it'.[10] The local can be marketed on the global scene and filtered through global perspectives and attitudes, which can give it global reach and visibility, while at the same time complicating its 'pure' local status. As Robins summarizes,

> The global–local nexus is about the relation between globalizing and particularizing dynamics in the strategy of the global corporation, and the 'local' should be seen as a fluid and relational space, constituted only in and through its relation to the global.[11]

Therefore, in Robins's words, '[i]t is important to see the local as a relational, and relative, concept'.[12] And when we add to this already complicated picture of local/global interrelations the third important dimension, that of the 'national', the situation becomes very complex indeed.

Conscious of these interactions and complexities, can we make our specific, localized readings of Shakespeare yet more nuanced and particular as we grapple with 'the problem' of 'the placing of Shakespeare in English culture'?[13] Can we extend our understanding of the tensions between seeing Shakespeare as a 'universal' writer and seeing him as a property of a particular nation to a micro-level of regional reception, reinvention and appropriation? One aspect not explored in much depth in existing criticism is Shakespeare's position in locations which, while not seeking independence or devolution through political means, retain strong sense of being different, separate from official (privileged) strands of national culture. Because they do not fall neatly into the categories of either the 'nation' or the 'colony', these locations can become invisible and critically neglected. Through an investigation of World Shakespeare Festival events in Newcastle and Gateshead, this chapter seeks to address this imbalance, while engaging with broader theoretical issues of how powerful cultural icons participate in constructing and challenging the boundaries of socio-cultural centre and periphery, boundaries defined in terms of regional geography, class and politics.

The 'glocal' reworkings of Shakespeare which White identifies come from a wide range of 'local' places across the globe, which prompts him to reflect on a 'whole new terrain of "localized" Shakespeare', a 'phenomenon' he sees as 'intrinsically pluralistic, uncommodifiable, both independent and sceptical of foreign models'.[14] However, this celebratory interpretation of 'independent' localized Shakespeare is open to debate when we consider the complex interconnections between the local, the global and the national outlined above. And in the context of a region within an established nation-state, with no intentions of devolution but with a strong sense of separate cultural identity, this formulation becomes even more problematic. What does 'foreign' mean in such a situation? Can the culture of such a region be 'independent' (and from what)? And does the word 'uncommodifiable' for artists from such a region denote simply an optimistic 'art-for-art's-sake' freedom, or also the fact that they may have difficulties in taking their work to wider audiences, 'selling' it beyond their own region or to the globe because of perceived parochialism? In other words, is it possible for an adaptation or appropriation of Shakespeare in an English regional location to be both of that location and distant from, or 'sceptical' towards, a 'foreign' nation of which it is ostensibly a part? What happens when we think of and situate Shakespeare in *English* localities – for whom there may be critical and material separation from models and (well-resourced) institutions of 'Englishness', *and* from England's 'metropolitan bank of Shakespeare knowledge'?[15] What happens, then, when we put the local before the national *and* the global? To Orkin, quite a lot:

> [T]he kinds of knowledge that, especially, particular non-metropolitan locations – whether they are located within twenty-first century Europe and North America but outside the Shakespeare metropolitan academy, or beyond it – might afford, may themselves, in turn, offer additional opportunities for thinking about Shakespeare's plays.[16]

We might add that such knowledge could also generate opportunities for thinking about the locations staging or making those plays.

This chapter can't answer all of the questions outlined above, but by raising them it can remind us what is at stake. Precisely because it is hard to demarcate the 'local' in an age of globalization, this chapter is not a place for short-sighted and exclusionary 'local theatre for local people'. Nor is it a patronizing lament for benighted neglected provinces: it is proof of a locale's energy that it can sustain more than images of itself in the culture it hosts and produces. To think of this another way, if Stratford or London do not need theatre solely by or for people in Stratford or London, why should anywhere else? Lastly, following Robins's insights regarding the relational nature of the local and the global, this chapter does not seek to 'idealize the local'. As Robins argues, 'We should not invest our hopes for the future in the redemptive qualities of local economies, local cultures, local identities'.[17] It is not in isolating and celebrating the 'pure' local but in the analysis of the relationships between the local, the national and the global that fruitful insights into modern engagement with Shakespeare lie.

We have therefore sought to see the 'local' in relation to the 'national' and the 'global' because this is how the world works. And yet, noticing that this is how the world works is not equivalent to seeing these processes as natural or non-political. On the contrary, they are mediated through relations of capital, materiality and (self-)exploitation. As Robins points out, 'The local and "exotic" are torn out of place and time to be repackaged for the world bazaar. So-called world culture may reflect a new valuation of difference and particularity, but it is also very much about making a profit from it.'[18] In this competitive environment, 'some localities are able successfully to "switch" themselves in to the global networks, but others will remain "unswitched" or "unplugged"', a position which often corresponds to those regions' political and economic marginalization.[19] Robins argues that '[i]n order to position itself in the new global context, the region must re-image and, ultimately, re-imagine itself'.[20] This, however, is doubly problematic for regions which already occupy ambivalent positions in relation to dominant strands of national culture, which can hinder their access to cultural and material capital necessary to enter the global market.

This chapter explores Shakespeare's role in this re-imaging and re-imagining of a locality's self-identity and 'packaged' form. In his study of amateur Shakespeare, Michael Dobson gives an example of this process happening in another northern English city. He cites Frank Brogan, the founder of a project, launched in 2002, to perform 'each of Shakespeare's plays in turn across two decades' in York. Brogan's words give an indication of what is at stake in these questions for Newcastle upon Tyne, just an hour north of York by train:

> This is what The York Shakespeare Project is all about. A whole community involving itself in productions of excellence and innovation. A whole community showing itself, through the work of Shakespeare, to the world.[21]

In 2012, the World Shakespeare Festival helped bring the global to English localities like Newcastle, but did it – could it – facilitate the reverse process? Did it – could it – help such localities become recognized as important players on the national and global stages? Or did these events manifest the paradox that while Shakespeare may belong to the world, the institutions through which Shakespeare is transmitted, nationally and globally, do not?

Local contexts

During 2012, Newcastle and Gateshead played host to a range of official, franchised, branded events in the World Shakespeare Festival: Oily Cart's version of *The Winter's Tale* for pre-school children, *In a Pickle* (at the Northern

Stage); the Royal Shakespeare Company's so-called 'African' *Julius Caesar* (at the Theatre Royal); a Tunisian revisioning of *Macbeth* by the company Artistes, Producteurs, Associés, called *Macbeth: Lëila and Ben – A Bloody History* (at the Northern Stage); dreamthinkspeak's fabulously fractured rendering of *Hamlet* as *The Rest is Silence* (at the Northern Stage); and a production of *West Side Story* (at The Sage Gateshead). In addition, a number of amateur performances were mounted, some under the auspices of the RSC's Open Stages project and some independently. Apart from *West Side Story*, which will be discussed in more detail later, none of the professional shows was created specifically for the North East – they all premiered and ran elsewhere before coming to the region (*Julius Caesar* in Stratford, *The Rest is Silence* in Brighton and London, *Macbeth: Leïla and Ben* in London, and *In a Pickle* in Stratford and London). Moreover, none of them engaged directly with the North East on the level of setting, costuming or dialect. While two of the productions were strongly localized, they were concerned with places elsewhere – an unspecified African country in the case of *Julius Caesar* and Tunisia in the case of *Macbeth: Leïla and Ben* – and there was no clear rationale as to why these particular shows of all the Festival's repertoire were chosen to be presented in the Newcastle and Gateshead area. In this respect, the World Shakespeare Festival in the North East had a global dimension, but its own locale seemed to have fairly minimal significance. One could be forgiven for feeling that Shakespeare was on tour rather than at home in the region, with companies from elsewhere bringing random offerings to the locals.

That said, the vast majority of 'official' productions in the Festival took place in London (notably the Globe to Globe season at Shakespeare's Globe) or Stratford-upon-Avon, with only a handful in other locations (Edinburgh, Brighton, Birmingham and Bridgend). So the role played by Newcastle and Gateshead attests to the vitality of their theatrical culture, and the viability of holding so many events there. Yet even as those involved in organizing such productions in the North East rightly heralded the way they were catering for the demands of sophisticated, open-minded audiences, they also implicitly acknowledged Newcastle's peripheral location in relation to more established centres of Shakespearean theatre, that is Orkin's 'metropolitan bank of Shakespeare knowledge'.[22] As Amy Fawdington, the Northern Stage's Communications Manager, put it, 'We're one of very few regions outside London that are partners in the festival and are proud to be able to bring such fresh and innovative productions to audiences in this part of the country, *who might not otherwise get to see them*'.[23]

It is also important to remember that this feast of Shakespearean fare came a year after a temporary cultural famine (suiting an age of 'austerity menus') had been announced. Michael Boyd, then Artistic Director of the Royal Shakespeare Company, wrote in 2011:

> As a result of the demands placed on us by the opening of the newly transformed Royal Shakespeare and Swan Theatres and the need to absorb a 6.9% cut in funding for 2011/12, we have taken the decision to concentrate on our work in Stratford-upon-Avon.

As the press release disclosing this announcement made clear, since 1977 the RSC's so-called Newcastle Season 'has generally been considered one of the cornerstones in the RSC annual calendar, and a crucial part of the company's aim to make its work geographically accessible to all parts of the British public'.[24] In that 2011 announcement, and after, the RSC indicated its commitment to its relationship with Newcastle the following year, and beyond.[25] Yet the decision not to hold a Newcastle season in 2011 provoked much consternation locally and nationally.[26] Some respondents promoted an image of the North as homogeneous, separatist and disdainful of non-Northern cultural patronage: 'Let the "Luvies" stay in Stratford. This ain't what we want up here!'[27] Others, however, summed up the decision as '[a] truly Shakespearian tragedy!'[28] Whatever the responses, a raw nerve had been prodded. And so the decision underlined how important, but also vexed and fragile, such relationships can be. They involve assumptions concerning cultural capital, privileged perspectives and metropolitan power, exposing strains in bodies cultural and political. The complexity of the relationship between Newcastle and the 'metropolitan bank' of Shakespeare was caught well by Laura Fraine, in a blog for Newcastle's *Journal*, which began by citing Sir Ian McKellen, who had performed in the RSC's first Newcastle season, and in the city many times since:

> 'These national companies are national. They belong to us all. They don't belong to London, they don't belong to Stratford upon Avon. We pay for them with our taxes.' [...] Much as we need innovative productions [...] the people of the North East also deserve the chance to see great, classic theatre. We deserve the best. We may have to visit London for many of Britain's cultural treasures, such as the national museums [...] but theatre travels. It's a huge shame that this year [2011] it won't.[29]

In reflecting on the World Shakespeare Festival, we might add to McKellen's and Fraine's observations. A city like Newcastle, in an area like the North East of England, deserves to be able to show to the world that it can support innovative, challenging, inclusive theatre, *because* it can. During the Festival, it *did*. But perhaps one thing missing from what the region enjoyed during the World Shakespeare Festival was the region itself. In other words, it was a privilege, stimulating and enlightening, to see how Tunisians were using Shakespeare to rethink their lives, and using their lives to restage Shakespeare, and to be able to see that somewhere far from Tunisia (or London, or Stratford-upon-Avon). But what opportunities did the World Shakespeare Festival present for someone from Jarrow, Fenham, South Shields or anywhere in the greater

Newcastle–Gateshead conurbation, to rethink *their* lives using Shakespeare? Where was the chance for a local reshaping of a canonical play? Where was *this* little bit of the 'World' in the World Shakespeare Festival?

Local Shakespeares?

We might cite several examples of the tensions such questions set up, some more or less significant or trivial than others. In *In a Pickle* there was a poignant scene where the many children in the audience were invited into the performance area and asked to comfort the crying baby Perdita. The actors suggested the children could consider what they thought might help soothe her. The children, quite sensibly, said 'milk': so everyone passed pretend milk to the baby, and everyone seemed to love the game because the baby was pretend, the milk was pretend, and everyone knew it, yet the children were doing theatre-work *by* pretending. But when the actors asked what else might help, one child said 'a dodie', leaving the actors baffled. A few of the parents and carers present translated what is a regional dialect term – 'she means a dummy' (or 'pacifier' for North American readers of this). As one brand of English met another in a Shakespearean medium was something lost in translation? Speaking afterwards, one of the actors said she hadn't known what the children were talking about, 'but maybe I should have because I'm from Darlington [about 40 miles/65 km from Newcastle]'. This suggests an awareness of the nuances of language but also how easily they can be forgotten.

Another example comes from scheduling the fringe events surrounding The Sage's hosting of *West Side Story*. Some peripheral events worked hard to draw people in, and encourage participation: there was, for example, a sold-out singing workshop where people could learn to do songs from the show, and then put on a performance for friends and family. Yet other events connected to *West Side Story*, such as a scheduled discussion of gang culture, were cancelled. The promotional material for that discussion stated:

> From *Romeo and Juliet* to riots of August 2011, gangs have existed in many forms throughout history. Is the portrayal of gangs in the arts representative of those in the real world? Join a panel of specialists, chaired by Nicholas Owen (BBC News presenter) to explore the subject of gangs and urban culture addressed in both West Side Story and Romeo & Juliet [*sic*], and to establish whether these themes are still relevant in today's gang culture.[30]

The cancellation seemed strange.[31] Patrons of The Sage have no difficulty attending and enjoying debates about contemporary issues of national significance – BBC Radio 3 regularly holds 'Thinking Allowed' seasons there. In this case, however, The Sage was confronted with 'low ticket sales'.[32] Perhaps, then, the event was cancelled because it wasn't entirely relevant for the local context: was this another case of local contexts disappearing behind national or 'metropolitan' concerns?

Like any other major conurbation, Newcastle–Gateshead is blighted with its share of socio-economic inequality and injustice. Many people in the area endure widespread, deep-rooted and cross-generational deprivation, disadvantage and disenfranchisement. Indeed, in many regards, the North East of England has worse social conditions than most other parts of the country (according to indicators such as underage pregnancies, people in receipt of out-of-work benefits, young adults not in employment, education or training, working-age adults on low pay, or communities experiencing fuel poverty).[33] But at least in terms of a key indicator like income, Newcastle and Gateshead are also relatively more equal than lots of other cities, which means the gaps between rich and poor are not as stark as in, say, the capital, where rioting in the summer of 2011 was intense:

> London is one of the most unequal cities on earth: the richest 10 per cent is worth 273 times more than the poorest 10 per cent. [...] In London, the rich and the poor live almost on top of each other. On a daily basis the least well-off are able to see what they will never have.[34]

In comparison, as of 2011, the year of the riots, in the North East of England around 21 per cent of the population were in the poorest fifth of the population by income, while around 14 per cent were in the richest fifth. This means that most people in the North East of England (around 65 per cent) are in the middle three-fifths; in turn, this means the gap between the richest and the poorest is among the smallest for any region in the UK.[35]

Clearly, in any period riots, unrest and uprisings have 'more than just one explanation'.[36] But, as Owen Jones has observed of the events of 2011, 'rising inequalities and systemic injustices appear to collude with a general erosion of popular hope for the future, and a sense of social wellbeing and collective sentiment'.[37] Conversely, less inequality means more social cohesion and stability.[38] The North East's relative lack of inequality goes some way to explaining why, perhaps, when much of the rest of the country rioted, Newcastle and Gateshead did not [for discussion of the riots elsewhere, particularly in London, see Prescott and Hampton-Reeves's chapters in this volume]. Several months after the summer disturbances, there were some concerns that there might be a repeat of the events similar to the Meadow Well riots to the east of Newcastle in 1991, with 'a failure to tackle unemployment in the region's youth' highlighted as a potential cause.[39] Yet when the introduction to a 2012 collection of essays analysing the causes and effects of the riots asked 'What Happened, Where?', Newcastle or Gateshead still did not feature in the answer.[40] In turn, perhaps this goes some way to explaining why there was not much appetite for a debate in the region about the relationship between gang culture, recent English riots, *West Side Story* and Shakespeare. Understanding such relationships might have been of great concern to people in London, but not so much in the North East.

Local (amateur) Shakespeares?

The amateur strand of the 2012 celebrations can afford us an even fuller and more complex picture of the North East's involvement in the World Shakespeare Festival. As Dobson points out, studying amateur theatre provides an insight into 'how successive groups of people have committed themselves to incorporating [Shakespeare's] plays into their own lives and their own immediate societies, and it makes visible a whole range of responses to the national drama which other reception histories have missed'.[41] Crucially, it helps us to understand not only the 'purely local' concerns and responses to Shakespeare, but also the complex interactions between local and national, individual and institutional, 'popular' and 'high' aspects of culture.[42]

In case of the World Shakespeare Festival these interactions were embodied most visibly in the involvement of the RSC's Open Stages project with amateur theatrical groups across the UK. The RSC embarked on the project in 2011–12, aiming to 'embrace, develop and celebrate amateur theatre, re-forging the bond with the world of professional theatre'.[43] It established links with ten regional 'partner theatres', representing Northern Ireland, Scotland, Wales and several locations across England.[44] These partner institutions facilitated contact with amateur groups in their areas. The groups themselves registered their interest in the Open Stages scheme with the RSC and, if accepted, produced their shows under its auspices. Eventually, regional showcases were hosted by the partner theatres, and some productions were selected for the national showcases at Stratford. The RSC found the project worthwhile, and has re-launched it for 2013–16, with incoming Artistic Director Gregory Doran reflecting on how its first run 'has enabled the RSC to engage with, and celebrate amateur, grass roots theatre making'.[45] Let us consider how the scheme worked in the North East of England.

The 'partner theatre' for the Open Stages in the region was The Sage Gateshead – a somewhat unusual choice, since it is primarily a music venue rather than a theatrical organization. This may be the reason why the most prominent production associated with the Open Stages in the North East was a musical – *West Side Story*, directed and choreographed by Will Tuckett, which ran at The Sage from 4–7 July 2012. It was an ambitious and impressive undertaking, with new choreography and a full-size live orchestra. It proved very successful, attracting large audiences and receiving a five-star review in the *Guardian*, which praised its drive, energy and dynamism.[46] Its minimalist staging, departing from the customary 1950–60s New York look, made it into an 'Anywhere Story', relevant to contemporary audiences and applicable to groups of disaffected young people in any location or community. In this respect, The Sage's production was definitely a global adaptation of Shakespeare. What it was not, however, was a 'North East Story'. The image on the programme's cover presented a hybrid city skyline, in which The Sage Gateshead's instantly recognizable silhouette was combined with generic poor city dwellings and New York City's water towers, promising a fusion of global and local interests (Figure 9). However, not only were there no references to the locale in the show's actual staging or costuming, but, more importantly, the region was conspicuously absent in the composition of the cast which, to our knowledge, did not include anybody based in the North East. The ensemble was recruited through the process of open auditions, advertised locally and nationally. Interestingly, the auditions at Newcastle's Dance City were only the first stage of the process. Those applicants who completed them successfully were invited to the second audition in London, on the basis of which the final selection for the show took place.[47] One of the participants reflected on her experience of getting through the local heat:

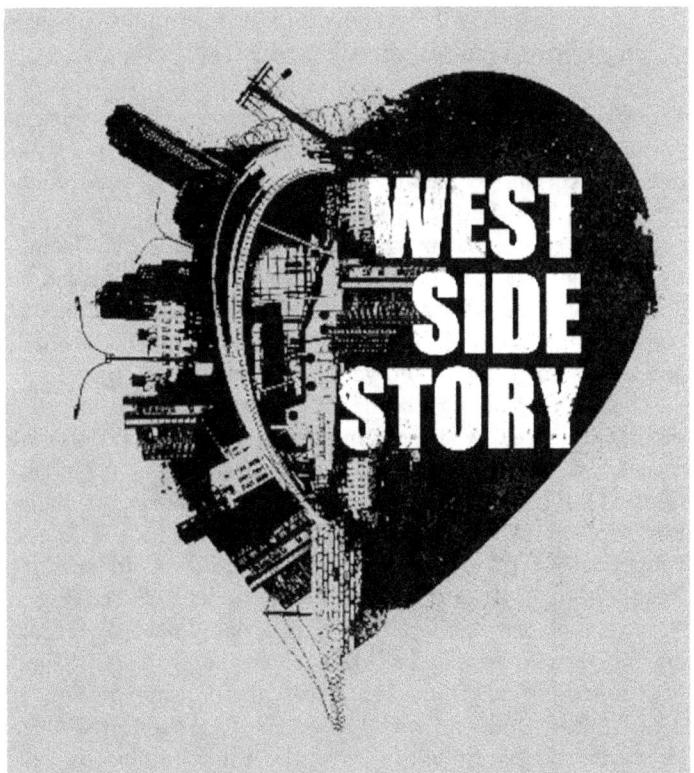

FIGURE 9 *Publicity image for* West Side Story *at The Sage Gateshead. Designed by Andy Lovatt and reproduced courtesy of The Sage Gateshead.*

[T]hat evening I was called by the producer of the show who asked me to get a train to London the following week, and prepare a song to sing in the audition. Naturally, this news resulted in hysterical squealing from my flatmates [...]. The excitement soon subsided however as I was hit by the reality that I was going to have to a) prepare a song, b) get tickets to London (not cheap!), and c) prepare myself to become humiliated in front of not only the entire production team of the show, but also a room of disgustingly talented musical theatre graduates.[48]

While some of the anxieties expressed here may be universal to young artists across the world, point b) foregrounds important concerns specific to the arts outside of the UK's metropolitan centre. Aspiring performers wanting to 'make it' – even in a show created specifically for the North East – are confronted by the material reality of having to cover the considerable costs of progressing via London. Moreover, once there, they compete against applicants who most likely have trained at prestigious institutions and venues outside of the region.

This last point was borne out by the eventual selection of the show's cast. The résumés included in the programme revealed that the performers were graduates of such institutions as Guildford School of Acting, Central School of Ballet, Bird College, Arts Educational School (London and Tring), Dance School of Scotland, Laine Theatre Arts, Italia Conti Academy of Theatre Arts, and D&B College of Performing Arts. The closest to the North East geographically were one performer who started her training at the Northern School of Contemporary Dance in Leeds (before moving on to Bird College) and one who graduated from Preston College. However, most were educated in the South of England and some as far afield as New York, Paris and New Zealand, and all had considerable prior performance experience in the UK and, in some cases, abroad. This begs the question not only of how well the show fitted with the RSC's Open Stages brief of celebrating and developing grass-roots, amateur theatre, but also queries the rationale for producing it at The Sage Gateshead. In an interview, the London-based choreographer/director Will Tuckett explained that part of the reason this *West Side Story* would be new, bold and different was that it was being made 'specifically for the stage *here*'.[49] However, his comments about the building, the acoustics and the stage itself demonstrate that by 'here' he meant The Sage, rather than the city of Gateshead or the North East. In the end, the venue and the musicians involved – the Northern Sinfonia under the direction of the Gateshead-born John Wilson – were the only visible local elements of the production. The components which are at the heart of approaching Shakespeare through the musical theatre – acting, singing, dancing, choreographing and directing – were all outsourced. This created an impression that you need imported practitioners to produce a high-quality show in the region, and that the promise of promoting local talent which this project seemed to offer was somewhat tokenistic.

The North and the World?

Interestingly, it was precisely the hope of showcasing their work and being recognized beyond the region that attracted some of the local participants to the World Shakespeare Festival and the Open Stages project. Amateur drama societies such as Newcastle's The People's Theatre do not need special encouragement to 'do Shakespeare' – in fact, The People's has presented at least one Shakespeare play every season since the 1920s. What the Open Stages project seemed to offer, however, was an opportunity to be associated with and appreciated by the established, nationally acclaimed institutions such as the RSC. One of the participants commented on how she initially thought that the RSC was interested and wanted to be involved, but when nobody from the company came to see their production 'it certainly felt far North'.[50] The Open Stages' regional showcase at The Sage Gateshead had a feeling of anticlimax, with only about five groups presenting extracts of their work to a small audience, which did not include a member of the RSC. In this respect, the amateur involvement with the World Shakespeare Festival in the North East may seem disappointing. However, it provides a fascinating insight into what local drama practitioners want and need, how they wish to engage with Shakespeare and with the nationwide and global theatre scene, and what opportunities they currently have to achieve their goals.

Two productions staged during the Festival serve as particularly apt illustrations here: *Quick Bright Things* by Alison Carr and *Rodney and Julie J.* by Victoria Baker, two brand new plays taking cue from and reworking Shakespeare's classics. *Quick Bright Things*, created for the RSC's Open Stages project and performed at The People's Theatre, offered an imaginative glimpse into Helena's life before and after the action of *A Midsummer Night's Dream*. *Rodney and Julie J.*, written and directed by Baker for her final year show at Newcastle College, premiered at the College's Peter Sarah Theatre and was subsequently invited for a one-off performance at The Sage Gateshead, as part of the fringe events surrounding *West Side Story*. It transferred *Romeo and Juliet* to a modern-day setting of '[T]wo household supermarkets, both alike in dignity and price', with Rodney working for Tesco and Julie J. for the rival Asda.[51] Both productions were innovative appropriations, rather than straightforward stage versions of the original plays, demonstrating a confident, non-reverential attitude to Shakespeare.

Most importantly for the purposes of this chapter, neither performance was set specifically in the North East or referred directly to the region. *Quick Bright Things* did not stipulate its geographical location, foregrounding theatrical spaces instead: it was performed in promenade style, with the first part set in the greenroom bar, the second on the main stage, and the third in a dressing room. The author explained that she wanted to 'get inside the play and inside the theatre' and make the production a 'theatrical experience'.[52] In effect, preparing a show for the Open Stages project gave Carr an occasion to play with theatrical form, using Shakespeare not as a revered classic, but as a springboard for experimentation and creativity. In doing so, she simultaneously showcased The People's Theatre itself – a long-established outfit with its own venue, located in an adapted cinema and boasting two stages and impressive backstage apparatus many amateur drama groups can only dream of.[53]

Similarly, *Rodney and Julie J.* did not specify the locale

in which its action took place, opting instead for a neutral setting 'in fair common land, where we lay our scene' (p. 1). The author/director indicated that she did not wish to limit the meaning and appeal of the play to one region, but rather to make it relevant to wider audiences.[54] Certainly, turning the protagonists of *Romeo and Juliet* into employees of rival supermarkets makes the play easily transferrable to any area in Britain and – with a small change from Tesco/Asda to the names of prominent local retail chains – to other countries in the Western world. What is specific to *Rodney and Julie J.* is not its geographical but its social setting. The main characters are unqualified, underpaid and disaffected low-grade workers – 'bloody shelf stacking part timers / And that hot headed cleaner Tyrone' (p. 4) – who hate their jobs and 'can't wait to get out of this dump' (p. 12). Rodney and Julie J.'s relationship focuses not so much on romance as on a prospect of improving their situation, with Rodney declaring: 'She makes me feel like I could do something with my life, go somewhere, be something. We could elope to college [...] and get some qualification thingies' (pp. 14–15). As the tone suggests, their story is closer to a grim farce than to a high tragedy: Rodney ends up breaking Tyrone's arms, is given a community service sentence, which prevents him from going to college, and Julie J. decides she will be 'better off without him' and goes on her own (p. 26). Romeo's death is transformed into Rodney getting a job at McDonald's, and his romantic last words into 'thus with a kiss I fry', as he kisses not Julie(t) but his McDonald's badge (p. 29).

Thus, by including references to multinational corporations and addressing problems endemic to a social group spread across wide geographical areas, *Rodney and Julie J.* targets global, rather than purely local, audiences and concerns (a point borne out by the group subsequently preparing the play for presentation at the 2013 Edinburgh Fringe Festival). This is indicative of the goals of theatre practitioners in the North East: they do not wish to be pigeonholed as regional, but to add their voices to national and global artistic debates and developments. Doing Shakespeare in innovative ways seems to offer an opportunity to achieve this, but in practice it proves tricky, since initiatives such as the Open Stages can create the feeling of established Shakespearean institutions 'dipping their toes' in the region rather than genuinely recognizing its achievement. Moreover, well-meaning schemes aiming to promote local art can create a feeling that its only value lies in its regional 'flavour', a museum-like quaintness. The author of *Quick Bright Things* made it clear that the last thing she wanted was to 'bang the Northern drum' in order to be recognized. She reflected: 'If we did "Cleopatra in the mine" maybe we would get noticed, but do we want to be seen in the South as just that?'.[55] It is not tokens and stereotypical representations that the artists in the North East need, but real opportunities to present their work in the global arena on an equal footing. And, as the auditions for the *West Side Story* demonstrated, these opportunities are few and far between.

Conclusion

What then is the position and perception of Shakespeare in the North East? As the discussion above demonstrates, asking this question generates complex responses. Shakespeare has been successfully presented and reworked by amateur companies in the region for years, yet when it comes to prestigious events, the practice seems to be to defer to outside institutions and 'experts'. In consequence, as one local theatregoer commented, there is a feeling that 'Shakespeare is a Southern thing'. He explained that he meant not so much Shakespeare himself, as the presentation of his plays in the region by such companies as the RSC: 'They come here and grace the North with their presence at the Theatre Royal. I enjoy Shakespeare when they come but it's still like sending missionaries to Africa'.[56]

To use a slightly facetious analogy, bringing Shakespeare to the North East seems to be like taking coals to Newcastle.

There is talent to burn there, in the form of long-established groups like The People's Theatre, but does the perception persist that experts and resources from elsewhere are needed to ensure an acceptable standard? Moreover, it is difficult for the local talent to move beyond the region and achieve recognition and success on the national and global arena. This is at least partly due to the entrenched perception of cultural authority being located in the metropolitan centre and diminished on the local 'periphery'. In this sense, perhaps it is not Shakespeare himself but Shakespeare as an institution, a guarantor of cultural capital, that is 'a Southern thing'.

When it comes to *actual* capital, it appears that throughout the history of state-funded cultural production in England, there has always been a tendency to privilege the national over the regional, the large-scale over the small-scale, 'quality' over 'amateurism'. As John Carey puts it in his polemic *What Good are The Arts?*,

> In England [...] public policy has not favoured the view that the making of art should be spread through the community. When the Council for the Encouragement of Music and Arts, which later became the Arts Council, was set up in 1940, it had to choose between promoting art by the people or art for the people. [...] The council chose the latter course.[57]

Much has changed, yet much has stayed the same: Orkin's 'metropolitan bank of Shakespeare knowledge' is still well-funded, even in trying times. In an article published during the World Shakespeare Festival, economic recession and ongoing debates and protests about cuts to publicly funded services and institutions, Lyn Gardner, one of the *Guardian*'s drama critics, reflected on the material conditions of cultural production now: 'British arts funding is not a level playing field. [...] It's always those at the top of the pyramid that are most likely to attract private sponsorship, and who are best equipped to survive a downturn.' Gardner's positive suggestion is to 'put money into the bottom of the pyramid, not the top – it is only by funding the bottom that we can create the future'.[58] Her comments were picked up by Andrew Cowie in a blog entitled 'Subsidised Shakespeare'. Cowie notes that as a recipient of Arts Council funding (the fifth-highest regularly funded, in fact), the Royal Shakespeare Company is privileged, but also responsible for generating and supporting productions that meet both high aesthetic standards *and* high standards of community and regional engagement.[59] Cowie eloquently explains how, through schemes such as Open Stages, the RSC is achieving these aims, but still ends with a set of questions: 'is Lyn Gardner right and if the Arts Council is serious about diversity and participation, might they be better off giving £1 million a year to a diverse group of sixteen different companies? Or half a million to 32 companies? Or a quarter of a million to 64 companies?'[60]

Perhaps such a shift in arts resourcing would mean that the sort of questions we have asked in this essay would become less pressing: if a North-Eastern theatre received £250,000, that might facilitate local productions involving local people for local, national and global audiences. Even if this did not happen, perhaps a change in the material conditions of cultural production is imminent anyway:

> At a time when the British government is making vague noises about a 'big society' in which the voluntary sector is to take over services formerly provided by the state, a time when threatened budget cuts are calling the very survival of subsidized theatre into question, it may be that the amateurs will have to step into the breach once more.[61]

Whatever the ideological problems and material fate of the 'Big Society' that could make such survivals possible, we might recollect the epigraph with which this chapter began, and ask one final question: in an era of austerity and globalization, do we want (or, indeed, can or should we have) 'cultural localism' by default or design?

As we try to answer that question, we might end by considering some of the implications of the preceding discussion, and recollect the terms and ideas with which we began it. Our starting position was that the local, global and national aspects of culture are constructed in relation to one another, and that the complex relations between them are predicated upon tangible political and economic factors. Our subsequent examination of the World Shakespeare Festival in the North East of England reveals that there is more to 'glocal' Shakespeare than current criticism accounts for. Most importantly, the interactions between the global, the national and the local are even more complex than we have thought. The national and the local in particular seem capable of assuming different definitions depending on where these definitions are made. From a global perspective, 'national' drama of, let's say, England, can be seen as a *local* drama – one among many national approaches. Yet from the perspective of somebody based in the North East, that 'national' drama may feel much more like a global (universalizing?) or even hegemonic construct – a standard imposed from the outside and made very difficult to achieve for regional practitioners. The 'local' in the sense of regional, on the other hand, can be dismissed by the metropolitan centre as parochial and unsophisticated. Figures invested with cultural capital, like Shakespeare, provide grounds on which these definitions and boundaries can and will be tested and debated.

Indeed, the debate continues. In autumn 2013, Newcastle's buses bore the advertising legend: 'Shakespeare returns to Newcastle'. This slogan actually heralded the return of the full season of *RSC* productions at Newcastle's Theatre Royal, a practice established in 1977 and interrupted, as we have seen, in 2011 due to a 6.9 per cent cut in funding and the opening of the new Royal Shakespeare and Swan Theatres.[62] This return was, of course, welcomed by the city and the company. But if you were an educator, theatre practitioner or student working on or with Shakespeare in the city, you might have legitimately queried the claim that the adverts on the buses made: yes, the RSC's season had been missing, but does that mean that Shakespeare was absent from Newcastle? Is the RSC Shakespeare? Is there no Shakespeare in the North without them? Evidently, it seems we have a long way to go before all the voices in these debates are given equal prominence and recognition.

Notes

1   Kevin Robins, 'Tradition and Translation: National Culture in Its Global Context', in *Enterprise and Heritage: Crosscurrents of National Culture*, ed. John Corner and Sylvia Harvey (London: Routledge, 1991), pp. 21–43 (p. 36).

2   The Royal Shakespeare Company website, http://www.rsc.org. uk/about-us/history/world-shakespeare-festival-2012/ [accessed 19 July 2013].

3   See, for example, Jonathan Bate, 'Shakespearean Nationhoods', in *Shakespeare in the New Europe*, ed. Michael Hattaway, Boika Sokolova and Derek Roper (Sheffield: Sheffield Academic Press, 1994), pp. 112–29; *This England, That Shakespeare: New Angles on Englishness and the Bard*, Willy Maley and Margaret Tudeau-Clayton (eds) (Farnham: Ashgate, 2010); *Shakespeare and National Culture*, ed. John J. Joughin (Manchester: Manchester University Press, 1997), especially Joughin, 'Introduction', pp. 1–15, Graham Holderness and Andrew Murphy, 'Shakespeare's England: Britain's Shakespeare', pp. 19–41, and Willy Maley, '"This sceptred isle": Shakespeare and the British problem', pp. 83–109. Other useful developments of this topic include Andrew Hadfield, *Shakespeare, Spenser and the Matter of Britain* (Basingstoke: Palgrave Macmillan, 2004); Jean Howard and Phyllis Rackin, *Engendering a Nation: A Feminist Account of Shakespeare's English Histories* (London: Routledge, 1997); David J. Baker and Willy Maley (eds), *British Identities and English Renaissance Literature* (Cambridge: Cambridge University Press, 2002); Richard Helgerson, *Forms of Nationhood: The Elizabethan Writing of England* (Chicago: University

of Chicago Press, 1992, reprinted 1994); Willy Maley and
Rory Loughnane (eds), *Celtic Shakespeare: The Bard and the
Borderers* (Farnham: Ashgate, 2013); and Terence Hawkes,
'Bryn Glas', in *Post-Colonial Shakespeares*, ed. Ania Loomba
and Martin Orkin (London: Routledge, 1998), pp. 117–40.

4   See, among others, the essays collected in Loomba and
Orkin (1998); Peter Hulme and William H. Sherman (eds),
'The Tempest' and Its Travels (London: Reaktion Books,
2000); Thomas Cartelli, *Repositioning Shakespeare: National
Formations, Postcolonial Appropriations* (Abingdon:
Routledge, 1999); Catherine M. S. Alexander and Stanley
Wells (eds), *Shakespeare and Race* (Cambridge: Cambridge
University Press, 2000); Ania Loomba, *Shakespeare, Race, and
Colonialism* (Oxford: Oxford University Press, 2002).

5   Martin Orkin, *Local Shakespeares: Proximation and Power*
(London: Routledge, 2005), p. 1.

6   Ibid., p. 2.

7   R. S. White, 'Introduction', in *Shakespeare's Local Habitations*,
ed. Krystyna Kujawińska Courtney and R. S. White (Łódź:
Łódź University Press, 2007), pp. 5–10 (p. 5). According to
White the term 'glocal' was 'anticipated [...] in a different
context' by Richard Burt in 'Shakespeare, "Glo-cal-ization,"
Race, and the Small Screens of Popular Culture', in
*Shakespeare the Movie II: Popularizing the Plays on Film,
TV, Video and DVD*, Burt and Lynda E. Boose (eds) (London:
Routledge, 2003), pp. 14–36.

8   White, 'Introduction', p. 5.

9   Robins, 'Tradition and Translation', p. 34.

10 Mark Thornton Burnett, *Filming Shakespeare in the Global
Marketplace* (Houndmills: Palgrave Macmillan, 2007), p. 48.

11 Robins, 'Tradition and Translation', p. 35.

12 Ibid., p. 35.

13 Peter Holland, *English Shakespeares: Shakespeare on the
English Stage in the 1990s* (Cambridge: Cambridge University
Press, 1997), p. 154. Holland is discussing the productions of
and responses to Northern Broadsides, a company with strong
roots in its region. See also Carol Chillington Rutter, 'Rough

Music: Northern Broadsides at Work at Play', *Shakespeare Survey* 56 (2003), pp. 236–55.
14 White, 'Introduction', p. 9.
15 Orkin, *Local Shakespeares*, p. 1.
16 Ibid., p. 2.
17 Robins, 'Tradition and Translation', p. 35.
18 Ibid., p. 31.
19 Ibid., p. 35.
20 Ibid., p. 39. On Newcastle's attempt to do this in the late 1980s and early 1990s, see ibid, pp. 39–40.
21 Frank Brogan, cited in Michael Dobson, *Shakespeare and Amateur Performance: A Cultural History* (Cambridge: Cambridge University Press, 2011), p. 213.
22 Orkin, *Local Shakespeares*, p. 1.
23 Amy Fawdington, Communications Manager at the Northern Stage, cited in Carla Washbourne, 'Preview: World Shakespeare Festival', Keep Your Eyes Open website, 29 June 2012, http://www.kyeo.tv/2012/06/29/preview-world-shakespeare-festival/ [accessed 29 July 2013]; emphasis ours.
24 RSC Press Release, '2011 Newcastle Season', 25 January 2011, http://www.rsc.org.uk/about-us/press/releases/2011-newcastle-press-release.aspx [accessed 23 April 2013].
25 'Royal Shakespeare Company retains Newcastle connection', *The Chronicle*, 4 July 2012, http://www.chroniclelive.co.uk/news/local-news/royal-shakespeare-company-retains-newcastle-1367270 [accessed 23 April 2013].
26 See, for example, Gordon Barr, 'Cash cuts force RSC to miss out Tyneside', *The Chronicle*, 25 January 2011, http://www.chroniclelive.co.uk/news/north-east-news/cash-cuts-force-rsc-miss-1394166 [accessed 23 April 2013]; and Mark Brown, 'Cuts mean Royal Shakespeare Company's Newcastle season is not to be', *Guardian*, 26 January 2011, http://www.guardian.co.uk/culture/culture-cuts-blog/2011/jan/26/cuts-royal-shakespeare-company-newcastle [accessed 23 April 2013].
27 'Winlatonlad', 'Comment', 29 January 2011, in response to Barr, 'Cash cuts'.

28 'Offshor714', 'Comment', 25 January 2011, in response to Barr, 'Cash cuts'.

29 Laura Fraine, 'RSC No-Show', *The Journal Blog Central*, 26 January 2011, http://blogs.journallive.co.uk/journalblogcentral/2011/01/rsc-no-show.html [accessed 23 April 2013].

30 '*West Side Story: Fringe Events*, 1st June–7th July', The Sage Gateshead promotional brochure (2012). The other cancelled event was 'Amateur Shakespeare with Michael Dobson', as confirmed in email communication from Rebecca Tempest at The Sage to Monika Smialkowska (22 May 2013).

31 This cancellation might bear comparison with cancelled African Globe to Globe productions, as discussed by Colette Gordon later in this volume (p. 197).

32 Tempest, email to Smialkowska.

33 See the data up to 2011 aggregated, indexed by geographic region and analysed by The Poverty Site, http://www.poverty.org.uk/summary/regional.shtml [accessed 29 July 2013].

34 Owen Jones, *Chavs: The Demonization of the Working Class* (London: Verso, 2012), p. xxiii.

35 See 'Income Inequalities: Graph 7', The Poverty Site, http://www.poverty.org.uk/09/index.shtml [accessed 29 July 2013].

36 Daniel Briggs, 'Concluding Thoughts', in *The English Riots of 2011: A Summer of Discontent*, ed. Briggs (Hook: Waterside Press, 2012), pp. 381–401 (p. 385).

37 Quoted in Simon Winlow and Steve Hall, 'Gone Shopping: Inarticulate Politics in the English Riots of 2011', in *The English Riots*, ed. Briggs, pp. 149–67 (p. 149). As Owen Jones notes elsewhere: 'Nearly two-thirds of the young rioters lived in England's poorest areas' (*Chavs*, p. xxii).

38 For the most comprehensive articulation of this fact see Richard Wilkinson and Kate Pickett, *The Spirit Level: Why Equality is Better for Everyone* (London: Penguin, 2010).

39 Adrian Pearson, 'Tyneside at Risk of Meadow Well Repeat', *The Chronicle*, 7 December 2011, http://www.chroniclelive.co.uk/news/north-east-news/tyneside-risk-meadow-well-riots-1408057 [accessed 25 July 2013].

40 Briggs, 'Introduction', in *The English Riots*, pp. 9–25 (p. 13).
41 Dobson, *Shakespeare and Amateur Performance*, p. 2
42 Dobson encourages the questioning of these categories, together with the strict distinction between 'amateur' and 'professional' theatre.
43 The announcement for the project on the World Shakespeare Festival's website, http://www.worldshakespearefestival.org.uk/projects/open-stages.aspx [accessed 23 July 2013].
44 The full list of the partner theatres, as published in the 'Final Progress Report from the Royal Shakespeare Company: Open Stages 2011–12' includes: National Theatre of Scotland; the Lyric Theatre, Belfast; Contact Theatre, Manchester; The Sage, Gateshead; Royal Shakespeare Company; New Wolsey, Ipswich; Hall for Cornwall, Truro; the Nuffield Theatre, Southampton; Questors, London; and Sherman Cymru, Cardiff. See the RSC's website, http://www.rsc.org.uk/search.aspx?q=progress%20report [accessed 23 July 2013].
45 Quoted on the RSC's website, http://www.rsc.org.uk/explore/projects/open-stages [accessed 23 July 2013].
46 Alfred Hickling, '*West Side Story* – Review. Sage Gateshead', *Guardian*, 6 July 2012, http://www.theguardian.com/music/2012/jul/06/west-side-story-review [accessed 23 July 2013].
47 An advert issued on the website of the National Operatic and Dramatic Association on 1 January 2012 did not mention the regional auditions at all, stating instead: 'Auditions will take place in London from 23–27th January. Applicants must be available in London on these dates.' See http://www.noda.org.uk/news/rsc_open_stages_ [accessed on 25 July 2013].
48 Charlie Burt, 'I'd like to be in America! Charlie Burt tells us about her experience of auditioning for a big musical production', *The Courier Online*, 12 March 2012, http://thecourieronline.co.uk/id-like-to-be-in-america/ [accessed 24 July 2013].
49 'Choreographer/Director Will Tuckett talking about auditions for *West Side Story* at the Sage Gateshead', The Sage Gateshead website, http://www.thesagegateshead.org/news-list/

west-side-story-auditions-january-2012 [accessed 25 July 2013]. In the video interview, Tuckett stressed 'here', hence our emphasis.

50 Alison Carr, interview with Monika Smialkowska (23 July 2013).

51 Victoria Baker, *Rodney and Julie J.* (Newcastle: 2012), unpublished script, courtesy of the author, p. 1. Further references in-text.

52 Carr, interview with Smialkowska.

53 The People's Theatre celebrated its centenary in 2011. It opened in 1911 in Percy Street and moved to its current venue (Stephenson Road) in 1962.

54 Victoria Baker, interview with Monika Smialkowska (10 April 2013).

55 Carr, interview with Smialkowska.

56 The respondent (interviewed by Smialkowska, 23 July 2013) was a man in his late forties, Newcastle born and bred, coming from a working-class family and currently employed as a civil servant.

57 John Carey, *What Good Are the Arts?* (London: Faber and Faber, 2005), p. 156. As Carey suggests, for more on this see Robert Hewison, *Culture and Consensus: England, Art and Politics since 1940* (London: Methuen, 1997).

58 Lyn Gardner, 'Why major theatre institutions should be left to die', *Guardian*, 20 August 2012, http://www.theguardian.com/stage/theatreblog/2012/aug/30/major-theatre-institutions-die [accessed 25 July 2013].

59 Cowie observes that the RSC received a grant of £16,413,895 in 2011–12 (down from £17,639,392 the previous year); see 'Subsidised Shakespeare', *Blogging Shakespeare*, http://bloggingshakespeare.com/subsidised-shakespeare [accessed 25 July 2013].

60 Cowie, 'Subsidised Shakespeare'.

61 Dobson, *Shakespeare and Amateur Performance*, p. 12.

62 See 'Newcastle loses out to RSC budget cuts', *BBC News*, 25 January 2011, http://www.bbc.co.uk/news/

uk-england-tyne-12281448 [accessed 8 October 2013]; Ian Youngs, 'RSC Returns to Newcastle After Cuts', *BBC News*, 8 February 2013, http://www.bbc.co.uk/news/entertainment-arts-21382076 [accessed 8 October 2013].

6

Shakespeare, Spectatorship and the 'Olympic Spirit'

Stephen Purcell

'Ladies and gentlemen', said the announcer, 'we now have the victory ceremony for the men's 400 metres, T38. The medals tonight will be presented by the Right Honourable George Osborne MP, Chancellor of the Exchequer.'

The boos rang out through the 80,000-capacity Olympic Stadium, and across the airwaves.

Video clips of George Osborne's reception at the Paralympics on 3 September 2012 made the national news and went viral on social media. The propriety of the crowd's response was much debated, and an article on the *Guardian*'s website the following day surveyed a number of Games spectators for their thoughts on the matter. While some interpreted the crowd reaction as a valid response to Osborne's recent and controversial changes to disability benefits – this was the Paralympics, after all – others felt it was bad form. Arguing that '[p]eople have a democratic right to express their opinion', charity worker Carolyn Allan suggested that the booing 'reflected the mood of the people'. Londoner Robert Dulin, on the other hand, noted that though he did not agree with Osborne's politics, he felt that 'the true spirit of the Games went out the window yesterday'.[1] These conflicting responses give a good sense of the various tensions at the heart of popular conceptions of Olympic spectatorship: that it is simultaneously democratic *and* harmonious, expressive of both national and identity politics, but characterized by collectivism and goodwill. The Olympic crowd is evidently a forum in which we construct an identity for 'ourselves' as a group – however tenuous, fleeting and unstable that identity may be.

This chapter will explore some of the ways in which the World Shakespeare Festival played a role in this process of myth-building. It will draw on my own experiences as a spectator at a range of WSF performances, considering the ways in which various productions interacted with the group identities enacted by their audiences in order to engage in a collaborative authorship of the performance. Where some performances clearly worked hard to foster a sense of unity among their audiences, others were unafraid to play to different constituencies in different ways. National and cultural identities played a major role in this, as we shall see; the demographic composition of different audiences also meant that these group identities varied enormously even between performances of the same production. Audiences at the WSF were unusually active in performing the identities requested of them, and these identities were generally negotiated rather than imposed entirely by the stage.

Universality and diversity

The London 2012 Festival (of which the WSF was a major part) had fairly clear aims for its audiences. The expectation that a Cultural Olympiad should 'serve to promote harmonious relations, mutual understanding and friendship among the participants and others attending the Olympic Games' was expressed clearly in the 1995 edition of the Olympic Charter; in an oddly paradoxical sub-clause, any such programme of cultural events was expected to symbolize 'the universality and the diversity of human culture'.[2] Interestingly, the 2010 edition of the Olympic Charter abandoned all such objectives, stipulating merely 'a programme of cultural events which must cover at least the entire period during which the Olympic Village is open'.[3] Nonetheless, the spirit of the 1995 charter lived on in the stated aims of the London 2012 Festival, which included ambitions to 'inspire and involve the widest and most inclusive range of UK communities', to 'connect future generations [...] with their peers around the world', to develop 'an enlightened policy of cultural diversity and inclusion', and to 'offer a platform for the many different communities of the United Kingdom to unite around shared celebrations'.[4]

It is relatively easy to assess the Festival's success in achieving these outcomes on the most straightforward statistical level. The Institute of Cultural Capital's *London 2012 Cultural Olympiad Evaluation* makes extensive use of the 'London 2012 Audience Survey' conducted by Nielsen/LOCOG, which polled 1,868 audience members across eight projects in the London 2012 Festival; this figure included 804 audience members of the World Shakespeare Festival at Globe to Globe.[5] Asked to rate the 'atmosphere' at the event they had attended, audiences judged the London 2012 Festival warmly: 95.5 per cent awarded seven out of ten or higher, with 52.1 per cent giving full marks.[6] When asked whether they agreed or disagreed that '[e]vents like this help the local community to come together', a smaller majority, 56.8 per cent, agreed, with 25.4 per cent neutral and the remainder disagreeing.[7] This lower rating may have been due to the fact that many spectators had travelled a long way to attend Festival events – 53.7 per cent of the Globe to Globe audience, for example, had to travel for more than an hour in order to get to the performance.[8] The Festival seems to have been fairly successful in attracting new audiences: 44 per cent of the Royal Shakespeare Company's World Shakespeare Festival audience in Stratford-upon-Avon, for example, and 80 per cent of the Globe to Globe audience in London, were new to the theatres.[9] The report's authors note, however, that certain events, including Globe to Globe, 'drew significant audiences who were regular participators or attendees at cultural activity': 98.6 per cent had engaged in other 'cultural activities' (such as 'theatre, cinema, music and exhibitions') three or more times in the last 12 months, compared with a national average of 63.5 per cent.[10] A surprisingly low proportion of respondents (7.1 per cent) reported themselves as having come from outside the United Kingdom.[11]

The report's qualitative data indicates that some audience members did see the Festival – and Globe to Globe especially – as expressive of an 'Olympic spirit'. One spectator, for example, saw the Globe to Globe Festival as a model of how to 'advance and showcase the Olympic spirit', while another commended the way in which Globe to Globe 'drew in so many different people from many different countries. Fits the Olympic spirit'.[12] A third example is even more explicit: 'The point of the Olympic Games is to bring the world together as one, and presenting Shakespeare's complete works using companies from as many countries is a wonderful companion to that'.[13] Clearly for some spectators, the very fact of an international Shakespeare festival was indication enough of the Olympic Charter's desired 'universality and diversity', and it may be that the specific workings of particular productions added to this feeling. Having said this, over a quarter of the Globe to Globe audience surveyed were unaware that the Festival was connected to the Olympics, and other Globe to Globe attendees reported themselves, for example, as being 'not that interested in the Olympic Games'.[14]

Intercultural celebration at Globe to Globe

The Globe to Globe Festival was probably the World Shakespeare Festival's most overt manifestation of the 'Olympic spirit'. Shakespeare's Globe theatre's unique architectural configuration tends to encourage a sociable and interactive relationship between performer and audience (and between spectator and spectator), and this was especially manifest at Globe to Globe. As Paul Prescott has argued, the Festival's performances 'could frequently be interpreted only via the reactions of fellow audience members':

> Watching one's own reactions to the play was often a matter of watching other people's, a reminder of what extraordinary value for money the theatre can offer when a single ticket grants you access to two shows: the one onstage and the one everywhere else.[15]

This was certainly true of my own experiences as both spectator and reviewer; in several cases, I found myself unable to detach the meaning of a production from my experience of its communal reception. When the family reunions at the end of *The Comedy of Errors* were greeted with boisterous cheering, it reminded me of what must be a very real desire for such reconciliation among the Afghan expatriate community. The Greek *Pericles* made its audience laugh and cry with its tale of triumph over adversity, and incorporated direct references – in English – to the Greek financial crisis.

Spectators' reactions were central in reviews, especially those featured on the *Year of Shakespeare* website and in its follow-up book.[16] The analysis that follows draws extensively on these reviews, since *Year of Shakespeare* was one of the few comprehensive accounts of the Festival (only the *Guardian* and *The Arts Desk* provided comparable coverage at the time). While its reviews provide invaluable information about spectators' responses, it should be noted that they were often written by critics (myself included) who were not necessarily part of the 'in-group' to whom all of a production's various cultural references were available. This decentring of the critic as privileged possessor of all the codes and conventions of performance was perhaps one of the Festival's most radical side-effects.

The extent to which Globe to Globe's inter-spectator communication was possible varied from production to production. Sarah Olive's reviews for *A Year of Shakespeare* testify to the fluctuating numbers of comprehending spectators at any given performance: 'half' of the audience at the Russian *Measure for Measure*, for example, seemed to her to be Russian speakers, while there were 'noticeably smaller numbers of Swahili speakers at the matinee of *Merry Wives* the same day'; the mixed composition of the audience for the latter made her resist the potential 'to read the action as taking place in a particular locality', so that she preferred to see the production as one that 'transcended language and appealed to a global community'.[17] This was not always the case, however. Several commentators worried that the nuances of a production would be lost on an English-speaking audience: a joke about German ex-President Christian Wulff in *Timon of Athens* made Emily Oliver wonder 'whether non-German-speaking spectators struggled to understand the stage action', while Adele Lee suspected that 'there was some significant political commentary' embedded in the Cantonese-language *Titus Andronicus* 'on which English-speaking spectators missed out'.[18] During the Belarusian *King Lear*, I certainly noticed that an exchange between two guards that has no direct equivalent in Shakespeare's text was drawing laughter from the small sections of the audience who were evidently following the language. I could not help but notice my own exclusion from the production's systems of meaning at that moment.

Among some audiences, there was an unmistakeable sense of national pride and celebration. Some companies, including the National Theatre of Albania and the Dhaka Theatre from Bangladesh, brought their national flags onto the stage with them during their curtain calls, to cheers from their audiences; Thea Buckley noted a similar cheer at the word 'Urdu' during the introduction to the Pakistani production of *The Taming of the Shrew*.[19] Rose Elfman's in-depth survey of Globe to Globe audiences provides numerous examples of spectators who saw their involvement in a production as expressive of pride in their cultural origins [see her chapter in this volume, which includes the survey itself as an appendix]. Such active involvement was not always celebrated by those on its margins, however. Georgie Lucas found the audience applause during the Armenian *King John* 'almost oppressive' – so much so that she 'started to wonder if the audience was on commission', and found herself frustrated by 'the kind of blind approval in which the shift in tone accompanying the threat of wholesale and bloody annihilation becomes so garbled that it elicits applause'.[20] Peter J. Smith, meanwhile, complained that spectators at the Indian *Twelfth Night* 'whooped, cheered, jeered, clapped and waved their arms at the tiniest invitation', transforming what he sees as a 'painful play about grief and the embarrassment of love' into 'a carefree romp'.[21]

Some spectators evidently took on a kind of dramaturgical role on behalf of their fellow audience members. Several of the *Year of Shakespeare* reviews cite conversations with other spectators as a source of information about a production; Sonia Massai's account of *The Tempest* is especially evocative, noting that the Bangla-speaking spectators made other members of the audience 'feel like welcome guests' as they 'generously shared information about the company, the props they used and the significance of specific gestures and dance routines'.[22] Erin Sullivan writes about a conversation with two Arabic-speaking spectators at *Richard II*, during which they informed her that the production contained 'subtle references to modern Palestinian politics' that audiences unfamiliar with the culture might miss: 'In their costuming and behaviour, Richard and his followers signalled the Fatah party, they suggested, and Bolingbroke in his bomber jacket and red beret Hamas'.[23]

Elfman's survey shows that Festival spectators frequently relied on the reactions of other spectators in order to make sense of the performance. The responses of a Dutch spectator to the Palestinian *Richard II* might be indicative: this spectator apparently 'understood the gravity and the context' of Ashtar Theatre's production 'through the active response of some audience members'. One moment in particular stood out for this spectator, as it did for many of the production's reviewers. At the end of Act 2, scene 4, as the Welsh Captain explained to Bagot (replacing Salisbury in this scene) that the Welsh forces had dispersed and fled, a group of masked men entered the stage wielding bloodied white flags; their rallying cry was met by other masked men and women stationed all around the auditorium, who then mounted the stage waving red, green and black flags. As Yuval Ben-Ami's account for the web magazine +972 explains, these colours were highly symbolic:

> The Palestinian flag fell apart. National identity has shattered. Over its smithereens, on Juliette's balcony [*sic*], stands an actor waving a golden flag stained with blood. Only this flag remains when the stage is vacated. This is a brief, stunning moment that will prove difficult to forget.[24]

Despite its bleak undertones, the moment was met with audience applause and cheering at both the matinee and the evening performances; some spectators had, furthermore, brought Palestinian flags along themselves, which they waved during the applause at the end of the show. For Elfman's Dutch spectator, this was the most surprising part of the performance: 'The political reality – audience, with Palestinian flags, and reacting to the Welsh uprising. Also screaming "Free Palestine" after the performance.' This spectator concludes the survey with the observation that '[t]he moment with the flag, and the audience's reaction to it, was really captivating and I felt like suddenly I understood the context a lot better'. The audience at this moment was clearly participating in a kind of collaborative authorship of the performance, rendering its politics ambiguous but highly charged.

Audience performance in Renegade's *The Winter's Tale*

Of all the Globe to Globe shows, it was perhaps the Nigerian company Renegade Theatre's *The Winter's Tale* that gave most prominence to the performances of its spectators. The actors tended to deliver their lines directly to the audience, as if they were seeking the crowd's mandate for their assertions; the Yoruba-speaking audience members tended to be highly vocal in their responses to such moments, loudly registering approval, disapproval, appreciation or scepticism as appropriate. There is evidently a rich vocabulary of vocal interjections in Nigerian culture, since identical noises could frequently be heard across the whole auditorium at particular moments. As Julie Sanders explains, in the Apidán theatre tradition from which Renegade draws inspiration, 'spectators are accorded the status of "co-actors" and frequently asked to fill in the gaps in retellings of traditional scenarios and tales'; during the evening performance at Shakespeare's Globe, 'the Yoruba-speaking section of the audience warmed to their task'.[25] Indeed, of the 16 audience members of *The Winter's Tale* who responded to Elfman's survey, 11 identified 'the reactions of the other spectators' as having helped them to understand the performance – at 69 per cent, by far the highest proportion of any production in the survey. Significantly, the remaining five spectators were all Yoruba-speakers themselves. A British-Nigerian audience member with 'a few words' of Yoruba described the sound of the language as having made him or her cry, and declared that 'the audience participation was amazing'.[26]

A fuller account of the performance may help to explain how this audience engagement worked in practice. The description that follows is based on my own experience as an audience member of the performance at the Globe on the evening of Friday 25 May, and on the video recording of the same performance that was made for Arts Council England's digital platform The Space (www.TheSpace.org).[27] The audience at this performance evidently included a large proportion of Yoruba-speaking spectators, many of whom were presumably British-Nigerian (as Tom Bird notes in his interview for this volume, the Globe had made a deliberate effort to advertise performances to ethnic communities in London). The production's call-and-response sequences were predicated on a confidence that numerous spectators would be conversant in Yoruba, as was the decision to have the show narrated by a singer in the guise of Time ('Ìgbà') – these passages of narration were summarized only very broadly on the English-language surtitles at each side of the stage. The production also clearly anticipated an audience who would be prepared to adopt the role of 'co-actors'. This projected audience matched the audience as it performed itself at the Globe on the evening I saw the production, but less so the audience of the previous day's matinee; the video taken of this performance for the Globe's archive records a far more muted response. In this video, the show seems strangely incomplete, like a studio sitcom with parts of the laughter track missing. As much as the performance constructed an identity for its audience, this identity was clearly partly reliant on cultural factors beyond its control.

Ìgbà (Motúnráyọ̀ Oròbíyi) began her storytelling from the Globe's balcony. Shakespeare's play was substantially re-ordered, opening with the abandonment of the baby Olúọlá/ Perdita. As the two clowns discovered the infant and the gold that had been left with her, they shared their surprise with the audience, to applause. Ìgbà then narrated the gap of 16 years, introducing us to Ògún/Polixenes (Ọlárótìmí Fákúnlé), the god of iron, who waved his rifle threateningly at spectators. The festival scene that followed was very festive indeed: Olúọlá (Olúwatóyìn Alli-Hakeem) entered from the yard, singing and dancing, flirting with audience members as she passed, and Fọláwẹwọ́/Florizel (Joshua Adémọ́lá Àlàbí) performed his love for her as another song and dance. The two then danced together, soliciting audience applause for their showier moves. His brazen appreciation of her undulating form provoked playfully disapproving laughter from some quarters of the audience (noticeably some of the older British-Nigerian women near me). The stage filled up with dancers, and the actors brought a few audience members up on stage to dance with them, to laughter and applause from the rest of the house.

Ògún's angry revelation of his true identity brought this carnivalesque section of the play to an abrupt end, but the sense of reciprocity remained as the story took its darker turn. Adéagbo/Camillo (Ọlásúnkànmi Adébáyọ̀) told the young lovers the story of Ṣàngó/Leontes, the god of thunder, and Ṣàngó's wife Ọya/Hermione. At this point, the play segued into a flashback; we were presented with Ṣàngó and Ọya themselves (Ọláwálé Adébáyọ̀ and Kẹ̀hìndé Bánkolé), and invited to judge their behaviour. Ṣàngó's jealousy upon Ọya's mildly flirtatious conversation with Ògún was shouted and mugged to the audience, to laughter. When he accused her of infidelity, alleging that Ògún had fathered her child, he pushed her belly with the blunt tip of his axe, and spectators made an audible moan, a collective expression of disapproval and perhaps also disappointment. The couple's argument played out at a frantic pace, punctuated by the occasional silence, during each of which audience members would make their own vocal contributions to the debate. Ṣàngó presented the case against his wife directly to the audience, to loud murmurs of dissent ('OH-oh!'); as he twice delivered the accusation 'She's an adultress' (2.1.80 and 2.1.90), these objections became even louder.[28] When Ọya appealed to the audience in her own defence, her words were met with interjections from the audience that affirmed both her innocence and the righteousness of her anger; the speech which in English begins with 'No, by my life' (2.1.97–102) became almost a call-and-response sequence.

A similar dynamic continued through the scenes that followed. Féyígbẹ̀san/Paulina (Idiat Abísọ́lá Ṣóbándé) was applauded as she swiped at a sycophantic Lord during her confrontation with Ṣàngó, while Ṣàngó himself strutted, roared and threatened spectators with his axe in fury, at one point running down into the yard. His violent anger towards the baby was met with gasps and sighs of outrage. The following transcript (translated back into Shakespeare's English) gives some sense of the rather ambivalent political energy that the audience response added to the scene:

> ṢÀNGÓ. *(to Antigonus)* Take up the bastard,
>   Take't up, I say. Give't to thy crone.
> FÉYÍGBẸ̀SAN. *(to Antigonus)* For ever
>   Unvenerable be thy hands, if thou
>   Takest up the princess by that forced baseness
>   Which he has put upon't!
> AUDIENCE. *[laughter as Antigonus hesitates]*
> ṢÀNGÓ. He dreads his wife.
> AUDIENCE. *[laughter]*
> FÉYÍGBẸ̀SAN. So I would you did.
> AUDIENCE. *[loud murmurs of assent: 'mm-HM!']*
> FÉYÍGBẸ̀SAN. Then 'twere past all doubt
>   You'd call your children yours.
> AUDIENCE. *[further loud murmurs of assent]*
> (2.3.76–82)

Happy to laugh at the emasculation of Antigonus (who was not given a Yoruban name in the production), the audience nonetheless endorsed Féyígbẹ̀san's defiance of patriarchal authority quite unambiguously. There was loud applause and cheering for her as she exited, leaving Ṣàngó seething.

The final scene brought this audience involvement to an appropriate climax. The now-repentant Ṣàngó, whose remorse had been greeted with stern approval from the participating audience members, was presented with the statue of his dead wife. The spectators seemed playfully cynical for a few moments: there was laughter as Féyígbẹ̀san scolded Ṣàngó for trying to touch the statue, and then more laughter as she performed an incantation, with increasing vigour, in order to bring it to life. As Ọya began to move and stepped down off her plinth, however, the audience's scepticism seemed to dissolve, and they – we – erupted into applause and cheering. But the production had one more surprise. During Ṣàngó's final self-congratulatory speech, Ọya returned to her plinth, resumed her pose, and became a statue once again, and Ìgbà informed us that she had become the spirit of the whirlwind. The audience laughed, applauded and cheered some more. As the cast took their bows, they took pictures of the audience on their smartphones, and several spectators reciprocated; I would be reminded of this celebratory exchange of flash photography two months later, as I watched the Olympics Opening Ceremony on television. In both cases, the activity made explicit what had been implicit throughout the rest of the performance: that this was an 'event' for performers and spectators alike, in which both groups participated in a collective act of identification and celebration.

I am aware that in writing this account of 'the audience's' performance, I have been somewhat imprecise. The audience was, of course, composed of a large number of individuals who responded in different, undocumented ways. My own shifting between first- and third-person plurals in the account above indicates, too, that it was possible to move between a detached awareness of the dominant crowd reaction and participation in it with some fluidity. The Yoruba-speaking spectators who interjected so vocally throughout the show by no means made up a majority of the audience as a whole; Elfman's survey suggests that Yoruba-speakers were outnumbered by non-speakers at a ratio of around 2:1 (though the small sample size makes such statistics unreliable). The production's interactivity was dependent on this vocal minority; this meant that those members of the audience without an understanding of Yoruba became highly dependent on their fellow spectators for their comprehension of the performance. The sense of 'the audience' as a character generated by the Yoruba-speaking participants was palpable, and this was a character that became intermittently available, through active listening and participation, for even non-Yoruba-speaking spectators to perform.

Home crowds at the Globe and the RSC

The 'Olympic spirit' is, as we have seen, just as much about national pride as it is about 'universality', and nowhere is this more evident than in the responses of the home crowd to the national teams. Like the Olympic Games, the World Shakespeare Festival provided an opportunity for British spectators to affirm a sense of their own national identity. The enactment of this identity, though, tended to foreground its own construction as *performance*, and in more than one production, the group performance requested of the audience seemed to result in some degree of scepticism or disjunction. Indeed, of the respondents to the Nielsen/LOCOG survey, only 51 per cent agreed that 'London 2012 Festival gives me a sense of national pride'; 24 per cent were neutral, and the remainder disagreed.[29]

The Globe to Globe Festival concluded with an English-language production of *Henry V* by the resident Globe company. Like *The Winter's Tale*, *Henry V* cast its audience in a central role, though unlike *The Winter's Tale*, this was an overtly fictitious one: in this case, that of the play's English army. Jamie Parker's Henry delivered the 'Once more unto the breach' speech (3.1.1–34) straight to the audience; since there were barely any other characters onstage, the fictional role that was being asked of us was clear, and Parker spoke the whole thing from an extension that jutted from the centre of the stage into the yard, putting him right in the middle of the building. This Henry was unmistakably a man of the people. When I saw the production later in the summer, he picked a 'good yeoman / Whose limbs were made in England' from the groundlings, clasping him heartily by the shoulder as he invited him to 'show us here / The mettle of your pasture' (3.1.25–7). Parker delivered the speech with such quick-fire energy and thrilling momentum that a large number of audience members joined in the cry at the end (goaded, no doubt, by the presence of Bardolph, Nym, Pistol, the Boy and others in the crowd):

HENRY. Cry 'God for Harry – '
AUDIENCE. God for Harry!
HENRY. '...England – '
AUDIENCE. England!
HENRY. '...and Saint George!'
AUDIENCE. And Saint George! (3.1.34)[30]

Henry then left the stage to applause. The effect of this participation, and more like it throughout the show, was to whip the audience up into pseudo-patriotic fervour: later, upon the delivery of the news that 'The day is yours' (4.7.84), a spectator behind me cried out 'Yes!', almost as if Andy Murray had just won the tennis. There were frequent bursts of applause, sometimes mid-scene; I was worried for a moment that the report of the numbers of French and English dead in Act 4, scene 8 would be responded to as though the score were being announced at the end of a sports event, but the production's focus on Henry's grief at this moment skilfully avoided any such crassness. Henry's line 'I love France so well that I will not part with a village of it' (5.2.173–4), however, got a huge laugh, and the production cut the Chorus's pessimistic epilogue – in which we learn that after Henry's early death, his heir and successor 'lost France and made his England bleed' (l. 12) – in favour of a feel-good jig.

On one level, then, the production was clearly asking its audience to enact a kind of jingoistic patriotism. This patriotism was English rather than British – the Scottish Captain

Jamy (Chris Starkie) was played as deliberately incoherent, and the Welsh Fluellen (Brendan O'Hea) as a fool. Indeed, in a July interview with the *Independent*, Parker noted that at one performance, 'two guys in the gallery turned up with a St. George's flag'.[31] When Abigail Rokison criticized the production for doing 'little to contradict' the nationalistic reading of the play and for feeling 'like an extension of the sort of patriotic fervour which has been abundantly evident in England this year', the user-submitted comments beneath her review on the *Year of Shakespeare* website commended the production's 'balance' and its 'healthy, uplifting patriotism'.[32] But I wonder whether, flag-waving aside, the production also left space for scepticism about English national pride. Following 'Once more unto the breach', Paul Rider's Bardolph entered the stage directly parodying Henry's speech, repeating the King's instruction to 'imitate the action of the tiger' before giving his own half-hearted impression of a tiger's growl, and garbling misquotations of the speech's most famous lines. Later, when Henry ordered his soldiers to kill their prisoners (4.6.37), the audience fell silent. We had been asked to *pretend* to be a patriotic English army, but this play-acting did not necessarily require us to endorse Henry's actions for real, and there were multiple opportunities for us to step out of role. The Globe audience was by no means uniformly English, after all. Whereas *The Winter's Tale* had encouraged its spectators to judge its characters, *Henry V* asked us only to play.

As we saw in the Globe to Globe Festival, the 'Olympic spirit' might manifest itself as an invitation to 'outsiders' to become part of the 'in-group'. But the keen sense of national identity fostered by the Olympics can work against this. The home crowd defines itself in large part by what it is not: visiting teams may be welcomed, even celebrated, but they often remain distinctly 'other'. The postcolonial politics of the World Shakespeare Festival came to the fore in Iqbal Khan's *Much Ado about Nothing*, one of the Royal Shakespeare Company's major contributions to the World Shakespeare Festival. This production set the play, according to its programme, in contemporary Delhi, but it seemed to assume an audience which was largely British and non-Indian rather than the ethnically diverse one anticipated by Globe to Globe. This audience was thus presumed to have no access to Indian culture other than through the lens of the tourist, so this was the fictional role we were asked to play.

The production transformed the entire foyer of Stratford-upon-Avon's Courtyard Theatre into an impressionistic recreation of modern Delhi, dressing the space with barrels, kettles, bins, fairy lights, scarves, parasols and posters. A rickshaw stood in the middle of the foyer, and bicycles hung from the ceiling. As the audience entered the building, the show's cast strolled the foyer and auditorium, greeting both playgoers and one another in character as tourists, policemen and local salespeople (Peter Kirwan recalls being asked if he would 'like hotel. Very nice hotel').[33] One pushed a bike, another took photographs, while a third carried heavy shopping bags. A soundtrack of blaring horns filled in the impression of a busy Indian city centre. The audience was invited into this pastiche of Delhi as consumers of 'India' the commodity: the RSC shop was selling some of the colourful beads, scarves and garlands for real.

As the production started in earnest, this play-acting began to deconstruct itself and the audience's role in proceedings became less clear. While the immersive pre-show set us up as part of the stage-world, for most of the show we became a conventional audience, sitting in darkness while the cast acted as though we were not present. There was no recommencement of audience interaction in the foyer during the interval. However, as Hero and Claudio's wedding scene started, five or six audience members were brought up onto the stage, invited to sit down on cushions, and offered snacks by the cast. They, and the rest of us, had become guests at the wedding: at the same moment, the auditorium was illuminated by fairy lights and the overhead house lights, and the whole building had been suddenly re-engendered as fictive space. Leonato (Madhav Sharma) and the Friar (Robert Mountford, here re-named 'Panditji') addressed us through a microphone, and Claudio (Sagar Arya) used the same hand-held prop to perform his public denunciation of Hero (Amara Karan). Clearly, we were being asked to play the role of shocked spectators. But this was a self-conscious, even disingenuous form of role-playing; the scene itself demanded a sense of astonishment from the fictional wedding guests, but no audience member who had been following the plot could have been remotely surprised by Claudio's false revelation. Some spectators, in fact, conspicuously refused to act – when I saw the production, one woman onstage was grinning widely throughout the whole exchange, as if to demonstrate the fun she was having.

The production's uncertainty over the role it desired its audience to play was reflective, perhaps, of an ambiguity over its cultural identity. It was not, it seemed, really sure how 'Indian' it wanted to be. Whereas Globe to Globe's productions had been performed almost entirely by non-British actors in their native languages, Khan's *Much Ado* largely retained Shakespeare's text, and the cast were British Asians. Some concessions were made to Indian culture: Beatrice could 'see a temple by daylight' (2.1.74–5), Claudio would 'rather hear the tabla and the pipe' (2.3.14–15), and Benedick went 'foremost in report through India' (3.1.97). Clearly references to churches, tabors and Italy were deemed incompatible with the Indian setting. But the play's many references to 'Messina' were unchanged, and characters referred to their 'doublets' and their 'swords' despite the evident absence of such anachronisms. The production seemed to suggest that Shakespeare's play had been mapped onto modern India to make a near-perfect fit, while at the same time demonstrating the wide gap that separated the two. Kevin Quarmby's review for *British Theatre Guide* criticized it as 'a parody or pastiche of "internationalism", with apparently second generation British actors pretending to return to their cultural roots in a decidedly colonial way'.[34] Kate Rumbold, however, pointed out that the RSC 'often sets plays in foreign locales, without the expectation that every member of the production team and cast be from that country'.³⁵ I wonder whether the production's positioning of its audience contributed to Quarmby's uneasiness. We were invited into its world as outsiders, to observe its conflicts from an amused distance; these conflicts were held up as part of a lifelike re-creation of modern India, but which was in fact a distinctly English concoction draped in Indian kitsch, almost like a theme park. As I left the theatre at the end, audience members were taking photos of each other on the rickshaw-style tricycle in the foyer.

Sporting audiences and intermedial performance

While Globe to Globe was characterized by a strong sense of unity – both within many of its audiences and in its own identity as a festival – the broader World Shakespeare Festival suffered from a sense of geographical and temporal dislocation. Globe to Globe took place in a single, shared-light location over a mere six weeks, whereas the World Shakespeare Festival was spread over several months and numerous locations across the country. This fragmentation meant that inevitably the 'Olympic spirit' was less emphatically present in other productions and their audiences. It is not, however, an inappropriate lens through which to view the broader Festival's various experiments with spectatorship. Bertolt Brecht called the sporting audience 'the fairest and shrewdest audience in the world', and suggested that audiences at boxing matches provided a model for the critical and detached stance he wished to encourage in the theatre.³⁶ Many of the World Shakespeare Festival's audiences were distinctly 'sporting' in this respect, alternately engaged and detached, and actively involved in forming both personal and public judgements on the events of the play.

Dreamthinkspeak's *The Rest Is Silence*, an immersive adaptation of *Hamlet*, made a thought-provoking attempt to problematize the act of spectatorship itself. Audience members were ushered into a dark, square, mirrored studio, and left alone with one another for the first few minutes. The mirrors forced an unusual kind of attention onto the audience, both as a group and as individuals; I found myself scanning the crowd for 'performers', self-conscious that I was probably being watched in this way myself by other spectators. It soon became evident, though, that the performance was to take place behind the mirrors, which lit up to reveal a set of domestic rooms behind one-way glass. Now we were spies, eavesdropping on the characters' private conversations, but dimly aware of our own reflections as we did so. At numerous points, the action would spill over into multiple rooms, and at these moments, spectators were faced with a choice as to which characters we most wished to scrutinize. The sounds of the characters' voices were relayed to us, slightly distorted, via hidden microphones, as if the rooms were bugged. Thus, the characters never spoke to us directly. Even in soliloquy, they would speak into what for them were simply mirrors, so that we were listening in on their most private thoughts. This rendered all the characters, but especially Edward Hogg's Hamlet, strangely impenetrable, unknowable and unreadable; it was easy to believe that this Hamlet had 'that within which passeth show' (1.2.85). This complete inhibition of actor–spectator interaction left the audience oddly adrift, forced to engage with the piece without explicit guidance from the stage, and aware that their own choices would be under scrutiny by their fellow spectators.

Just as audiences watched the Olympic Games themselves via a combination of live and digital media, so too was it possible to experience the World Shakespeare Festival. Tim Crouch's *I, Cinna (The Poet)* was streamed to schools on 2 July 2012; TR Warszawa's *2008: Macbeth* was streamed on the *Guardian* website on 13 August; the National Theatre's *Timon of Athens* was broadcast to cinemas across the world on 1 November. Certainly the latter two were fairly standard examples of the growing genre of live-streamed theatre, relaying the performance as it happened to a remote and dispersed audience. But both *I, Cinna* and *Timon* were broadcast to audiences in intensely *social* spaces – the former to schools and the latter to cinemas. A sense of 'conversation', then, was not entirely impossible.

That was certainly my experience of *I, Cinna (The Poet)* when I watched the webcast with a group of 41 Year 8 students (12- to 13-year-olds) during an educational outreach event at the University of Warwick's Business School on the morning of 2 July 2012. Their teacher prefaced the screening with a discussion about citizenship, ethics and responsibility, following which he loaded the RSC's *I, Cinna* webpage and projected it onto a large screen at one end of the room. TV presenter Konnie Huq opened the broadcast from a studio in London, saying hello to a list of participating schools, before conducting a live interview with writer/director Tim Crouch and actor Jude Owusu [see Tracy Irish's interview in this volume for further discussion of both the production and the webcast]. The play itself – a one-man show for young audiences – had been pre-recorded. The dialogue, however, implied conversation even as the medium worked against it: 'Pick up your paper and pens. Yes? Got them? Good! Let's write together, you and me'.[37] Cinna's 'Good!' would have made no sense, of course, had the students answered 'No!' to his previous question, but fortunately there were no such interjections from this class. When Cinna explained to his audience, looking straight into the camera, that a 'republic' is 'a place where everyone is equal', he asked: 'Is your country a republic? Is this a republic, in here, in this place? Are we equal here?'[38] The students around me made no reply – mainly, I am sure, because replying to a recorded film is self-evidently not part of a genuine conversation – but I wonder whether an ambiguity over the subject of Cinna's question contributed to their uncertainty. 'This place' was simultaneously a classroom, Warwick Business School's Teaching Centre, Cinna's Rome, the stage set and a London studio, each of which implied different sorts of hierarchical power structures.

Despite the temporal and geographical remoteness of the production, though, certain moments in the broadcast prompted activity and conversation among the young spectators around me. The students gasped as Cinna performed an 'augury' by slicing open a chicken, groaning in mock-disgust at a close-up, and giggling at their own reactions. When Cinna instructed them to write one word to describe 'the leader of your country', he followed it up with the question, 'Who wrote a bad word then?'.[39] The students laughed, and some murmured to one another, but there were no replies loud enough for me to hear. The line 'Pick up your pens' created a rush of activity every time it was uttered, and Cinna's final task for his audience – to write a poem about his death in just three minutes – resulted in an intense hush as the students busily scribbled away, some of them whispering to one another but most of them concentrating in silence. They applauded the film at the end, following which they were given three minutes to formulate questions for a live Q&A session with Crouch, Owusu and children's author Malorie Blackman. Their teacher, though, used this time for his own follow-up discussion, so he muted the first few minutes of the webcast Q&A. The makers of the piece were clearly keen to foster a genuine conversation with their remote viewers; in response to a question about whether or not freedom is worth killing or dying for, Crouch asked viewers to send in their own ideas about what they would kill or die for. Obviously, though, they had time to answer only a handful of the audience-submitted questions, and none of the questions submitted by my group made it to the London studio.

Refusing to play

In August, the Wooster Group/RSC collaborative production of *Troilus and Cressida* saw the 'Olympic spirit' break down almost completely. It met a hostile reception from critics and audiences more generally: the *Guardian*'s Michael Billington described it as a 'strangely infertile' production which did 'nothing to enhance our understanding of the play'; the *Independent*'s Paul Taylor, 'a mass of alienation effects in search of a play'.[40] Writing for *WhatsOnStage*, Simon Tavener condemned the production as 'one of the worst pieces of theatre I have seen on a professional stage', and the user-submitted comments beneath his review tended to concur, with 30 of the 40 awarding the show the lowest possible rating of one star.[41] When Jane Shilling gave the production a more positive write-up, all eight of the user-submitted comments on the *Telegraph*'s website disputed her conclusions.[42] Even its co-director Mark Ravenhill, in a strangely self-congratulatory tweet, noted that 76 audience members walked out during the first preview performance.[43]

This marked absence of audience goodwill was provoked by the production's deliberate dismantling of theatrical convention. The two companies had rehearsed separately, Mark Ravenhill directing the RSC cast in Britain as the Greeks, and the Wooster Group playing the Trojans under the direction of Elizabeth LeCompte in New York. Ravenhill and his cast made some bold and unusual interpretative decisions, exploring the Greek soldiers' various crises of masculinity – Achilles, Patroclus and Thersites spent sections of the play in drag, for example, while Ajax wore a fancy-dress wrestler outfit. Nonetheless, the *style* of performance in the Greek scenes was broadly typical of the RSC, focused as it was on concept, character and clarity.

The Wooster Group adopted a very different strategy, doing all they could to ensure that their performances as the Trojans were generated externally. Four small screens at each corner of the stage played clips from a diverse selection of films (including *Atanarjuat*, a 2001 film about an Inuit tribe, and Elia Kazan's 1961 film *Splendor in the Grass*). The performers copied the movements of the actors in the film clips, lifting their arms, brushing back their hair, convulsing or even wobbling with the camera as their screen counterparts did the same. Such actions were clearly not directly connected to the text, which the Wooster Group delivered by copying the vocal score which was being relayed to them via their earpieces. In the Trojans' performances, therefore, the connections between text, intonation and action were almost completely arbitrary – though there was a certain logic to the choice of film clips, in which fight scenes were generally used for arguments, or love scenes for the title characters' exchanges. A kind of game was being attempted: the Wooster Group seemed to be challenging the audience to do the work of interpretation entirely by themselves. Sometimes, when the two companies appeared together onstage, an odd sort of synthesis emerged, in which the character-driven RSC actors attempted to make some kind of narrative sense of the Woosters' randomly generated performances. I was especially struck by a scene between Scott Handy's Ulysses and Scott Shepherd's Troilus, when Handy seemed to respond to Shepherd's wild movements as if they were symptoms of Troilus's disturbed mind.

The production's reception, though, indicated that its audiences were largely unwilling to play the game of theatrical signification as the Wooster Group had attempted to redefine it. To return to the sports metaphor, it was as if the Woosters and the RSC were playing by different rules; in their determination not to adopt the codes and conventions of the host company (and nation?), the Woosters risked being seen as unsportsmanlike. Clearly in the minds of many audience members, the production had somehow failed to honour the promise implicit in an RSC-produced *Troilus and Cressida*; I found more to enjoy in the production than Paul Prescott did, but I very much agreed with his objection that 'ticket prices should have been cut, expectations managed and the contract between artists and spectators redrawn'.[44]

The Wooster Group's refusal to privilege the British audience was in many respects the opposite of the largely inclusive attitude of the visiting Globe to Globe companies, and of the cultural self-affirmation offered by the in-house Globe and RSC productions. *Troilus and Cressida* and its reception deconstructed easy notions of the Brits as magnanimous hosts: a celebration of cultural difference would only extend so far, and the Wooster Group pushed it to breaking point. Indeed, many of the user-submitted comments beneath the *WhatsOnStage* review characterized the production as a contrast between incompetent Americans and their superior British counterparts, complaining, for example, that '[t]he Americans were out of their depth' or that '[t]he American Trojans could not speak the verse'. 'I felt sorry for "our lot"', wrote one spectator; another reported feeling a sense of 'relief when the Brits got back on stage'.[45]

The Wooster Group's decentring of the privileged 'host' spectator, then, was of a very different order to the analogous decentring which took place at Globe to Globe. The former provoked hostility; the latter was widely interpreted as a manifestation of 'the Olympic spirit'. At Globe to Globe, spectators who did not speak the languages or fully understand the conventions of the visiting productions seemed generally unthreatened by their own inexpert status, using the reactions and encouragement of the 'in-group' spectators to assist them as they engaged with the production's systems of signification. Comfortable group identities were often ruptured by Festival productions, whether intentionally or not: *The Rest Is Silence* and *I, Cinna (The Poet)*, for example, asked spectators to reflect upon their own individual choices, while audiences at *Henry V* or *Much Ado about Nothing* were encouraged to perform group identities which would turn out to be unstable or untenable. What the Festival productions seem to have had largely in common, though, was an emphasis on collaborative and sociable forms of meaning-making, and it was where this was most markedly absent that so many spectators withdrew their goodwill. In the modern Shakespearean audience, as in the Olympic crowd, the twin goals of communal togetherness and individual agency, of 'universality' and 'diversity', work in a constantly fluctuating dynamic, both with and against each other.

Notes

1 Amelia Gentleman and Owen Gibson, 'George Osborne should have expected to be booed, say Paralympic spectators', *Guardian*, 4 September 2012, http://www.guardian.co.uk/politics/2012/sep/04/george-osborne-booed-paralympic-games [accessed 26 October 2013].

2 International Olympic Committee, 'Olympic Charter' (Lausanne: IOC, 1995), http://www.olympic.org/Documents/Olympic%20Charter/Olympic_Charter_through_time/1995-Olympic_Charter.pdf, p. 67 [accessed 26 October 2013].

3 International Olympic Committee, 'Olympic Charter' (Lausanne: IOC, 2010), http://www.olympic.org/Documents/Olympic%20Charter/Olympic_Charter_through_time/2010-Olympic_Charter.pdf, p. 80 [accessed 26 October 2013].

4 Beatriz García, 'London 2012 Cultural Olympiad Evaluation' (Liverpool and London: Institute of Cultural Capital, Arts Council England and LOCOG, 2013), http://www.artscouncil.org.uk/what-we-do/our-priorities-2011-15/london-2012/, Appendix 1.1, p. 5 [accessed 26 October 2013].

5 Ibid., Appendix 1.4, p. 10.

6 Ibid., p. 88.

7 Ibid., p. 89.

8 Ibid., p. 128.

9 Ibid., p. 91.

10 Ibid., p. 100.

11 Ibid., p. 84. In Rose Elfman's survey of Globe to Globe spectators, 48 per cent identified their nationality as something other than British in answer to the question 'What country are you from?' The reason for this discrepancy may be that the ICC's survey asked respondents where they had come from in order to attend the Festival, whereas Elfman's asked them to identify their country of origin. The divergence between the two figures would seem to suggest that Globe to Globe audiences included a large proportion of people who live in Britain but were born elsewhere.

12 Ibid., p. 185.
13 Ibid., p. 185.
14 Ibid., pp. 179, 180.
15 Paul Prescott, 'Nightwatch Constables and Domineering Pedants: the past, present and future of Shakespearean theatre reviewing', in *A Year of Shakespeare: Re-living the World Shakespeare Festival*, ed. Paul Edmondson, Paul Prescott and Erin Sullivan (London: Bloomsbury, 2013), pp. 12–30 (p. 23).
16 Paul Edmondson, Paul Prescott and Erin Sullivan (eds), *Year of Shakespeare*, http://www.yearofshakespeare.com/ [accessed 26 October 2013], and *A Year of Shakespeare: Re-living the World Shakespeare Festival* (London: Bloomsbury, 2013).
17 Sarah Olive, '*Measure for Measure*', in *A Year of Shakespeare*, p. 125, and '*The Merry Wives of Winsdor*', ibid., p. 134.
18 Emily Oliver, '*Timon of Athens*', in *A Year of Shakespeare*, p. 202; Adele Lee, '*Titus Andronicus*', ibid., p. 207.
19 Thea Buckley, '*The Taming of the Shrew*', in *A Year of Shakespeare*, p. 188.
20 Georgie Lucas, '*King John*', in *A Year of Shakespeare*, p. 99.
21 Peter J. Smith, '*Twelfth Night*', in *A Year of Shakespeare*, pp. 221–2.
22 Sonia Massai, '*The Tempest*', in *A Year of Shakespeare*, p. 197.
23 Erin Sullivan, '*Richard II*', in *A Year of Shakespeare*, p. 172.
24 Yuval Ben-Ami, 'A Palestinian king in London: On Ashtar's *Richard II*', *+972 Magazine*, 27 May 2012, http://972mag.com/a-palestinian-king-in-london-on-ashtars-richard-ii/46913/ [accessed 26 October 2013].
25 Julie Sanders, 'Creative exploitation and talking back: Renegade Theatre's *The Winter's Tale* or *Ìtàn Òginìntìn* ('Winter's Tales')', in *Shakespeare Beyond English: A Global Experiment*, ed. Susan Bennett and Christie Carson (Cambridge: Cambridge University Press, 2013), pp. 241–50 (p. 247).
26 Elfman notes that this audience's willingness to participate extended to her survey, too: she reports that she was

'approached by groups of people who actively wanted to take it – as if their roles as "co-actors" extended beyond the performance itself into the process of documenting its reception' (email to the author, 15 September 2013).

27 *The Winter's Tale*, The Space, http://thespace.org/items/e0000pru [accessed 23 October 2012; no longer available].

28 These lines, of course, were delivered in Yoruba: I have translated them back into Shakespeare's English with reference to the video made available on The Space. This and all subsequent references to Shakespeare are from *The Oxford Shakespeare*, Stanley Wells, Gary Taylor, John Jowett and William Montgomery (eds) (Oxford: Clarendon Press, 1986).

29 García, 'London 2012', p. 184.

30 Transcribed live from the matinee performance on 8 July 2012.

31 Alice Jones, 'We happy two: Jamie Parker and Tom Hiddleston tackle Shakespeare's *Henry V*', *Independent*, 19 July 2012, http://www.independent.co.uk/arts-entertainment/theatre-dance/features/we-happy-two-jamie-parker-and-tom-hiddleston-tackle-shakespeares-henry-v-7956970.html [accessed 26 October 2013].

32 Abigail Rokison, '*Henry V*', *Year of Shakespeare*, 14 June 2012, http://bloggingshakespeare.com/year-of-shakespeare-henry-v [accessed 26 October 2013].

33 Peter Kirwan, '*Much Ado about Nothing* (RSC) @ The Courtyard Theatre', *The Bardathon*, 12 August 2012, http://blogs.nottingham.ac.uk/bardathon/2012/08/12/much-ado-about-nothing-rsc-the-courtyard-theatre/ [accessed 26 October 2013].

34 Kevin Quarmby, '*Much Ado About Nothing*', *British Theatre Guide*, http://www.britishtheatreguide.info/reviews/much-ado-about-rsc-courtyard-t-7732 [accessed 26 October 2013].

35 Kate Rumbold, '*Much Ado About Nothing*', in *A Year of Shakespeare*, pp. 151–2.

36 Bertolt Brecht, *Brecht on Theatre*, ed. and trans. by J. Willett (London: Eyre Methuen, 1977), pp. 6, 8.

37 Tim Crouch, *I, Cinna (The Poet)* (London: Oberon Books, 2012), p. 17.

38 Ibid., p. 21.
39 Ibid., p. 22.
40 Michael Billington, 'Troilus and Cressida – review', *Guardian*, 9 August 2012, http://www.theguardian.com/stage/2012/aug/09/troilus-and-cressida-review [accessed 5 March 2014]; Paul Taylor, '*Troilus and Cressida*, Riverside Studios, London', *Independent*, 31 August 2012, http://www.independent.co.uk/arts-entertainment/theatre-dance/reviews/troilus-and-cressida-riverside-studios-london-8099436.html [accessed 5 March 2014].
41 Simon Tavener, '*Troilus & Cressida* (RSC)', *WhatsOnStage.com*, 9 August 2012, http://www.whatsonstage.com/reviews/theatre/london/E8831344532501/Troilus+&+Cressida+(RSC).html [accessed 13 September 2012; comments no longer available].
42 Jane Shilling, '*Troilus and Cressida*, RSC and The Wooster Group, Swan Theatre, Stratford-upon-Avon, review', *The Telegraph*, 9 August 2012, http://www.telegraph.co.uk/culture/theatre/theatre-reviews/9464579/Troilus-and-Cressida-RSC-and-Wooster-Group-Swan-Theatre-Stratford-upon-Avon-review.html [accessed 26 October 2013].
43 Mark Ravenhill, 'Only 76 walk outs during last night's first preview of our RSC/Wooster Group Troilus and Cressida. Are we being radical enough?' (tweet), 4 August 2012, https://twitter.com/markravenhill/status/231669684947275776 [accessed 26 October 2013].
44 Paul Prescott, '*Troilus and Cressida*', *A Year of Shakespeare*, p. 217.
45 The binary recurred in numerous user-submitted comments, of which the following are a further selection: 'The only saving grace was the RSC members [...] the Americans were simply awful [...] Every time the flaccid Americans came on stage, I wanted to laugh [...] It was a relief when the Brits got back on stage [...] there is a reason why Americans shouldn't do Shakespeare [...] If there had been two curtain calls, one for the Greeks and one for the Trojans I would have booed the Trojans [...] The Brits were pretty good, but the show was fatally undermined by the self-indulgent twaddle

of the Wooster Group [...] the Americans were atrocious'. User-submitted comments beneath Tavener, '*Troilus & Cressida* (RSC)' [accessed 13 September 2012; comments no longer available].

7

Expert Spectatorship and Intra-Audience Relationships at Globe to Globe 2012

Rose Elfman

The 37 companies presenting Shakespeare in translation at the 2012 Globe to Globe Festival confronted significant challenges in engaging Globe audiences. By touring to a London theatre, they would face large numbers of spectators who would not understand the productions' spoken languages, performance conventions or references local to their 'home' contexts. At the Globe, moreover – a theatre founded with the goal of restoring 'authentic' performance conditions for the original texts – many spectators would likely possess powerful expectations regarding the works in English. These potential gaps in understanding presented political as well as artistic concerns.

As Karen Fricker, Dennis Kennedy and Ric Knowles have argued, a touring performance may lose many of its original resonances through decontextualization, particularly when framed within an international theatre festival.¹ Furthermore, this displacement can also encourage audiences to adopt reductive, self-serving attitudes toward the country that produced the performance. Using the metaphor of the 'market' to describe spectators' engagement with touring productions, each of these scholars asserts that superficial desires to consume alterity can easily foreclose intercultural exchange. Thus Knowles argues that 'festivals increasingly function as National showcases, in which the "Culture" of nations [...] is on display for a world and audience that is thereby constructed as an international market'.[2] Touring, it would seem, risks reducing a production to a generalized spectacle, while putting the spectator in a position of power as a consumer of the 'nations on display'.

Within the Globe, such concerns intensify. W. B. Worthen argues that in this theatre, Britain's colonial legacies, global economic forces and the authoritative weight of Shakespeare in English converge to bolster British spectators' perceptions of national superiority at the expense of touring performers.[3] Writing of the 1997–2001 Globe to Globe series, in which companies from India, Japan, South Africa, Cuba and Brazil presented Shakespearean translations/adaptations at the Globe, he asserts that due to a combination of privilege and ignorance, spectators consistently belittled this work as inferior to English standards of production. Although publicists promised a rigorous exploration of the ways that Shakespeare has been 'adapted and illuminated' worldwide, he writes, the milieu of the Globe encouraged a dismissive and proprietary gaze:

> [I]n practice these local purposes are precisely obscured by Globe performativity. At the Globe, performance tends to essentialize rather than multiply Shakespeare. The force of the [touring productions] is to confirm European fantasies [...], reified against the whitewashed background of tourist privilege, the privilege to decide others' meanings, the privilege of *owning* Shakespeare.[4]

When a touring translation is presented in a theatre dedicated to the historical Shakespeare, Worthen suggests, spectators miss important aspects of its meaning due not only to inhabiting a different geographical context, but also to their investment in the superiority of the plays as performed in English. When 'foreign' performers appeared on this authoritative stage, the argument goes, spectators viewed them as 'subaltern, sweaty others' better appreciated for exotic 'culture' than for artistic achievement.[5]

Worthen's account has several limitations, notably the fact that he bases his conclusions entirely on the words of professional reviewers without acknowledging the heterogeneity of audiences or documenting other kinds of spectator response. Yet his scepticism regarding the Globe's intercultural potential is characteristic of the dominant scholarly narrative surrounding these productions. Rob Conkie suggests, for example, that the Globe invited the translated performances for the sake of making its own productions appear more 'authentic' in contrast, while Kate McLuskie's essay on *uMabatha: The Zulu Macbeth* argues that market forces required this South African production to heighten its 'exotic' value in order to appeal to predominantly white audiences at the Globe.[6] Together with the festival scholarship described above, these writers seek to demonstrate that cross-cultural performances often serve to reinforce, rather than challenge, the self-satisfaction of privileged audiences. As they imply that this effect intensifies the more closely spectators identify with the cultural authority that Shakespeare wields in English, they suggest that the power dynamics at the Globe preclude meaningful engagement between spectators and touring performances.

My project here is to complicate that narrative.[7] As my fieldwork at the 2012 Globe to Globe Festival shows, touring performances of Shakespeare-in-translation can and do engage audiences in productive ways despite – indeed, *because* of – their geographical displacement. When the productions left their 'home' contexts to perform in a theatre that typically privileges English-speakers and celebrates English texts, they posed significant challenges to those norms by appealing to an array of distinct epistemologies. For audience members who could not speak the languages of translation, these performances estranged the viewing process. As they grappled with the difficulty of constructing meaning, they reported more complex experiences of reception than the consumerist dynamics described above. More significantly, such productions can confer authority upon members of underrepresented diasporic communities. Both the 'marketplace' model of festival spectatorship and Worthen's characterization of 'Globe performativity' depend on audiences receiving touring productions as wholly foreign. Yet in 2012, thanks in part to the Globe's efforts to recruit spectators from the language communities represented onstage,[8] audiences included large contingents of people who *could* speak the languages of translation, and whose reactions to the dialogue made their group presence a visible and audible component of the performance event [for a related analysis of this, see Steven Purcell's preceding chapter in this volume]. As these groups demonstrated informed responses to the production, they conspicuously displaced English-speakers as 'expert' spectators at the Globe.

Using audience surveys to compare the responses of spectators who could speak a production's language to those who could not, I examine the effects of this festival environment on both groups of audience members. First, I demonstrate that the two groups employed distinct methods to understand the productions, with language-speakers concentrating on dialogue and the non-language-speakers on the corporeal work of the performers. I suggest that the Festival event privileged the competence of language-speakers, while requiring non-speakers to develop experimental viewing strategies. Furthermore, the divergence in understanding between these two groups became obvious to spectators on both sides. Thus language-speakers assumed positions of relative authority on the productions, while non-language-speakers were confronted with the gaps in their knowledge. Language became a frame through which different groups were privileged, publicly, in turn.

Consequently, ignorance of a production's references was no longer the default position for Festival audiences, and the enthusiastic reactions of more knowledgeable spectators highlighted the limits of such an approach. Rather than simply consuming a performance's 'exoticism' or rejecting it as un-Shakespearean, many spectators who could not understand the productions became more aware of how their cultural positioning shaped their responses. Questioning their own interpretative abilities, many looked to others for guidance. Conversely, many spectators able to speak the languages found the event powerful due to the rarity of seeing aspects of their heritage represented in mainstream London artistic production. My observations also suggest that many enjoyed adopting roles as 'experts', as they explained the performances to other spectators. By marginalizing normative spectators while privileging those who are often marginalized, therefore, the Festival undermined the power imbalances that, as so many scholars have argued, face touring translations of Shakespeare at the Globe.

Methods

I approached the Festival with the aim of using an ethnographic approach to compare the reception processes of spectators on both sides of the language gap. Although logistical constraints shaped my methods significantly, I collected both quantitative and qualitative information regarding spectators' backgrounds, expectations and viewing experiences. My primary research instrument was a written survey, developed in conversation with Globe staff. This presented a combination of multiple-choice and open-ended questions. Due to limited resources and my desire to collect a standardized pool of data, the survey was in English only and asked the same questions for all productions; a sample copy appears at the end of this chapter. I administered the survey by approaching spectators in the lobby immediately after each performance. In an effort to include a wide range of perspectives, I listened for people speaking a variety of languages to their companions before inviting them to participate.

The data analysed in this chapter reflect a total of 195 responses, encompassing 20 of the 38 productions at the Festival.[9] Although all respondents needed to know some English to complete the surveys, the results represent comparable numbers of spectators claiming competence in the given performance's language (44 per cent) and those with little or no knowledge of it (53 per cent).[10] In an effort to honour the complexity of spectator experience, I also include anecdotal observations that illuminate or complicate statistical trends. Since the surveys represent a tiny, self-selecting portion of the Festival's 85,000 ticket-buyers, my conclusions remain speculative.[11] However, this approach has enabled a multivocal account of reception that complements other methods such as reading published reviews or theorizing from one's own experiences as a spectator, as Steven Purcell does in this volume. Whereas Worthen's focus on critics led him to imply that the touring productions faced audiences that were uniformly invested in conservative notions of British national identity and Shakespearean performance, my methods treat the diversity of spectator experience as key to festival reception dynamics. Audience members who could speak a production's language demonstrated the depth and vitality of informed responses, while also influencing the reactions of others.[12]

Reception processes: Foreknowledge vs experimentation

A central component of Worthen's argument is that at the Globe, spectators' preconceptions regarding the greatness of the English plays obstruct their ability to appreciate the creativity of touring performers. As he demonstrates, constant comparison to an imagined ideal caused some critics to reject translated performance for its 'antinomian otherness, its intractable inability to do right by Shakespeare'.[13] For general audiences at Globe to Globe 2012, however, knowledge of Shakespeare proved to be less important than the work of the actors in helping them to understand a performance. This becomes apparent by comparing responses to the multiple-choice survey question, 'Which of the following factors helped you to understand the performance?'. Although language-speakers and non-speakers employed different strategies to interpret Festival productions, both relied more heavily on the phenomena of the performance than on prior knowledge of the story or the playwright. Furthermore, while non-speakers were likelier than speakers to indicate that prior knowledge of Shakespeare was helpful, they were also likelier to admit that they did not understand fully, or as well as other spectators. Instead of smugly rejecting the adaptations as improper Shakespeare, viewers valorized the artistic mastery of the performers while acknowledging the limits of their own points of view.

The chart below demonstrates the frequency with which language-speakers and non-language-speakers indicated that various elements helped them to understand the production. For the purpose of this analysis, I combine into one group the respondents who had indicated 'fluent' or 'good enough' knowledge of the language, and into another group those who had indicated knowing 'none' or 'a few words' of it. This categorization erases some important differences, but allows me to distinguish those able to engage thoroughly with the spoken text of a production from those with minimal linguistic access. The answer choices are arranged from left to right in descending order of popularity among respondents overall.

Since the groups of language-speaking and non-language-speaking respondents were not of equal size (86 and 104, respectively), the chart plots their answers in terms of *percentages* of respondents in the same fluency group, rather than the raw total of responses. Thus the first bars on the

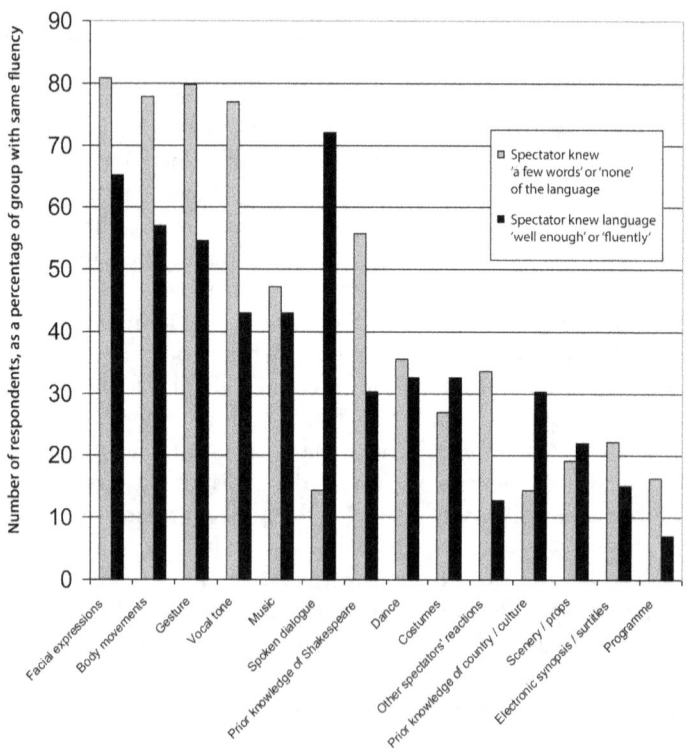

'Which of the following factors helped you to understand the production?'

FIGURE 10 *Correlations between spectators' language fluency and their modes of understanding a production.*

left, above 'Facial expressions', indicate that 81 per cent of spectators who spoke 'none' or 'a few words' of the language selected 'facial expressions' as an element that helped them to understand the production; 65 per cent of spectators who spoke the language 'well enough' or 'fluently' indicated that facial expressions had helped them to understand. Since spectators were encouraged to select multiple elements, the high percentage for 'facial expressions' does not necessarily mean that individual spectators deemed this the most helpful factor. Rather, it means that spectators identified it as helpful more consistently than other elements. The trends indicate emphases in group, rather than individual, responses.

The most striking pattern to emerge is that for spectators who did not speak the language of a production, the actors' work became paramount. Facial expressions, body movements, gesture and vocal tone nearly tied as the most commonly helpful element among this group, each selected by 77–81 per cent of respondents with little to no fluency. The actors' presentation of their bodies surpassed other visual elements, such as costume and scenery/props, in popularity among these respondents. This suggests, perhaps, that this group of spectators perceived the performers' movements as 'universal' behaviour; their focus on the human body implies that they saw it as a shared form that moves in essentially recognizable ways. Elements such as dance and costume, on the other hand, might seem more overtly codified according to unfamiliar conventions, and thus less accessible. Whatever the reason, the performers' bodies and voices were credited more consistently with enabling understanding than any other factor of the performance, including design elements, framing devices such as programmes and surtitles, and prior knowledge of Shakespeare.

For language-speaking spectators, on the other hand, the spoken dialogue was the factor most consistently selected as helpful. This element created the largest divergence between speakers and non-speakers. 72 per cent of language-speakers indicated that dialogue helped them to understand, as opposed to 14 per cent of non-speakers (and nearly all of these were spectators who spoke 'a few words' rather than 'none'). While it is not surprising that language-speakers found the dialogue more helpful than non-speakers did, it is remarkable that this group did not deem any other performance elements helpful to the same extent. Although the categories of actor behaviour that non-speakers had relied upon were still among the most likely to be selected, this did not occur with the same emphasis. 'Facial expressions' made a relatively strong showing at 65 per cent, but 'gesture' and 'body movement' were reported helpful by just above 50 per cent of language-speakers. 'Vocal tone' dropped lower still, to about half the usefulness it enjoyed among non-speakers. Apart from dialogue and three other elements, which I will address shortly, non-speakers outweighed speakers in their use of every other category.

A few possible explanations present themselves. First, those fluent in the languages of the various productions might be less comfortable in English, making these spectators more likely to misread the survey. Some respondents might not have understood that they could choose multiple options, for example. This would explain a puzzling aspect of this data: 28 per cent of respondents who claimed to know the translation language did *not* indicate that dialogue helped them to understand the performance. Another clue may come from the unusually large gap between speakers and non-speakers in regard to vocal tone. For speakers of a language, the primary value of speech may appear to be its semantic content, with sound treated as secondary to meaning. For non-speakers, however, the act of listening to opaque speech seems to have estranged the reception process, prompting them to focus on the actors' delivery of language rather than the words themselves.

Spectators who do not share a production's spoken language may, therefore, develop new reception strategies, while also becoming conscious of this process during the performance. This hypothesis gathers support from some of the comments that survey respondents made, such as 'Not knowing the words [illegible] I concentrated on the actors', 'Need to focus on expressions and non verbal cues more', and 'Seeing Shakespeare in another language involves you more, like watching a silent film'. Whatever the reason, the disparity remained: those who understood the language were most likely to credit the script for their comprehension of the production, while those who could not understand the dialogue were most likely to credit the performers. In other words, language-speakers were more likely to deem important the element of the production that most obviously required foreknowledge to interpret. Non-language speakers, on the other hand, were more likely to derive meaning from the immediate phenomena of the performance: in particular, corporeal behaviours whose cultural codification might be less apparent.

The fact that language-speakers found dialogue helpful more than non-speakers did may seem obvious. However, I suggest that this finding belies a deeper epistemological gap between the two groups. Helen Gilbert and Joanne Tompkins argue that audiences commonly perceive spoken language as 'the fundamental and most important system through which a play "means"'; a spectator's relationship with language is central to his or her engagement with a performance event.[14] Spectators who understand the spoken language may not have cause to examine or question their overall interpretations of a performance, feeling confident in their foreknowledge and normal habits of perception. When confronted with an unfamiliar language, on the other hand, spectators seemed to become more aware of the need to experiment with new channels of seeing and listening. In bringing mixed audiences into sustained encounters with diverse languages, therefore, the Festival undermined non-speaking audience members' self-sufficiency as spectators, while inviting language-speakers to assume positions of authority as experts.

Indeed, the only other elements that language-speaking spectators identified as helpful at higher rates than non-speakers did were three that also required 'insider' knowledge from the production's home context. These included scenery/

props, costumes and prior knowledge of the country/culture. Spectators in either group might assume that body movements and facial expressions convey 'universal' actions and emotions, but articles of clothing (especially those evoking 'traditional' dress) and scenic objects (such as rugs, musical instruments and weapons – all commonly appearing throughout the Festival) could seem more obviously tied to a specific time and place. This might lead audience members to whom such elements are strange to conclude that they have a significance that they cannot access, while spectators to whom they are familiar would feel more confident identifying their relevance.

Non-speakers, on the other hand, were more likely than language-speakers to rely on external aids, particularly those relating to the plot of the original play. Other elements that non-speakers found helpful in greater numbers than language-speakers did included prior knowledge of Shakespeare, the programmes, the electronic synopses and other spectators' reactions. With the exception of Shakespearean foreknowledge, these elements position the spectator as an outsider to the performance event, one who requires mediating devices to make sense of it. Conversely, spectators who spoke the language were more likely to rely on the first-hand knowledge that they had brought to the theatre. While these aids helped non-speakers to follow the plot of a production (if they could read English), the Festival privileged those for whom such devices were unnecessary. As the following graph shows, language-speaking spectators were likely to have full confidence in their understanding of a performance's narrative, while non-speakers were unlikely to report this.

More importantly, this divergence in interpretative confidence appears to have been apparent to both groups. When asked 'How well do you think you understood the production in comparison to the other spectators?' respondents fell into patterns that reiterated the primacy of language. Exactly half (43/86) of the spectators who reported 'good enough' or 'fluent' comprehension of the spoken language also reported that they believed that they understood the production

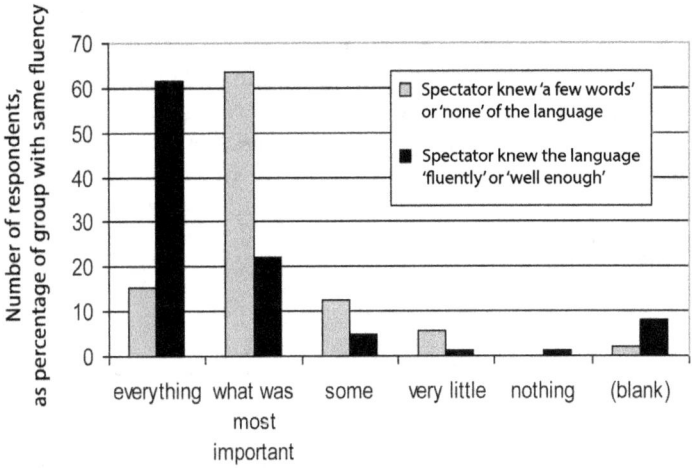

How much of the plot the spectator reported understanding

FIGURE 11 *Fluent vs non-fluent spectators' ability to follow the plot of a performance.*

'better than most spectators'; this was this group's most common selection for the question asking about their relative comprehension. Only six of this group (7 per cent) reported understanding 'less than most spectators'. These findings support my assertion that within the Festival environment, speakers of the visiting productions' languages held authority as expert spectators, supplanting normative London theatre-going audiences in this regard.

Not only did these spectators become aware of their superior knowledge in contrast to the majority audience, but non-speakers also recognized their *non*-expert status in large numbers. Although the majority (60/104, or 58 per cent) of spectators who spoke 'none' or 'a few words' of the language believed that they understood 'about as well as most other spectators', a significant minority (31/104, or 30 per cent) reported understanding 'less than most', while only eight (8 per cent) believed that they understood 'better than most'. With some exceptions, therefore, audience members on both sides of the language barrier appeared to believe that spectators with access to the production's language had an advantage that spectators without such access did not. While knowledge of the English language and Shakespearean texts might normally be the most valuable attributes within the Globe, the 2012 Festival undercut the superiority of spectators who brought *only* that to the theatre.

Intra-audience relationships

In the remainder of this chapter, I will trace the effects of this mutual recognition among Festival audiences. What happens when audience members identifying with each of the Globe's visiting performances conspicuously displace the English-speakers that the theatre normally privileges? This is a particularly pressing question at the Globe since the open-air environment makes spectators' reactions more apparent, while the theatre's architecture encourages interaction to an unusual degree. Not only could spectators observe each other's responses, therefore, but they could also engage strangers in conversation: as Steven Purcell points out in this volume, spectators who knew the language could adopt a 'dramaturgical role on behalf of their fellow audience members' (p. 139), explaining details of a production to less knowledgeable viewers around them.

These factors pose perhaps the biggest challenge to the 'marketplace' model of intercultural spectatorship. While the act of attempting to trace a narrative in a foreign-language performance may implicitly prompt spectators to recognize the limited and provisional nature of their expertise, interaction with audience members for whom the language is *not* foreign provides a much blunter indication. Furthermore, for many of the language-speakers I surveyed and observed, hearing and seeing their languages represented on the Globe stage enabled a sense of community based on the celebration of a shared and often underrepresented heritage. As the Festival honoured their languages and knowledges before global audiences in this famous theatre, spectators who might ordinarily feel marginalized were able to step, temporarily, into the centre. At least for the course of the Festival, access to the individual languages of translation – rather than knowledge of Shakespeare's English texts – became the central determinant of privilege within the Globe.

Exemplifying the impact of the language disparity on audience members' relationships with each other, non-speakers were nearly three times more likely than speakers of a language to indicate that other spectators' reactions helped them understand the production (34 per cent vs 13 per cent). Although 34 per cent is a minority of spectators within this group, it is a noticeable trend; furthermore, this number includes more than half of the non-language-speakers who reported understanding 'less than most other spectators'. When language difference made spectators less confident in their own responses, they were likely to look around for guidance, treating others' responses as more authoritative than their own. Spectators who spoke the language, however, enjoyed a greater perception of autonomy: they were most likely to trust their own reactions without believing that they needed outside help.

While survey respondents did not explain precisely what they understood from other spectators' reactions, my observations provide some possibilities. The laughter of audience members who understood the lines suggested the presence of verbal jokes if the humour was not obvious visually, while cheers and applause implied that something important had been said. Responses to music also held clues. By singing or humming along, audience members could indicate that a song pre-existed, rather than being original music, and was relatively well-known;[15] standing to sing as the first bar of music played suggested that the song was a national anthem.[16] Personally, once I could tell that neighbouring spectators understood a production's language, I became much more aware of their responses as well as of my own.

The more conspicuous language-speakers became, the more they had the potential to shape other spectators' experiences. As Susan Bennett writes:

> In almost all cases laughter, derision, and applause is infectious. The audience, through homogeneity of reaction, receives confirmation of their decoding on an individual and private basis and is encouraged to suppress counter-readings in favour of the reception generally shared.[17]

In a mixed audience such as at Globe to Globe 2012, a spectator faces competing choices of how to react. Yet although non-speakers may see their own uncertain impressions mirrored around them, expert spectators can illustrate a more 'correct' response.

The social pressure exerted by such an environment has potentially beneficial effects. In fostering self-consciousness and heightened awareness of others among audience members who did not speak the language, the Festival emphasized the need to listen and learn. The fact that so many of these spectators treated others' reactions as helpful to their own understanding suggests that in contrast to Worthen's self-satisfied critics, many audience members at the Globe in 2012 considered other perspectives while questioning their own. Conversely, the Festival encouraged people who knew these languages to enjoy hearing, speaking, singing and responding to them, with abandon, in a public space that ordinarily privileges English.

My own observations as a spectator, however, complicate this theory. Although many non-language-speaking audience members did seek help from the 'experts' around them, others simply turned to their companions to commiserate. In addition to overhearing comments such as 'It is a bit of a struggle, isn't it?', I was conscious throughout the Festival of spectators looking anxiously around when they did not share the in-group's laughter, trying to catch a sympathetic eye. Rather than stepping outside the comfort of their habits to fill gaps in their knowledge, these spectators seemed determined to find a community in which *not* understanding was normal.

The frustration of these spectators does not necessarily indicate the failure of the intercultural encounter. I agree with Rustom Bharucha when he argues that 'there are some unprecedented insights that can be gained from being silent, decentred, marginalized to the corners of a room, excluded from the intimacy of certain bondings. There are lessons in humility to be learned from being "left out".'[18] It is perhaps more pleasant to feel fully included as a spectator, and certainly much of the rhetoric surrounding both the Globe to Globe Festival and the Olympic Games emphasized unity and understanding rather than the difficult process of critiquing one's own privilege.[19] Yet by targeting spectators who would otherwise seldom experience such community in mainstream London theatre, the Festival provided the opportunity for 'insiders' and 'outsiders' to switch positions and see from the other's perspective. It is possible, therefore, that the experience of exclusion could teach empathy to typically privileged spectators, while reminding them that not every production has to cater to their tastes and knowledge. However, such effects are difficult to prove.

Another potential problem arising from English-speakers' displacement as 'experts' is that they may project their expectations about a production's home 'culture' onto other spectators. For example, two white British women sitting in front of me at the Company Theatre's *Twelfth Night*, in Hindi, struck up a conversation with a darker-skinned man seated nearby. They seemed to expect, based on his appearance, that he could function as a representative of both the performance and the country it came from. First, they singled him out as a non-typical Globe spectator, opening the conversation by asking, loudly and slowly, 'Is this your first time at the Globe?'. When he admitted that this was the case, they asked him where he was from; upon hearing that he came from Bangladesh, they proceeded to question him about the production. Despite his protestations that he could not speak for the performers since the troupe was based in Mumbai, India – and he spoke Bangla, not Hindi – they persisted in treating him as an 'expert': 'But I suppose there are more similarities if this [was] performed in Bangladesh than in England or France?'. His noncommittal 'maybe' did not stop them from asking questions such as 'Do you think there will be some dancing tonight? I'd really like to see some dancing in here'.

Throughout this conversation, the women's assumptions reinforced their own privilege: the production would represent an authentic, preferably spectacular, portrayal of culture; that culture would be foreign to them, just as the man appeared foreign to the Globe; the differences between 'foreign' cultures that they perceived as similar were not significant. The act of conferring 'expert' status on him, therefore, did not seem to cause them to revise their preconceptions; rather, they continued to treat him as an outsider. If, as Knowles suggests, festival contexts tempt spectators to view performances as representative of entire countries, then members of London's diasporic communities risked incurring an equally reductive gaze at the Globe.

Yet other anecdotes suggest more productive interactions. Reviewer Matt Wolf, for example, found himself seated next to a 'very kind Pakistani medic and her family' at Theatre Wallay's *The Taming of the Shrew*, in Urdu.[20] As Wolf relates a literary allusion in the production's script, he credits these neighbours for the information, as they 'enlightened [him] on that topic and quite a bit else'.[21] This exchange helped him to craft a more informed review for his readers; releasing some of his authority as an 'expert', he found both aid and pleasure in having a more knowledgeable spectator nearby. Still, without hearing the 'Pakistani medic's' side of the story, I do not know whether she enjoyed being in a position to teach him, was annoyed at being expected to do so, or felt something else altogether.

Many 'expert' spectators did, however, initiate communication to instruct their less knowledgeable neighbours. For example, during the Bitter Pill Company's *Merry Wives of Windsor*, in Swahili, there was a group of five Kenyan spectators sitting two rows in front of me. Throughout the production, one of these spectators turned to a British woman sitting behind him, giving her a running commentary. As she listened with apparent interest, he explained plot points and the significance of events such as the singing of the national anthem, while scribbling notes on his programme to illuminate translation nuances. In devoting such effort to helping a stranger engage with the production, the Kenyan spectator seemed to enjoy his position of authority.

Further showing how an 'expert' spectator might initiate an exchange while taking control of its terms was a woman sitting next to me at the Dhaka Theatre's *The Tempest* (in Bangla). I had already been observing her because of the 'inside knowledge' that her behaviour suggested: she laughed at spoken dialogue, hummed along with the live music and clapped at times that surprised me, particularly in response to the musicians. However, she opened friendly contact with me as well as with other spectators nearby, proffering a bag of almonds during the performance and insisting that we take some until our polite reluctance was overcome. After the curtain call, she asked each of us in turn what we had thought of the production. Hearing that a spectator had 'liked it' was not enough; she wanted to know why. When I returned the question, she said that the story had fit the style of performance well, then exited before I could ask anything else.

In this interaction, the neighbouring spectators and I became her informants, as she had initially become mine. It seemed important to her that spectators engaged with both her and the performance in ways that extended beyond mere niceness, and her questions nudged us to do so if we had not already. She did not *tell* outsiders how to understand the production, but rather was curious to know the real impressions we had formed. Like the Kenyan man above, she appeared to recognize and relish the authority that the Festival environment had granted her.

Beyond placing language-speaking spectators in a position of relative power over non-speakers, the Festival performed important work for some members of this group by honouring cultures, countries and languages that do not often receive prominent recognition in London. For some spectators who identified with these backgrounds, the Festival seemed to provide an opportunity for community and connection. While I do not claim that all members of these groups shared this desire, survey responses from language-speaking spectators to the question 'Why did you choose to attend this particular production?' included the following:

- To feel more connected to my country of origin.
- To see performance [*sic*] from my own country in London. Please more.
- To introduce the culture to my future in-laws who are from a different culture.

Comments conveying similar sentiments elsewhere on the surveys included:

- Hearing Yoruba spoken/sung is healing/soothing – made me cry in parts. Audience who understood Yoruba gushed with the performers – the audience participation was amazing.
- I am from India (that made it naturally easy). Me and another friend loved the Marathi bits.
- I really enjoyed the music/dance too – reminded me of my culture. I loved it! It made me cry, almost...

In these responses, the spectators suggest that a major component of the productions' power was their public presentation of a shared heritage. By touring, therefore, the productions did not simply lose meaning, but found local relevance in their encounters with spectators for whom the representation of these cultures *in London* filled a personal need. However ephemerally and imperfectly, the performances provided a community for some audience members who could not easily find it elsewhere.

Ultimately, the complexities of Globe to Globe 2012 cannot be resolved into a tidy narrative. Due to the accelerated schedule of the Festival, productions showed for two or three times at most; it is difficult to know how much such events contributed to lasting learning or relationship-building across specific cultures. Furthermore, spectators' desires, expectations and experiences are so diverse that claims for how they act or think remain provisional at best.

Still, the diversity of Festival audiences offered several challenges to the touring dynamics described by Worthen and Knowles. Rather than encouraging spectators to simply consume the exotic or compare a production unfavourably to English Shakespeare, the Festival demonstrated the importance of more informed responses. The visible and audible reactions of language-speakers confronted spectators who spoke only English with the limits of their authority as 'expert' audience members for Shakespearean performance, while also expanding their options for engagement. Non-speakers could more easily recognize that gaps in their understanding were due to their positioning rather than flaws in the performance; they could also ask questions rather than having to dismiss the work as incomprehensible. For language-speakers, overt participation provided a means of demonstrating their shared presence; the Globe became a forum in which to enjoy hearing, speaking and singing languages that might ordinarily achieve little public recognition in London. Moreover, the event conferred authority upon them as 'experts', privileging them over those who know Shakespeare best in English.

Albeit temporarily and imperfectly, Globe to Globe 2012 reversed the norms of London theatre in regard to what Christopher Balme calls 'the dynamic of inclusion and exclusion'.[22] Non-traditional audiences gained authority in the Globe space, while those who would ordinarily be privileged by English Shakespeare often felt they had to ask for help or risk being left out. The Festival contributed toward weakening the authority that 'Shakespeare' wields in English, in favour of a more inclusive vision of the plays as global possessions. By inviting multinational, multilingual audiences to appreciate Shakespearean adaptations from around the world, the Festival laid the foundation not only for the serious reception of 'foreign' Shakespeare in London, but also for the revision of consensus surrounding what (and who) is 'foreign' or 'familiar' to London in the first place.

Appendix: Copy of the survey questions distributed to Globe to Globe audience members (spacing and layout has been changed)

1. Where were you sitting/standing for this performance? (Indicate on Layout Plan)

2. How would you describe your ability to understand the spoken language of the performance?

    ☐ fluent   ☐ good enough   ☐ I know a few words
    ☐ I understood none of it

3. How well did you know this play in English?

    ☐ very well   ☐ moderately well   ☐ a little bit
    ☐ not well at all

    If you know the play, how did you become familiar with it?

    _____

4. How well do you know the country/ culture presenting this performance?

☐ very well ☐ moderately well ☐ a little bit
☐ not well at all

If you know the country/ culture, how did you become familiar with it? _____

5. What country are you from? _____

Which language(s) do you speak? _____

6. How well do you think you understood the production in comparison to the other spectators?

☐ Better than most people ☐ About the same
☐ Not as well as most people

7. Why did you choose to attend this particular production?

☐ Interested in the language/country

☐ Interested in this particular play

☐ Media or internet coverage of the Globe to Globe Festival

☐ Media or internet coverage of this company/ production

☐ Attending with friends/family

☐ Other/Comments: _____

8 Have you seen Shakespeare performed in languages other than English before?

☐ Yes, as part of this festival ☐ Yes, elsewhere
☐ No, never

If yes, were there key similarities or differences?

_____

9 What were you hoping for from this production? (Please mark all that apply)

☐ A peek into the country's traditional culture

☐ New insight into a Shakespearean play

☐ An example of contemporary artistic achievement

☐ Enjoyable entertainment

☐ A fun afternoon/evening with friends/family

☐ Other/Comments: _____

10 Which aspects of the performance surprised you, if any?

_____

11 Which of the following best describe your opinion about Shakespeare <u>before</u> attending this production? Please mark all that apply.

☐ Shakespeare's plays are **universal**; they speak to all people, places, and times.

☐ The value of Shakespeare's plays is in their **poetic language**.

☐ The value of Shakespeare's plays is in their **stories**

- [ ] Shakespeare's plays are **historical** documents that should be performed in authentic conditions.
- [ ] Shakespeare's work can be adapted meaningfully to **any** new context.
- [ ] Shakespeare's work can be adapted meaningfully to **some** other contexts
- [ ] Shakespeare's plays provide good **raw material** for artists to explore their own creativity.
- [ ] Other/Comments: _____

12 Did the experience of attending this production affect the opinion(s) you expressed in Question #11?

- [ ] yes, it made me question or change my opinions
- [ ] yes, it strengthened my opinions
- [ ] no, no effect

Comments: _____

13 Were you able to follow the plot of the production?

- [ ] I understood **everything**
- [ ] I understood **what was most important**
- [ ] I understood **some things** but had many questions
- [ ] I understood **very little**
- [ ] I understood **nothing**
- [ ] I did not try to follow the plot
- [ ] Other/Comments: _____

14 Which of the following elements helped you to understand this production? (Please mark all that apply)

- [ ] The spoken dialogue
- [ ] Vocal tone
- [ ] Facial expressions
- [ ] Gesture
- [ ] Body movements
- [ ] Music (if any)
- [ ] Dance (if any)
- [ ] Synopsis on electronic boards in theatre
- [ ] Scenery and/or props
- [ ] Costumes and makeup
- [ ] The printed programme (if any)
- [ ] The reactions of the other spectators
- [ ] Your prior knowledge of Shakespeare (if any)
- [ ] Your prior knowledge of the country or culture (if any)

Please draw (a circle) around the 1-2 elements that you found *most* helpful.

Comments: _____

Thank you very much for your time! If there is anything else you would like to mention about the production, please include it below.

Notes

1. Karen Fricker, 'Tourism, The Festival Marketplace and Robert Lepage's The Seven Streams of the River Ota', *Contemporary Theatre Review* 13:4 (2003), pp. 79–93; Dennis Kennedy, *The Spectator and the Spectacle: Audiences in Modernity and Postmodernity* (Cambridge: Cambridge University Press, 2009); Ric Knowles, *Reading the Material Theatre* (Cambridge: Cambridge University Press, 2004).

2. Knowles, *Reading the Material Theatre*, p. 181.

3. W. B. Worthen, *Shakespeare and the Force of Modern Performance* (Cambridge: Cambridge University Press, 2003).

4. Ibid., pp. 154–5.

5. Ibid., p. 154.

6. Rob Conkie, *The Globe Theatre Project: Shakespeare and Authenticity* (Lewiston: The Edwin Mellen Press, 2006); Kate McLuskie, 'Macbeth/*Umabatha*: Global Shakespeare in a Post-Colonial Market', *Shakespeare Survey* 52 (1999), pp. 154–165.

7. This article is adapted from a chapter of my doctoral dissertation, 'Global Shakespeare at the Globe: Challenging the Tourist-Spectator', available via ProQuest.

8. Tom Bird, personal interview, 18 February 2012, Santa Barbara, California. See also Bird's interview in this volume.

9. Copies of the completed surveys are housed in the Globe's archives.

10. The remaining three per cent of respondents left this question blank.

11. 'Shakespeare's Globe announces success of the Globe to Globe Festival as it completes its six week marathon', Shakespeare's Globe, 7 June 2012, http://www.shakespearesglobe.com/about-us/press/releases/globe-theatre [accessed 10 June 2012].

12. While this dynamic intensified in 2012 due to the Globe's efforts to recruit language-speaking spectators, it was also present in the earlier productions. As Globe researchers Elin Jeynes and Jessica Ryan suggested of the closing performance

of *uMabatha* in 2001, 'a group of Zulu audience members who understood the language and responded with "Yabo" and other native expressions during the performance' not only 'signaled the possible extent of the cultural differences' but also caused the other spectators to become 'more passive in order to observe this Zulu response'. See 'Umabatha', *Research Bulletin* 25, Shakespeare's Globe (2002), p. 12, http://www.shakespearesglobe.com/uploads/ffiles/2012/03/891356.pdf [accessed 20 January 2012].

13 Worthen, *Shakespeare and the Force*, p. 167.

14 Helen Gilbert and Joanne Tompkins, *Post-Colonial Drama: Theory, Practice, Politics* (New York: Routledge, 1996), p. 168.

15 This occurred at the Greek *Pericles* and the Bangla *The Tempest*, among others.

16 This occurred at the Swahili *Merry Wives of Windsor* and the Urdu *Taming of the Shrew*.

17 Susan Bennett, *Theatre Audiences: A Theory of Production and Reception* (New York: Routledge, 1997), p. 153.

18 Rustom Bharucha, *The Politics of Cultural Practice: Thinking through Theatre in an Age of Globalization* (Hanover: Wesleyan University Press, 2000), p. 3.

19 For example, a Globe brochure advertising the Festival states that 'Shakespeare is the language which brings us together better than any other, and which reminds us of our almost infinite difference, and of our strange and humbling commonality'; 'Globe to Globe 37 Languages 37 Plays', Shakespeare's Globe, 26 September 2011, p. 3, http://globetoglobe.shakespearesglobe.com/schedule [accessed 20 January 2013].

20 Matt Wolf, 'Globe to Globe: The Taming of the Shrew, Shakespeare's Globe', *The Arts Desk,* 28 May 2012, http://www.theartsdesk.com/theatre/globe-globe-taming-shrew-shakespeares-globe [accessed 29 May 2012].

21 Ibid.

22 Christopher B. Balme, *Decolonizing the Stage: Theatrical Syncretism and Post-Colonial Drama* (New York: Oxford University Press, 1999), p. 119.

8

'Mind the gap': Globalism, Postcolonialism and Making up Africa in the Cultural Olympiad

Colette Gordon

In our post-1994 euphoria we too often imagined we were the naughty prodigal finally 'returning' home to a mythical happy family of nations.

JEREMY CRONIN (2012)

Shakespeare's Coming Home
GLOBE TO GLOBE FESTIVAL (2012)

In the Opening Ceremony to the 2012 Olympics, Britain showed itself 'a nation secure in its own post-empire identity'. Thus it appeared in the *New York Times*, trailing the rider '… whatever that actually is' as a backhanded acknowledgement of the celebration's multicultural eclecticism.[1] But the Ceremony's thematizing of history as a glorious march of 'revolutions', beginning with industrialization, registered an awkward (dis)engagement with Empire. As host to the Olympics and the Cultural Olympiad, Britain offered participating countries, many of them former colonies, the chance to leave the postcolonial behind and stand with the host nation as proudly 'global'. Across the cultural celebrations, an eagerly rehearsed rhetoric of 'globalism' presented itself as overtaking and replacing postcolonialism under the celebratory banner of the Games. This featured prominently in the framing of Africa brought into the cultural celebrations via Shakespeare. All of the five countries that made up Africa at the Globe's Shakespeare celebration were formed through a history of British colonial domination. But the celebratory logic of ceremony and festival persuaded spectators that participation in the global now admits countries to modern Africa, displacing and replacing the postcolonial as the (nervous) condition of African modernity.

Reflecting on the postcolonial under the rubric of the global, this chapter explores the production and reception of Africa in cultural programming by the Globe Theatre, the Royal Shakespeare Company and the British Museum, and reflects critically on the discourse of authenticity around productions 'from Africa'. What follows is not a critique of the work of directors and creative teams, or of the Festival organizers and programmers – still less of the productions, which achieved a range of rich and complex effects. In each case, accounts of cultural value brought 'from Africa' (which tend to flatten and distort the real picture of African participation in the Festival) emerged spontaneously in discourse about productions, sometimes helped along by publicity materials, but often unbidden. Such perceptions reflect less the desires and fantasies of creators than the expectations of consumers. Attending to this process, the relatively small subset (*UVenas No Adonisi / Venus and Adonis, Wanawake wa Heri wa Windsor / The Merry Wives of Windsor, Itan Oginnitin / The*

Winter's Tale, Vakomana Vaviri Ve Zimbabwe / The Two Gentlemen of Verona, Cymbeline, Julius Caesar, 'Shakespeare: Staging the World') has more global implications. Noting how 'Africa' was admitted to the global space of the celebrations may provide a key point of reference for contextualizing and qualifying the global euphoria (euphoria *about* the global) of the 2012 Olympic moment in Britain.

Carrying a torch for Caliban

The 2012 Olympic Opening Ceremony worked like a national jukebox, privileging emotional pleasure and the vicissitudes of memory over order and hierarchy. While director Danny Boyle's show was fêted as 'a triumph of punk over pomp', a mode of eclectic nostalgia framed the stadium's presentation of British history as much as its celebration of British pop culture and music.[2] This was stadial history for a stadium audience, in which representativeness and comprehensiveness were beside the point. History was revolution and the Ceremony showcased 'Britain's revolution that changed the world': Industrialization, riding on the back of the Industrial Revolution. Boyle's bold vision delivered a Wagnerian spectacle of the nation forging the Olympic rings along with its identity, a potent demonstration of the harnessing of energy that apparently made the 'Isles of Wonder' a player in global history.

In one of the strangest episodes of an Olympic Ceremony noted for its off-key moments, a spry top-hat-and-tailed Kenneth Branagh intended to represent Isambard Kingdom Brunel stood among the belching towers and addressed the crowd of milling extras:

> Be not afeard. The isle is full of noises,
> Sounds and sweet airs that give delight and hurt not.
> Sometimes a thousand twangling instruments
> Will hum about mine ears, and sometime voices

That, if I then had waked after long sleep,
Will make me sleep again; and then, in dreaming,
The clouds methought would open, and show riches
Ready to drop upon me, that when I waked,
I cried to dream again.[3]

Branagh delivered his lines with a throat-swelling emotionality that recalled his iconic turn in the 1980s as Henry V, putting courage into the hearts of his 'band of brothers' and a disillusioned post-Falklands Britain.[4] Here Shakespeare's words were offered as a charm to dispel anxiety in the face of environmental destruction and rapid social change, soon to be enacted through the arrival of the Industrial Revolution and (invisibly in the Ceremony) the ambitions of Empire. The 'voices and thousand twanging instruments' of Industry are rumblings that 'delight and hurt not', a mere show of industrial light and magic, though – as he suggests in a slightly different key – they also offer to pour down riches. The speech holds out the double reassurance of entertainment and of profit. This is a white magic that follows a principle (profit) 'as lawful as eating'.[5] This was a gamble, even a provocation, given the crisis in British public spending, which might make certain sections of British audiences less than comfortable with a £27 million spectacle featuring a dancing unpaid NHS force and an army of suited speculators guiding the nation onward, while assuring the Commons that their wizardry is both harmless and capable of bringing massive gains.

However, the dissonance was stronger and more peculiar. Shakespeare's conjuring of sound and spectacle on an indeterminate magical island transferred with little obvious trouble to Boyle's 'Isles' as a general instance of Shakespeare's poetry and imagination (and a compact inscription for the Olympic bell). But the poetry and imagination is Caliban's, not Prospero's, an odd proxy for the king of industrial light and magic. Moreover, the famous lyricism of these lines has a political significance in *The Tempest* and resonates (as does the whole play) in a postcolonial context. The oppressed slave's tender paean to the Isle's natural 'magic', a magic that *predates* Prospero's rule, is perhaps the strongest argument for his rights – stronger than the claim of the colonizer, which he also voices: 'This Island's mine, by Sycorax my mother' (1.2.333–4). James Shapiro excused the 'odd choice' of speech as a simple appropriation of Shakespeare's 'beautiful' language, to 'talk about how magical a place the British Isles are'.[6] However, it is hard not to imagine there was some edge of ironic commentary involved in putting the speech into the mouth of the Victorian engineer. Danny Boyle, likened to Prospero, was clearly ready to acknowledge the role of immigrants, especially the forebears of black Britons, in building postwar Britain, with references to the NHS and the 'Windrush Generation', the history syllabus's synecdoche for British multiculturalism,[7] though that segment (which NBC in America chose not to broadcast[8]) was lost to many stadium viewers in the general 'Pandemonium', swallowed up by the spectacle of British advancement through industry.

In the stadial fantasy, modern industrialized Britain with its sky-climbing towers rises up from the ground of the English Commons with all the raw materials for development lying there already, under the green and pleasant fields, as they did for Milton's Satan. Modernization is achieved by an innocent (and somewhat baffled) industrialism – driven by a solid drum section and equally solid Protestant work ethic – that shows no awareness of colonialism or Empire. In this bright vision, Britain's Industrial Revolution functions as the historical trump card that eclipses Empire and the history of colonial expansion that made possible both the 'Isles' and their global success. In this moment of celebration, the global seemed to efface the postcolonial. But Shakespeare's mawkish appearance both as architect-apologist for modernization and the voice of the slave, asked audiences to mind the gap.

Making up Africa (Globe to Globe)

Shakespeare played a less eccentric and more central – one might say centrist – role in the Cultural Olympiad. The Bard promised to be the 'trump card' in the Olympic committee's plan to put 'art at the heart of the Olympics', with the RSC's World Shakespeare Festival leading the scheme.[9] But the RSC's 'World' initiative was eclipsed, in the media, and finally in the Olympiad's own reporting, by the ambitious programme of its partner, the London-based Shakespeare's Globe.[10] The Globe to Globe Festival (G2G), which presented '37 plays in 37 languages', played over six weeks on a single stage and offered its programming at the heart (geographical and temporal) of the London Olympic celebrations. Framed as a multicultural rather than a multinational project, rooted in London's language communities, G2G could align itself with the London Festival's ethos of inclusion and prevent its parade of difference from being received as a neocolonial update of the World Fair. Such emphasis on minority communities made G2G an interesting supplement to the Olympic Ceremony and a contrast to the RSC's more diffuse and arguably patchy internationalism, which for the WSF included a *Much Ado about Nothing* set in Delhi, critiqued for its failure to acknowledge 'the company's inevitable second-generation detachment from India', and the 'African' *Julius Caesar* discussed in the next section of this chapter.[11]

Part of the challenge for G2G and its gambit in staging '37 plays in 37 languages' was to present all of its productions, which showed for just two to three days, as events not to be missed. The productions that went to make up Africa in Globe to Globe's programming shared a baseline eventness as African productions, their coming from Africa feeding a sense of anticipation and excitement in audiences. While G2G drew attention to difference *in* the city, there remained fascination with the far-flung and distant perceived as constituting the Festival's 'worldness'. Hence the Festival carried an alternative tagline, which made space for national pageantry and acknowledged the appeal of ethnographic spectacle: 'Shakespeare's Coming Home'. Under this banner, audiences could imagine the Festival as a tribute to Englishness, in which representatives from the furthest corners of the globe bring back Shakespeare as England's due.

Such an investment in Africanness worked with but also against G2G's declared commitment to diaspora. This was epitomized in the contribution of 'Two Gents', the company that, while presenting a Shona version of *Two Gentlemen of Verona / Vakomana Vaviri ve Zimbabwe*, presented its own peculiar tale of two cities (Peter Kirwan and Charlotte Mathieson discuss the production's staging of 'meta-tourism' in its opening scene in their chapter for this volume). The Festival programme lists the company, generally billed as 'Zimbabwean' or 'from Zimbabwe', as coming 'from Harare/ London'. The Gents might have come to the Globe directly from Zimbabwe, had their brief planned appearance in Harare before the Festival not been cancelled due to funding difficulties. While one would imagine the company struggling to get to London, Two Gents had in fact been working to secure sponsorship to get the company from their home in London to Harare before Globe to Globe. The Two Gentlemen of Zimbabwe are three British residents: German-born director Arne Pohlmeier and émigré actors Tonderai Munyevu and Denton Chikura (supported in this project by a Shona translator). Since coming together in London, they have made trips to Harare to develop their productions, which play on the UK and international festival circuits. In 2010, their website described them as a 'cross-cultural theatre company', 'based in London and Harare'. The Globe took these claims further by putting Harare first, suggesting it as the company's primary base.[12]

While it would have been interesting to see the piece performed on Zimbabwean stages, it does not follow that a performance in Harare would be more 'authentic'. The company has a significant Shona-speaking audience in London and the UK. The 2011 National Census indicates that Shona is the second largest African language spoken in the UK.[13] *Vakomana Vaviri Ve Zimbabwe* and *Kupenga Kwa Hamlet*, the company's other Shakespeare repertoire piece, might attract a *larger* Shona speaking audience in London (from émigrés like Munyevu and Chikura) than in Zimbabwe. And its position as theatre of the diaspora does not make it inauthentic – although interestingly Munyevu has suggested that the company's work is better understood by 'Europeans' than by either Zimbabwean or British audiences.[14] It was fitting that G2G's programmers should have lent the stage to a London company actively engaging a diasporic audience and dealing with issues of exile and migration (the subject of their original play *Magetsi*), particularly given the high numbers of Zimbabwean-born nationals in the city. But, presenting companies drawn from cities around the globe, the Festival only incidentally showcased linguistically diverse work by diaspora companies in London. In this regard, *Vakomana Vaviri* was an important inclusion.

Unlike Two Gents, the South African Isango Ensemble did bring their staging of *Venus and Adonis* to London direct from a performance in Cape Town, where the company is based and where most of the actors hail from. But, even here, the statement that Isango brings theatre 'from South Africa' is more complicated than it first appears. Like Two Gents, Isango is effectively split between two locations and might equally receive a double billing: Cape Town/London. While the performers have their homes in Cape Town, mainly in the townships surrounding the city, and the company operates from temporary premises in the city centre, the 'Mother City' can more accurately be said to serve as a rehearsal space for Isango's international productions. The *company* finds its performing home in London, where it has its largest audience (at the Young Vic, Hackney Empire and now the Globe). Following repeated financial failure, several scandals, claims of exploitation, acrimony and litigation, and lacking a permanent rehearsal and performance space (after two expulsions), the many times re-formed company had all but ceased performing in South Africa.[15] The Cape Town premiere (more accurately a preview) of *UVenas no Adonisi* was not advertised and was open only to invited friends and family of the cast. The Cape Town 'premiere' of *La Boheme* (*Abanxaxhi*) advertised on the company's website, but elsewhere described as a 'sneak preview', seems to have been a similarly closed event, primarily for patrons.[16]

Like Two Gents, Isango was formed through a series of London-based interactions, when British director Mark Dornford-May, then director of Broomhill Opera (Wilton's Music Hall), met with South African millionaire Dick Enthoven in 2000 in London and expressed his interest in forming a company from performers in South Africa. The company was set up with Broomhill musical director Charles Hazlewood, with whom Dornford-May had visited South Africa in 1997, giving workshops in Umlazi – though the company's website claims that 'Mark Dornford-May and Music Director Pauline Malefane formed what is now the core of Isango Ensemble in Cape Town in 2000'.[17] After premiering at Spier Festival in South Africa, the company's productions transferred to Wilton's Music Hall and went on to tour internationally.[18]

When Enthoven withdrew his funding from the project, Dornford-May's continued work with a South African cast was underwritten by South African-born British producer Eric Abraham under his Portobello label.[19] And when that relationship soured, the company was helped to keep afloat by a successful 2007 season at London's Young Vic, where they received ardent support from another white South African-born Londoner, the theatre's artistic director David Lan, now a member of the company's international council and ambassador for Isango.[20] Two Gents came together in London in the same year, when Pohlmeier, recently arrived from South Africa, signed on to the Young Vic Directors' Programme set up by Lan.[21] Pohlmeier's idea was to use what he had learned about protest theatre in South Africa to direct a township-style Shakespeare two-hander. No official call went out, but Munyevu got in contact with Pohlmeier and rehearsed a scene for him. It was the impression the actor made when asked to perform in Shona for the (non-Shona-speaking) director that led to the project's focus shifting from South Africa to Zimbabwe.[22]

While all the G2G productions 'from Africa' used black actors (and *only* black actors), the majority had white directors. For South Africa there was British-born Mark Dornford-May; for Zimbabwe, German Arne Pohlmeier; and for Kenya, Daniel Goldman, director of the UK Tangram Theatre Company, with Sarah Norman, artistic director of London-based Bitter Pill Theatre Company, the company credited with *Heri Wanawake Wa Windsor* (a Swahili *Merry Wives of Windsor*).[23] In each case, the role of director is complex, assuming different functions according to the needs and makeup of the company and expressing varying (and loosely defined) areas and levels of power and creative control. The crediting of directors (and companies) then tells us very little about the specific creative process in each case, though it tells us something about theatre networks.

The Festival programme and coverage identified *Heri Wanawake Wa Windsor* as the work of 'Kenya's Bitter Pill Theatre Company'. But Kenya's Bitter Pill Theatre Company is a composite fiction, generated in a process of collapse and inversion similar to that yielding G2G's 'Harare/London'-based Two Gents. For this project, Norman and Goldman directed a group of Kenyan actors from The Theatre Company in Nairobi, established, owned and managed by Keith Pearson.[24] Goldman was brought in at short notice to replace the director and worked primarily to prepare the actors for the particular performance challenges of the Globe's stage, made more formidable by the lack of a strong audience language base. Norman suggested the project. Neither director speaks Swahili.[25] Bitter Pill, a company made up of British producers and performers, finds its primary link to Africa in Norman, who was born and schooled in pre-Independence Zimbabwe and proposed a Swahili *Merry Wives* for the Festival programme shortly after moving from the UK to Kenya.[26]

Norman has done significant work in Zimbabwean theatre and in Shakespeare. Before leaving Zimbabwe to study in the US, she co-founded the multiracial company Over the Edge (OTE) which between 1995 and 2002 produced successful small-scale Zimbabwean reinterpretations of Shakespearean and classical works, including a *Twelfth Night* that won the 'Spirit of the Fringe' at the 2000 Edinburgh Festival and toured in the USA. In London, prior to the Festival, Norman worked as associate director for Christopher Luscombe's 2010 Globe revival of his 2008 *Merry Wives*. This followed her own production of *Merry Wives* for Ovalhouse in 2009. This production, which was set in rural Zimbabwe and employed a Zimbabwean cast, left few records, but it seems important for understanding Norman's role in shaping *Heri Wanawake Wa Windsor*, translated and, in one report, 'localized in the Kenyan context' by actor Joshua Ogutu.[27]

Bitter Pill's website lists '*Merry Wives of Wedza*' among their productions.[28] Opening the link (www.bitterpillproductions.com/wedza.html) the title is amended to *Heri Wanawake Wa Windsor*. There is no Wedza in Kenya and no such word in Swahili. *Merry Wives of Wedza* (a district in the North East of Zimbabwe) was the name of Norman's 2009 Ovalhouse production. The collapsing of the Zimbabwean and Kenyan titles complicates the Globe's already complicated narrative. While the notes for *Heri Wanawake Wa Windsor* announce: 'Bitter Pill bring their version of *The Merry Wives of Windsor* from Nairobi to London', readers are told that the company's 'exuberant, African take on Shakespeare's comedy of failed courtship [...] first played at the Harare International Festival of Arts in Zimbabwe [HIFA], before travelling north to engage with the sun-soaked joys of the Swahili language'.[29] This conjures a rather bizarre scenario, in which the creation and development of this 'African take' on *Merry Wives* might have preceded involvement of Kenyan language and Kenyan actors. It seems unfeasible that the production would have been workshopped without Ogutu, its translator and star actor (playing three roles). But it is significant that, while the notes make space for Harare within the narrative of 'Nairobi to London', they still miss a station – Bitter Pill's website indicates that *Heri Wanawake Wa Windsor* was also workshopped in London, at Ovalhouse.[30]

Either the two discrete productions followed a strikingly similar path through HIFA and Ovalhouse – which would be interesting in itself – or the first showing of *Heri Wanawake* at HIFA recorded in the Globe notes was in fact a showing of *Wedza*. I have not been able to find any record of Ogutu's involvement at HIFA. If *Wedza* was the basis for the Kenyan *Merry Wives*, the project would have travelled from London (Norman's base) to Harare and (depending on whether workshopping happened before or after the Ovalhouse production) possibly back to London before arriving in Nairobi, its supposed point of departure. The latter reading seems confirmed by Sonia Massai's account, which also notes similarities with Christopher Luscolme's 2008 production for the Globe.[31] In this case, a full assessment of the production might grapple with the extent to which the Kenyan *Merry Wives* was a translation, not just from Shakespeare, but from a Zimbabwean setting, conceived for London audiences.

'Kenyan Bitter Pill' and 'Zimbabwean' Two Gents also traced overlapping paths on the international African theatre circuit, which took both companies through Ovalhouse and the Harare Festival. As companies cross in this way, the real terrain of theatre work becomes apparent and the distinction between British, Southern African and East African theatre programming in the Festival becomes difficult to maintain. What we begin to see is how several of the African productions in the Festival were populated by a network of Europe-based theatre-makers with access to and a stake in African theatre or its brand as it operates in London and the international circuit. Directors in this niche seem to move with ease between projects identified as African, while actors are more constrained. After G2G, Bitter Pill engaged a second African project, *The Harare Files*, based on women's stories from Zimbabwe, with an actor from Two Gents. In 2013, the

Two Gents went on a final tour, with Pohlmeier (now a Globe Education Practitioner) beginning new work with a company based in Yaoundé that combines classical (German) theatre and actors' Cameroonian heritage, and that is scheduled to tour in Germany in 2014.[32]

Pohlmeier's UK-sponsored South African experience allowed a transfer, through London, to funded work with Zimbabwean actors, language and heritage. Township theatre is part of the history and vocabulary of Zimbabwean theatre, which in the 1980s absorbed elements of South African protest theatre through contact with activist practitioners.[33] But, rather than developing out of this tradition in Zimbabwe, Two Gents appears, at least on the surface, to repeat the initial meeting between (white) protest theatre director-experts and Zimbabwean actors – if the émigré actors are to be positioned as Zimbabwean performers. The Zimbabwean actors for *Merry Wives of Wedza* were promised 'a likely continuing role if the project moves on', but *Merry Wives* moved on to work with Kenyans.[34]

It does appear that on the international festival circuit a generalized 'African' expertise, more readily accessed by Europeans than by Africans, becomes mobilized as a form of capital, that renders African 'experience' commodifiable and commensurable. Of concern is not that the Kenyan production at G2G was also a UK, and Zimbabwean, production, but that the continent's countries, languages and theatres may be interchangeable in the hands of African 'experts' provided that they can source the right actors – in this case all black – that bespeak their authenticity. This picture is however complicated, rather than simply compounded, by the crossing with Norman. Although interviews with Two Gents say nothing about OTE, the Zimbabwean multiracial group which in the last decade gathered UK audiences for its localized engagements with Shakespearean theatre, their work seems a clear aesthetic precursor to Two Gents' deft, humorous, small-scale, multilingual Shakespeares. Before Two Gents' Chikura emigrated to the UK, he had his start in the theatre with OTE in Harare.³⁵ The real, intersecting histories of such small theatre companies and their collaborations complicate and belie the division between white (European) theatre-makers and black (African) actors that appears – at least on the surface – in G2G's programming.

Though the marketing of the Festival may have given the impression of contributors bringing work directly from Africa, the productions discussed show how much of this work was actually coming from companies or key figures already in London. This highlights the financial constraints on companies trying to enter from outside the system. G2G favoured groups able to find and secure their own funding and/or draw a profit from a more extensive tour strategy. Only a select few would have the resources to convert this 'opportunity' into something profitable. This finds an interesting parallel in the RSC Open Stages project: Adam Hansen and Monika Smialowska note the substantial costs to participants for the Gateshead Open Stage in North East England, required to audition in London for a production which finally took only actors with training outside the region, primarily London (pp. 116–18). It should be noted that African theatre *has* a home in London – in particular though the efforts of Ovalhouse – which has fostered especially audiences for Southern African and West African theatre in London.

Of the five companies identified with Africa, two represented home-grown African theatre and collaboration – albeit with custom-made G2G productions. Nigerian Renegade Company and South Sudan Theatre Company (SSTC) both claim strong support at home. SSTC's directors indicated that *Cymbeline* in Arabi Juba (Juba Arabic) would be performed in Juba before the Festival in London (though interviews with SSTC members seem to contradict this claim).³⁶ In the year that followed, the company performed four times in informal venues in Juba, reportedly attracting a crowd of over 10,000 to one of their performances.³⁷ Director Wole Oguntokun's announcement that Renegade would perform *Itan Oginnitin* at the Musical Society of Nigeria in Lagos before heading to London is reported by Nigerian media to have been met with gratitude and cheers.[38] Of course, it is hard to read those cheers at a distance. As the SSTC actors who performed *Cymbeline* at the Globe to 'standing ovations' and 'glowing praise' (including a four-star *Guardian* review) prepared to return home, members of the cast expressed anxiety about the future their work would have in Juba.[39]

Two Gents entered the Festival with a reworked version of their founding production, ready to tour with two others, and the promise of a Globe launch for their next Shakespeare project.[40] Isango's custom-made *Venus and Adonis*, also booked for touring, secured the company a second week-long (solo) run at the Globe in 2013, further expanding its London audience base. For the troupes returning home – however triumphantly – the material benefits of Festival participation were less clear. As a newcomer and outsider to this system, SSTC relied on support from the British Council.[41] Oguntokun had strong pre-existing links with London theatre through the British Council; his company performed at the British Council-sponsored Lagos Theatre Festival in 2013.[42] At the end of 2012, Bitter Pill/Theatre Company Kenya's *Heri Wanawake*, which the company's strategic plan noted as 'self-financing', performed for a three-day run at Nairobi's Alliance Française, apparently to small audiences (around twenty people).[43] The 'local theatre' created for Globe audiences might prove unpopular or unsustainable back home. Companies creating it might require foreign funding for their home performances as much as for their performances in London. The actors for *Heri Wawakane*'s three-day run performed against a corporate banner.[44] Nevertheless, these groups articulate an ongoing commitment to creating theatre for incipient national audiences in Africa.

Africa is a country (*Julius Caesar* and the 'Robben Island Bible')

While the Globe generated excitement in audiences eager to welcome productions from Africa, the same willingness seems to have been extended to the RSC's very British *Julius Caesar*. The production located the action in an unspecified African state, combining the visual signifiers of a generic West African marketplace, with East African accents, West African music, and elements of South African political iconography. The sub-Saharan composite elicited some concern about staging Africa as a country, although the issue was not generally raised in reviews. What is more interesting is that the media seem to have been ready to receive this as an African production performed by an 'African cast' (as half a dozen news sources reported).[45] The confusion went beyond race. The RSC commissioned Richard Dowden, a specialist journalist on African issues, director of the Royal African Society, and author of a book on Africa (published under the label that formerly underwrote Mark Dornford-May's Isango group), to write an essay for the programme notes. The notes contain many of the points made by the director, Gregory Doran, in his press release. Dowden also published a review of the production on the Royal African Society website. The review conveys a striking, but familiar, tone of condescension. What is most striking, however, is the writer's apparent confusion of the Africanized production with an African production:

> I tried to imagine what it would be like. My first image was of African actors struggling to be like Romans speaking quaint 16th century English. It would be admirable but unconvincing. Black skins beneath white masks I had thought. An African Caesar would be almost as awkward as a European Othello.[46]

Putting aside his reading of Othello, Dowden's assumptions

about the 'African' cast look rather odd when he ties them to concerns about language, boiled down to the cruel and unusual spectacle of African actors struggling to speak Shakespeare's English lines with their added Roman whiteness. But Doran's production included a team of RSC veterans. Ray Fearon (Antony) has worked with the RSC since 1993, Jeffery Kissoon (Julius Caesar) since 1978 and Cyril Nri (Cassius) started his acting career at the RSC in 1982 in the role of Lucius.

If anything, what this pan-African project presented was a spectacle of black British actors struggling to be like 'Africans', to speak in accents that would be recognized as authentic within the ersatz African world of the play. Dowden recounts how viewing the production set him straight. But this corrected account is no less speculative:

> I could not have been more wrong. It was as if the play was written for those actors. Every gesture and intonation is African. So are the political themes: noble ideals leading good men to bloody murder, the coup against a tyrant followed by the falling out of the conspirators, petty jealousies, sly duplicity and secret plotting. All these themes have haunted African politics for half a century. Here are Idi Amin, Nelson Mandela, Robert Mugabe, Laurent Kabila and Colonel Gaddafi. Ashanti togas and wrap-around lappas make it even more authentically African as if the play was about a recent coup in Africa.

The journalist concludes with a statement that establishes the show's heavy citation of stock imagery from political news media coverage (African dictator, bloody coup, riots, demonstrations of power, etc.) as the measure of its own eventness. Following this logic, the African *Julius Caesar* is a news story because *Africa* is a news story, though Dowden also claims its universality:

> An all European cast could only to [*sic*] the play as a re-enactment of ancient history. This African production is

a news story [...] This production has taken *Julius Caesar* out of time and place, made it global and timeless.

Dowden pictures an 'all European' cast in opposition to Doran's all-African cast. But as already suggested, the RSC cast was, conspicuously, a showcase of black British acting talent.[47] It included actors born in Nigeria, Uganda, Ghana (as well as Trinidad and America), but, with the exception of Cyril Nri who was raised in Nigeria during the Biafran war, almost all had lived from early childhood in the UK, mostly in and around London.[48] Paterson Joseph (Brutus) recalls that the 'African' delivery of the lines – later limited to an 'East African' accent – 'seemed to tie in well with most of us'.[49] But for all the British performers, presumably it required some special effort. The cast also included volunteers from the 'black community' around Stratford and Birmingham, who were brought in as 'citizens of the city' to swell the crowd scenes.[50] It is a peculiar problem of this production that even as British blackness was made visible, it was simultaneously concealed in the generic performance of 'Africanness'.

In a press release, and in interviews, Doran cited a list of post-independence African dictators ('Amin or Bokassa, Mobutu or Mugabe') that might be seen as offering parallels for Rome's Caesar. By way of further support he invoked Tanzania's first president Julius Nyere translating *Julius Caesar* into Swahili, Apartheid actor and activist John Kani naming this 'Shakespeare's African play' and, most powerfully, Nelson Mandela imprisoned on Robben Island, inscribing his name alongside Caesar's: 'Cowards die many times before their deaths; the valiant never taste of death but once'.[51] In choosing to autograph these lines, Doran suggested, the nation's future leader was 'asserting that *Julius Caesar* spoke in a particular way to his continent'.[52] What way precisely remains unclear. But there is little to connect Mandela's appropriation of Caesar's stoic defiance to a vision of African history as an endless cycle of despotisms.

Mandela's autographed copy of the so-called Robben Island 'Bible' would appear again, prominently, in the British Museum's 'Shakespeare: Staging the World' exhibition, again part of the Cultural Olympiad. Always open on Mandela's signature, the book was arguably the exhibit's major drawcard. Capitalizing on excitement around the celebrations and the British playwright's global significance, the Museum made the broadest claims yet for Shakespeare's importance on the island. According to curator Dora Thornton, those political prisoners, who 'studied' and circulated Sonny Venkatrathnam's book, 'found a common bond in Shakespeare as they did in their fight against apartheid'.[53] In this scenario one imagines freedom fighters (rather than curators), 'reverently' dubbing their Shakespeare 'the Bible'. It is unsurprising, and indeed common, to see Shakespeare invoked as a comrade in struggles for political liberation, distinguishing the freedom fighter, with his high humanist ideals, from the guerrilla soldier or terrorist. In the 'irresistible' proposal the Globe received from South Sudan, its author, who would become the country's minister of culture, related how he would 'lie in the Bush under the stars reading Shakespeare plays to avoid thinking about the killing that would happen the next day'.[54] The 'Bible' tag came into use in wry reference to the book's cover, Venkatrathnam's wife having pasted it with Hindi postcards to allow it to pass as a religious text. In the exhibition, the moniker took on its own power, exploiting the cultural equivalence between Shakespeare and the Bible.[55] Offering the Robben Island 'Bible' as the ultimate fetish, the exhibition also used the tag to argue that the book was a source of spiritual sustenance and moral development, held in 'reverence' by African National Congress (ANC) members: 'used in the same way as the bible has been used down the ages: as a constant reference for debating the moral issues of the day'.[56]

While the book was on display in London, claims for its 'iconic' status and role in the struggle produced emphatic denials from ANC spokesman Jackson Mthembu and also from Ahmad Kathrada, the chairperson of the Robben Island

Museum, a fellow prisoner on the Island and a key figure in the cluster of stories told around the Robben Island Bible. According to the *Toronto Star*: 'Kathrada said he couldn't remember [...] the passage he signed. He [Venkatrathnam] asked a number of us to sign our name beside the passage that you find interesting of Shakespeare. And that was the sum total of my connection [...] I have no other connection [to the book].'[57] An earlier interview with Matthew Hahn, who penned a play about the Robben Island Bible story, shows Kathrada perplexed by his questions, along with two other former prisoners, who also could not remember the quotations they had signed.[58] The press, while it provided enthusiastic coverage of the exhibition and its star exhibit, remained quiet about Kathrada's querying of the 'Bible's' place in its narrative of struggle. What was glossed over is not necessarily the tale of a fake, a story told to increase the value of Venkatrathnam's artefact. As David Schalkwyk convincingly argues, the contradictions, elisions and general sense of bafflement in interviews with signatories are themselves telling. Memory is faulty, subject to stress and to later constructions. The 'truth' of what happened on the island, what Venkatrathnam's Shakespeare meant to imprisoned activists, is hard to recover now, even for those who were there, and who gave their signature.[59]

The 'Robben Island Bible' exemplifies how objects are created out of desires and expectations. A copy of Shakespeare disguised with Hindi images and circulated by its owner for fellow prisoners to sign before his release, becomes a spiritual focus and centre of debate, a moral workshop, a means of collective ethical reflection and instruction, a school of goodness, a 'bible' for the liberation movement.[60] The story of the Robben Island Bible writes itself. And it suited the mood and intellectual agenda of the 'Mbeki years' (1999–2008) following Mandela's presidency, when the book was first displayed. In 2012, that mood had shifted. Since Mbeki's ousting by his successor, Jacob Zuma, tensions within the ANC and between those who fought together against Apartheid had become visible in South African politics. Replacing the old unity of struggle, a more complex narrative had begun to re-form memories of the resistance to apartheid. Venkatrathnam attributes memorial failure among Robben Island signatories to personal shifts in ideology that have taken place since the ANC came to power and, in his view, the 'communists' became the 'biggest capitalists'.[61] As the Robben Island narrative starts to fracture, exposing tensions, refusals, uncertainties and shifts of allegiance, the new story enters – fascinatingly, howsoever unsettlingly – into the *present* of global, post-apartheid South Africa. But the media liked the old story.

'Post' it: The mythic past and the global future

UVenas no Adonisi was the opening performance at Globe to Globe, and there too the spectre of South Africa's present made way for the ghosts of Africa past and future. Beyond the baseline compromise between local multiculturalism and global internationalism registered in the Festival's two taglines ('37 plays in 37 languages' and 'Shakespeare's Coming Home') G2G performed – and favoured – a particular kind of Olympic balancing act: celebrating countries' entry into the 'global' while answering to expectations of authenticity. This was grasped immediately in Peter Kirwan's review for *Year of Shakespeare*. The successful Festival opener, it was noted, showed itself 'both recognizably South African and unmistakably global', 'aware of the future but celebrating an African heritage'. In summary:

> *U-Venas no Adonisi* was the perfect opening to the Festival, representative of its South African visitors while speaking to a broad and accessible multicultural audience [...] it offered a modern idea of Africa, globally aware but celebratory of its diverse heritages. Shakespeare's poem became a tribal story, a myth of essential human practices,

and a full standing ovation welcomed this newly timeless tale back to London.[62]

The review represents an attempt to establish an appropriate descriptive vocabulary and success benchmarks for the Festival in its first moments, and organizes itself around a set of dichotomies that appear natural in the context of the Festival, and which are repeated: 'celebrating an African heritage', 'a tribal story, a myth' – yet 'aware of the future', 'globally aware'.[63] In the ideal G2G production, with its 'modern idea of Africa', the old, tribal and universal form one side of the dichotomy, with the new, multiple and global on the other side. The tension is resolved, or transcended, through G2G, where the all-encompassing universal of Shakespeare's plays meets the all-encompassing global of the international theatre circuit. The ideal production must acknowledge past and future: or rather acknowledge the past as tribal, and the future as global. This rhetoric insists on uniting past and present, even as it severs them. One must ask: between heritage (myth) and the global future (reality), where is *history*? What do the G2G productions really tell us about the inherited past or the global future?

While the Olympics offered Britons an opportunity to celebrate their heritage and global future 'secure in their own post-empire identity', South Africans quietly observed their country's democratic majority with the celebration of Freedom Day. This was an occasion to celebrate, but also to reflect soberly on what had been achieved in 18 years of post-apartheid democracy. Among talk, alternately optimistic and despairing, of moving 'beyond apartheid', one commentator addressed the question of what it would mean to embrace the global reality. Jeremy Cronin reminded South Africans: 'In our post-1994 euphoria we too often imagined we were the naughty prodigal finally "returning" home to a mythical happy family of nations'. However, apartheid 'was not disconnected from a much longer global and local history [...] Treating apartheid as a stand-alone evil disconnects it, in the first place, from 500 years of colonial conquest, and from persisting patterns of global inequity and neo-colonial domination'.[64] This argues that South Africa did not become global when apartheid ended. Apartheid *was* global, and the country remains bound in global systems of inequality. Cronin's anatomy of global euphoria is surely worth remembering in the context of the Games, especially as the UK shifts its postcolonial identity into the register of the 'global', and offers this privilege to other countries.

So much for celebration of the global. What about authenticity? The greater part of G2G's African productions did not match with the 'from Africa' narrative associated with them. But such a narrow conception of authenticity is a red herring. If we attend to what the demand for authenticity conceals – the actual conditions of production of the companies that did participate – we find that beyond the couple that delivered a desired narrative of nation-building and home-grown theatre, *all* tell stories of the global in Africa, though less grand narratives: of dispersal, dependency, exile and exploitation.[65] It is worth attending to *these* stories, and worth noting that they do not only concern Africa. Amid the confusion occasioned by the RSC's pan-African palimpsest, discussion came down to a debate as to whether it should have involved greater coherence in costume, music, accents and historical markers, referencing a more specific location (i.e. greater authenticity). Writing for the *New Yorker*, prominent Nigerian-American author Teju Cole weighed in in favour of the production in this debate, finding its choices both effective and valid.[66] But the problem, I would argue, is not that the RSC's *Julius Caesar* imagines Africa as a country; rather, that it presents an African state cut off from history, a trend also in the G2G productions.[67] Doran's rendering of 'Modern Africa' contains few traces of what historically made it modern: the traumatic encounter with colonial power. Instead, the Arab Spring, evoked in relation to the production, is supposed to mark Africa as modern. Thus, in the 'all-black' *Julius Caesar* situated in post-independence Africa, colonial power is deftly erased. In an interview about the production, Doran remarked that '[p]ost-colonial Africa is just a concentration of history that allows us all a metaphor to apply to the rest of the world'.[68] The statement, addressing 'us', is intended to cue self-examination: 'How do we act in the face of tyranny? Is it right to assassinate?' But the production engages 'the rest of the world' in a peculiar way. The temporal-geographical locator 'modern Africa' with 'the backdrop of the Arab Spring' admits North Africa into the pastiche of Sub-Saharan Africa, while the set evoked for critics the toppled statue of Saddam Hussein in Firdos Square, but also the monuments of Lenin and Kim Il-Sung.[69] This gesture to the Arab Spring brings the production closer in time ('our' time) even as it keeps the world of the play at a distance. The UK is not subject to an Arab revolution. Nor it seems is it involved in the post-independence cycle of African despotisms, coups and civil wars. Outside of the history plays, it was Shakespeare's judicious habit to locate social commentary relevant to his London audiences in locations beyond censor. But in this 'African' *Caesar*, Shakespeare's anywhere but England becomes everywhere but England (the developed world).[70]

G2G invited African countries to cast off their pasts and stand proudly with the global crowd. As SSTC co-director and translator Joseph Abuk said: 'when we return to the South, we will be like other people in other places [...] We met 37 countries and participated with them. They considered us their equals. This will be a great thing for South Sudan.'[71] SSTC's *Cymbeline* was the pride of G2G's programming, perfectly balancing the appeal of global renewal and authenticity. In a swarm of articles emphasizing the country's newness (South Sudan gained independence in July 2011), the press made clear that, more than celebrating independence, by staging theatre in the unique regional lingua franca Juba Arabic, the company was offering communication and cohesion for an unstable and painfully fragmented region.[72] Though the history of Sudanese conflict is complex, and the production (backed by the British Council) invited Globe audiences to lend support to the (current political) winners, everyone could agree about the worthiness of this work. The *Independent* announced SSTC's performance in Juba Arabic as fulfilling an 'ambition to rise above the country's past'.[73] However, this vocal support maintained silence around Britain's role in the region's instability, most insidiously through aggressive language policy that in 1928 suppressed the Arabic lingua franca and installed English as the official language with support for six African languages. Purporting to preserve the 'African way of life', the policy functioned as part of a colonial strategy designed to exploit and exacerbate the division and inequality that allowed South Sudan to be marginalized and controlled.[74] Today, Arabi Juba's importance as an oral vernacular points to widespread illiteracy across the country and the legacy of an oppressive colonial educational policy in South Sudan that may be likened to Bantu education in South Africa.[75]

A large part of the symbolic and emotional work that 'making up' Africa performed at the Festival was in putting away the spectre of responsibility. Making it global meant making it *new*. In media coverage, shared 'experience' (the easily consumable) displaced shared history, and shared responsibility. Worth noting then is the element of resistance in SSTC's performance, observed by Kim Solga:

> Instead of standing apart from us to 'stand for' their work (and for their country) in an ordinary bow, the performers asked us at the curtain to join them in that work by joining in its welcoming. In Shakespeare's own house, the SSTC turned the tables on the Bard, using his *Cymbeline* as but a prologue to their intensely performative, personal celebration – and to the work that lies ahead of them as artists and citizens of a nation in difficult transition. Most importantly, they sang and danced and cheered that work as all of ours – as not just a source of 'global' pleasure, but also a site of global responsibility.[76]

Solga's account affirms my argument, but it goes beyond it too in recording how performers took the stage at G2G, demonstrating a creative agency that was essential in all the productions. To argue that the G2G productions were unrepresentative of countries or their histories would be beside the point. Neither the Festival participants, nor its organizers, were obliged to locate audiences within the context of the national histories of countries representing/represented. Of all things I am least concerned to show that productions were 'inauthentic'. The degree of distortion in accounts of the Festival might be attributed precisely to an overinvestment in authenticity.

Rather than trying to show that plays shown at Globe to Globe were inauthentic, I would argue that it is precisely in these material conditions that their authentic condition as African (and global) is to be found. In several cases, PR and press elided or simply failed to grasp this, sustaining an effect of authenticity demanding raced foreign bodies. But something obvious seems to have been missed here, in the essential definition of 'globalism'. To take a salient example, while the (re)ordering of cities to make up 'Harare/London' in G2G's notes for the Two Gents may have misled readers as to the company's London base, the collapsing of distance between cities it effects is apt – and an apt acknowledgement of conditions of production affecting the Festival as a whole.

G2G's focus on the global city London, linking to other urban centres worldwide, the attention paid to *cities* rather than countries of origin, acknowledges the cultural force of migrancy and gateway cities and points to a now widely held understanding of globalism as constituted by global flows of capital and labour concentrated in cities, cities that reflect global (economic) more than national affiliations. In this model, London joins New York and Tokyo among the great capitals of global capital directing those flows.[77] Although focus has shifted to 'global city regions' (where, it should be noted, 'glocalization' involves interplay not of the global and local but of the processes of globalization and urbanization), the simple framework of John Friedmann's 'world city hypothesis' well comprehends what was happening in 'Harare/

London', in the Festival's flows of people and resources.[78] The peculiar mixture of opportunity and exploitation in 'making up' Africa at G2G was both global and authentic, authentically global. Ultimately, the 2012 London Olympic celebrations may have been, if anything, a little too successful in transcending national boundaries, leaving us to consider how little there was to transcend – or how much still remains – beyond the 'global'.

Notes

1 Sarah Lyall, 'A Five Ring Opening Circus, Weirdly and Unabashedly British', *New York Times*, 27 July 2012, http://www.nytimes.com/2012/07/28/sports/olympics/in-olympic-opening-ceremony-britain-asserts-its-eccentric-identity.html?pagewanted=all&_r=0 [accessed 5 December 2013].

2 Bernadette Macnulty, 'London 2012 Opening Ceremony, first review', *Telegraph*, 27 July 2012, http://www.telegraph.co.uk/sport/olympics/london-2012/9433039/London-2012-Opening-Ceremony-first-review.html [accessesd 12 May 2013].

3 William Shakespeare, *The Tempest*, ed. Frank Kermode (London: Methuen, 1964), 3.2.133–41.

4 James Chapman, *Past and Present: National Identity and the British Historical Film* (London: I. B. Tauris, 2005), pp. 140–1.

5 William Shakespeare, *The Winter's Tale*, ed. John Pitcher (London: Arden, 2010), 5.3.109–10.

6 Michael Florek, 'Shakespeare passage features in opening ceremony', *USA Today*, 27 July 2012, http://usatoday30.usatoday.com/sports/olympics/london/story/2012-07-27/shakespeare-tempest-london-olympics-opening-ceremony/56548372/1 [accessed 6 January 2013].

7 Katherine Edwards, 'Gove's history curriculum needs to do more to teach equality', Guardian Teacher Network, 29 April 2013, http://www.theguardian.com/teacher-network/teacher-blog/2013/apr/29/gove-history-curriculum-more-equality [accessed 4 October 2013].

8 'NBC's opening ceremony mess', *Guardian*, 28 July 2012, http://www.theguardian.com/media/us-news-blog/2012/jul/28/nbc-opening-ceremony-cringeworthy-moments?CMP=twt_fd&CMP=SOCxx2I2 [accessed 30 April 2014].

9 Ruth Mackenzie quoted in 'RSC's Shakespeare Festival is Cultural Olympiad "trump card"', *Telegraph*, 6 September 2012, http://www.telegraph.co.uk/culture/cultural-olympiad/8744676/RSCs-Shakespeare-Festival-is-Cultural-Olympiad-trump-card.html [accessed 20 February 2014].

10 Ruth Mackenzie and Beatriz García, 'Reflections on the Cultural Olympiad and London 2012 Festival', Arts Council England (2013), http://www.artscouncil.org.uk/media/uploads/pdf/Reflections_on_the_Cultural_Olympiad_and_London_2012_Festival.pdf, pp. 9, 21 [accessed 14 December 2012].

11 Kate Rumbold, '*Much Ado About Nothing*', *Year of Shakespeare*, http://bloggingshakespeare.com/year-of-shakespeare-much-ado-about-nothing-at-the-rsc [accessed 20 May 2013].

12 Penelope Woods, 'Denton Chikura, Tonderai Munyevu and Arne Pohlmeier of Two Gents Productions in Conversation with Penelope Woods', in *Theatre and Adaptation: Return, Rewrite, Revisit*, ed. Margherita Laera (London: Methuen Drama, 2014), in press.

13 '2011 census: Quick statistics for England and Wales, March 2011', Office for National Statistics, 30 January 2013, http://www.ons.gov.uk/ons/dcp171778_297002.pdf [accessed 03 August 2013].

14 Christina Matzke, '"Stark Raving Sane" or Playing Kupenga Kwa Hamlet (The Madness of Hamlet) Tonderai Munyevu in Conversation', in *Kuvama Ukama – Building Bridges: A Tribute to Flora Veit-Wild*, Julius Heinicke, et al. (eds) (Heidelberg: Kalliope Paperbacks, 2012), pp. 361–71 (p. 371).

15 David Thomas, 'Evicted Fugard Actors in Crisis Talks', *Cape Times*, 24 November 2010, http://www.highbeam.com/doc/1G1-243451834.html [accessed 10 May 2013];

Philani Nombembe and Grace Johnson, 'u-Carmen director "exploiter"', *The Sunday Times*, 17 April 2011, http://www.timeslive.co.za/entertainment/2011/04/17/u-carmen-director-exploiter [accessed 10 May 2013]; Brent Meersman, 'A real-life drama at the Fugard', *Mail and Guardian*, 17 December 2010, http://mg.co.za/article/2010-12-13-a-reallife-drama-at-the-fugard [accessed 10 May 2013]; Colette Gordon, 'Shakespeare's African *nostos*: township nostalgia and South African performance at sea', *Africa Theatre*, 12 (2013), pp. 28–47.

16 Isango website, http://www.isangoensemble.org.za/shows/la-boheme/; http://www.theglobalfund.org/en/laboheme/ [accessed 7 September 2013].

17 Jonathan Lennie, 'Cape Crusaders: Isango Ensemble', *Time Out*, http://www.timeout.com/london/opera-classical-music/cape-crusaders-isango-ensemble [accessed 7 September 2013]; Mark Dornford, ZoomInfo, http://www.zoominfo.com/p/Mark-Dornford/150105181 [accessed 7 September 2013]; Isango website, http://www.isangoensemble.org.za/ [accessed 1 September 2013].

18 Isango website, http://www.isangoensemble.org.za/shows/the-mysteries/ [accessed 18 May 2014].

19 *Encyclopedia of South African Theatre, Film, Media, and Performance*, http://esat.sun.ac.za/index.php/Isango_Portobello [accessed 2 May 2014]; Meersman, 'A Real Life Drama'.

20 'David Lan on Isango Ensemble', Young Vic website, ' http://www.vam.ac.uk/content/articles/a/about-a-christmas-carol/ [accessed 5 May 2014]

21 Ovalhouse website, http://www.ovalhouse.com/participation/recent-successes [accessed 7 September 2013]; Woods, 'Denton Chikura, Tonderai Munyevu and Arne Pohlmeier of Two Gents Productions in Conversation'.

22 Ibid.

23 In 2012 'Bitter Pill' described itself, and was referenced, as 'an award winning theatre company in London' but it has since redefined itself as 'working across Europe and Africa'. Bitter Pill website, http://www.bitterpillproductions.com/ [accessed 10 May 2014].

24 Keith Pearson, Linkedin, http://ke.linkedin.com/pub/keith-pearson/20/169/131 [accessed 3 April 2014].

25 'An Interview with Daniel Goldman', Everyone Theatre, http://everything-theatre.co.uk/2013/06/everyone-theatre-interview-with-daniel.html [accessed 10 May 2014]; Emma Cox, '"The Girl Defies": A Kenyan *Merry Wives of Windsor*', in *Shakespeare Beyond English: A Global Experiment*, ed. Christie Carson and Susan Bennett (Cambridge: Cambridge University Press, 2013), pp. 53–62 (p. 55).

26 The Space, http://thespace.org/items/e00003u4?t=cvspv [accessed 7 July 2013; no longer available]; Cox, '"The Girl Defies"', p. 55.

27 'Review: Wanawake wa Heri wa Winsa', Maneno Matamu: a space dedicated to African languages and African Poetry, 22 December 2012, http://manenomatamu.wordpress.com/2012/12/22/review-swahili-merry-wives-windsor/ [accessed 1 May 2014].

28 Bitter Pill website, http://www.bitterpillproductions.com/futureproductions.html [accessed 5 September 2013].

29 Globe to Globe website, http://globetoglobe.shakespearesglobe.com/plays/the-merry-wives-windsor/english-20 [accessed 7 September 2013].

30 Bitter Pill website, http://www.bitterpillproductions.com/wedza.html [accessed 5 September 2013].

31 Sonia Massai, 'Ms-directing Shakespeare at the Globe-to-Globe festival, 2012', in *Women Making Shakespeare: Text, Reception and Performance*, Gordon McMullan, Lena Cowen Orlin and Virginia Mason Vaughan (eds) (London and New York: Bloomsbury, 2014), pp. 313–22 (p. 315).

32 'Frank McKone, 'Two Gents Productions Approaching End', *Canberra Critics Circle* blog, http://ccc-canberracriticscircle.blogspot.com/2013/03/two-gents-productions.html [accessed 3 December 2013]; Young Vic Director's Programme, http://directors.youngvic.org/index.php?pid=25&did=501 [accessed 27 November 2013].

33 See Owen S. Seda, 'Transculturalism in Post-Independence Zimbabwean Drama: Projections of Zimbabwean Theatre at

the Onset of a New Millennium', *Zambezia*, 31:1–2 (2004), pp. 136–47 (pp. 138–9).

34 'Looking for Zimbabwean Actors in London', *Zimbabwe Situation*, http://www.zimbabwesituation.com/may21_2009.html [accessed 1 May 2013].

35 'Denton Chikura' on Amanda Howard Associates website, http://www.amandahowardassociates.co.uk/cv/chikura-denton.pdf [accessed 1 December 2013].

36 Christine Matzke, 'Performing the Nation at the London Globe – Notes on a South Sudanese *Cymbeline* "We will be like other people in other places"', *Shakespeare in and out of Africa* (*African Theatre 12*), ed. Jane Plaistow (2013), pp. 61–82.

37 Ester Liberato and Ségolène Malterre, '"Fear no more the heat of the sun": Shakespeare in S. Sudan', *France 24* (*Observers*), 1 July 2013, http://observers.france24.com/content/20130628-curtain-opens-south-sudanese-theatre [accessed 8 July 2013].

38 Mary Ekah, 'Nigeria: Art Meets Charity', *This Day*, 2 June 2012, http://www.thisdaylive.com/articles/art-meets-charity/117138/ [accessed 20 February 2014].

39 Toby Collins, 'South Sudan Theatre Company perform Cymbeline in London', *Sudan Tribune*, 9 May 2012, http://www.sudantribune.com/spip.php?article42545 [accessed 3 December 2012]; Ari Bloomekatz, 'South Sudan Troupe Sees New Country's Struggle in Shakespeare', *Los Angeles Times*, 16 May 2012, http://articles.latimes.com/2012/may/16/entertainment/la-et-globe-to-globe-shakespeare-20120512 [accessed 20 December 2012]; Matzke, 'Performing the Nation at the London Globe'.

40 The Moors Project, Two Gents Productions website, http://www.twogentsproductions.com/shows/the-moors-project [accessed 15 December 2013].

41 SSTC website, http://www.southsudantheatre.com/supporters [accessed 1 May 2014]. SSTC and Renegade Theatre Company performed in Bangalore as part of the Ranga Shankara Theatre Festival.

42 Oguntokun was an official consultant to the British Council and to the National Theatre for its 2009 production of Wole

Soyinka's *Death and the King's Horseman*. Wole Oguntokun, LinkedIn, http://www.linkedin.com/pub/wole-oguntokun/42/b42/7a5 [accessed 15 December 2013].

43 'The Theatre Company Strategic Plan 2012-2014', http://theatrecompany.net/wp-content/uploads/2012/08/Strategic-Plan-TTC-2012-2014-webcopy-.pdf [accessed 1 May 2014]; Joel Magu, 'Wanawake Wa Heri Wa Winsa a great masterpiece', *Star*, 10 January 2013, http://www.the-star.co.ke/news/article-102278/wanawake-wa-heri-wa-winsa-great-masterpiece [accessed 7 September 2013]; Maneno Matamu, 'Review'.

44 Maneno Matamu, 'Review'.

45 *Birmingham Press*, 22 June 2012, http://www.thebirminghampress.com/2012/06/22/review-an-african-tale-by-shakespeare/; *Tab Norwich*, 19 October 2012, http://norwich.tab.co.uk/2012/10/19/review-julius-caesar; Noah Millman, 'The Coup', *New Conservative*, 24 April 2013, http://www.theamericanconservative.com/millman/the-coup/; *African Style Daily*, 10 June 2013, http://africastyledaily.com/art/2013/06/10/aad-reviews-julius-caesar/; Ben Brantley, 'The Caesar Wears an African Cloak', *New York Times*, 14 April 2013, http://theater.nytimes.com/2013/04/15/theater/reviews/julius-caesar-at-the-harvey-theater.html?pagewanted=all [all accessed 3 August 2013].

46 'Shakespeare And Africa – Richard Dowden Reviews An Africanised Production Of Julius Caesar', *African Arguments Online*, 4 July 2012, http://africanarguments.org/2012/07/04/shakespeare-and-africa-richard-dowden-reviews-an-africanised-production-of-julius-caesar/; republished on Dowden's own blog as 'Shakespeare – African and universal', http://188.65.113.19/country-profiles/1008-richard-dowdens-blog.html [both accessed 1 May 2013].

47 For the full cast see RSC press release, http://www.rsc.org.uk/about-us/press/releases/pan-african-julius-caesar.aspx [accessed 22 June 2013].

48 Valerie Gladstone 'African Caesar', *NY Press*, 10 April 2012, http://nypress.com/african-caesar/ [accessed 3 June 2013].

49 Rebecca Cain, 'Paterson Joseph talks to Freetime about

Shakespeare and Peep Show', *Bucks Free Press*, 31 August 2012, http://www.bucksfreepress.co.uk/leisure/latest/9902463.print/ [accessed 6 June 2013].

50 'Volunteers required to join RSC's Julius Caesar cast', *BBC News*, 3 April 2012, http://www.bbc.co.uk/news/uk-england-17587691 [accessed 3 June 2013].

51 See RSC press release. William Shakespeare, *Julius Caesar*, in *The Arden Shakespeare Complete Works* (London: Arden Shakespeare, 2001), 2.2.32.

52 RSC press release.

53 Dora Thornton, 'When the World Came to London', British Museum blog, 11 July 2012, http://blog.britishmuseum.org/2012/07/11/when-the-world-came-to-london/ [accessed 8 September 2013].

54 Ros Wynne Jones, 'Cymbeline: From war-ravaged South Sudan to the Globe Theatre', *Independent*, 2 May 2012, http://www.independent.co.uk/arts-entertainment/theatre-dance/features/cymbeline-from-warravaged-south-sudan-to-the-globe-theatre-7704215.html [accessed 5 March 2013].

55 Stephen Greenblatt, *Shakespearean Negotiations: The Circulation of Social Energy in Renaissance England* (Oxford: Clarendon Press, 1988), pp. 161–3.

56 Dora Thornton (exhibition curator) quoted in John Battersby, 'South Africa: African Freedom and Shakespeare's World', *All Africa*, 12 July 2012, http://allafrica.com/stories/201207120221.html [accessed 20 February 2014].

57 Anita Li, 'African National Congress disputes 'iconic' status of Robben Island Bible displayed in British Museum', *Star*, 19 July 2012, http://www.thestar.com/news/world/2012/07/19/african_national_congress_disputes_iconic_status_of_robben_island_bible_displayed_in_british_museum.html [accessed September 2012]. For Kathrada's centrality, see Matthew Hahn's play *The Robben Island Bible*.

58 See David Schalkwyk, *Hamlet's Dreams The Robben Island Shakespeare* (London: Methuen, 2013), pp. 18–20.

59 Ibid.

60 Thornton, quoted in Battersby.

61 Quoted in Schalkwyk, p. 20.
62 Peter Kirwan, '*Venus and Adonis*', *Year of Shakespeare*, 25 April 2012, http://bloggingshakespeare.com/year-of-shakespeare-venus-and-adonis [accessed 4 August 2012].
63 Ibid.
64 Jeremy Cronin, 'How History Haunts Us', *The Sunday Times*, 29 April 2012, http://www.timeslive.co.za/local/2012/04/29/how-history-haunts-us [accessed 29 April 2012].
65 See Gordon, 'Shakespeare's African *nostos*'.
66 Teju Cole, 'An African Caesar', *New Yorker* blog, 22 April 2013, http://www.newyorker.com/online/blogs/books/2013/04/julius-caesar-gregory-doran-brooklyn-academy-music.html [accessed 11 July 2013].
67 See also Natasha Distiller, 'Tony's Will: *Titus Andronicus* in South Africa 1995', *Shakespeare International Yearbook 9* (2008), pp. 152–70.
68 'Julius Caesar director Gregory Doran: Africa lends itself well to Shakespeare', *Metro*, 13 August 2012, http://metro.co.uk/2012/08/13/julius-caesar-director-gregory-doran-on-transporting-shakespeare-to-africa-534520/ [accessed 4 August 2013].
69 RSC Programme Notes; 'Volunteers required', *BBC News*; Chase Quinn, 'Brooklyn Academy of Music stages all-black "Julius Caesar"', *Grio*, 23 April 2013, http://thegrio.com/2013/04/23/brooklyn-academy-of-music-stages-all-black-julius-caesar/; Zachary Stewart, 'Julius Caesar', *Theatremania*, 15 April 2013, http://www.theatermania.com/new-york-city-theater/reviews/04-2013/julius-caesar_64899.html; Sandra Lawson, '*Julius Caesar*', *Plays to See*, http://playstosee.com/page.php?sad=play&id=772 [all accessed 3 July 2013].
70 This worked differently in a more peripheral location like Newcastle where, as Hansen and Smialkowsa argue, the proffered resistance to a London-centred anatopism was a salutary feature of the programming. However, the RSC's ersatz African rendering of *Julius Caesar* is a poor example of this localism, where the RSC is perceived as gracing the

North with Shakespeare 'like sending missionaries to Africa' (p. 122).

71 Nadia Mayen, 'South Sudan troupe give historic Shakespeare performance', *Al Arabiya News*, 7 May 2012, http://www.alarabiya.net/articles/2012/05/07/212711.html [accessed 3 June 2013].

72 Ari Bloomekatz, 'South Sudan Troupe Sees New Country's Struggle in Shakespeare', *Los Angeles Times*, 16 May 2012, http://articles.latimes.com/2012/may/16/entertainment/la-et-globe-to-globe-shakespeare-20120512 [accessed 20 February 2014]; Barbara Wilcox and Larry Friedlander, '*Cymbeline* in South Sudan: Lessons for a New African Nation' [unpublished conference paper].

73 Jones, 'Cymbeline: From war-ravaged South Sudan'.

74 See Ali Abdel Gadir Ali, Ibrahim A. Elbadawi and Atta El-Batahani, 'Sudan's Civil War: Why Has it Prevailed for So Long?', in *Understanding Civil War: Africa*, Paul Collier and Nicholas Sambanis (eds) (Washington: World Bank Publications, 2005), pp. 193–220 (p. 196).

75 Colette Gordon, 'Sharing History: South Sudan Theatre Company's *Cymbeline* at the Globe', *Year of Shakespeare*, 17 June 2012, http://bloggingshakespeare.com/year-of-shakespeare-sharing-history-south-sudan-theatre-companys-cymbeline-at-the-globe#sthash.sh3He9BF.dpuf [accessed 5 September 2013].

76 Kim Solga, 'The South Sudan *Cymbeline*', Shakespeare's Globe blog, 3 May 2012, http://blog.shakespearesglobe.com/the-south-sudan-cymbeline-reviewed-by-kim-solga/ [accessed 4 August 2013].

77 John Friedmann, 'The World City Hypothesis', *Development and Change*, 17.1 (1986), pp. 69–83; Saskia Sassen, *The Global City: New York, London, Tokyo* (Princeton: Princeton University Press, 1991).

78 Alan Scott (ed.), *Global City Regions: Trends, Theory, Policy* (Oxford: Oxford University Press, 2001).

9

A Tale of Two Londons: Locating Shakespeare and Dickens in 2012

Peter Kirwan and Charlotte Mathieson

In 1847, the sale of a key piece of Shakespearean heritage to the American showman P. T. Barnum, who wished to purchase, disassemble and ship the house on Henley Street known as Shakespeare's birthplace to the United States, was halted. One of the key players among the committee of fundraisers who found the £3,000 necessary to keep the house in its original location was Charles Dickens, already by this point a celebrated novelist inextricably connected to the physical and cultural hub of London. Dickens had experienced first-hand the value of the Shakespeare birthplace on a visit to the region in 1838, writing in his letters of how 'we sat down in the room where Shakespeare was born, and left our autographs and read those of other people and so forth'.[1] Although his fiction jests at those who are over-inspired by an almost spiritual investment in Shakespeare's birthplace, Dickens's role in saving the house from international export is nonetheless indicative of the increasing cultural value ascribed to literary places as sites of national significance throughout the nineteenth century as authors became solidified as national symbols through the rendering of literary locations as tourist destinations – a practice that would later render 'Dickens's London' a key site in the literary tourist landscape.

Dickens's involvement in the purchase of the Shakespeare birthplace represents a meeting-point of Britain's two most prominent writers which serves to underscore the centrality of place in the creation and performance of Britain's national literary heritage. In 2012, the use of literary places in a wider project of national identity formation came to the fore in the concurrent celebrations of Dickens and Shakespeare that formed part of the Cultural Olympiad: the World Shakespeare Festival (introduced elsewhere in this volume) and Dickens 2012, 'an international celebration of the life and work of Charles Dickens to mark the bicentenary of his birth' that included hundreds of historical, literary, theatrical, cinematic, architectural, educational and heritage events throughout the year.[2] Both Festivals were international in scope, but it was London that formed the centre-point of these events. Neither Dickens nor Shakespeare were born in London but both are inextricably associated with the city through their careers and, as the city's most famous literary exports, both were employed prominently within the context of London's 2012 celebrations that created a national legacy and positioned that legacy on the global stage.

Yet the role played by these two authors in shaping London's cultural capital was marked by a demonstrable tension in the global politics that underscored the Festivals. Reflecting the breadth and diversity of both authors' works and cultural afterlives, both Festivals appropriately encompassed a significant international constituency, the World Shakespeare Festival taking an explicitly global focus while Dickens 2012 incorporated events from around the world.

Yet despite this global reach, both Festivals continued to assert the prominence of London as cultural centre and privileged this space as the location of authorial meaning; an investment that carried particular weight in a year – that of the Queen's Diamond Jubilee – already preoccupied with the cultural construction of 'Britishness'. In this chapter, we interrogate the local and global resonances of Shakespeare and Dickens in the Olympic year and question the assumptions and politics of literary place – in this context London – governing the cultural memory of these authors.

London: E20, GB

In March 2011, as the Olympic Park in the regenerated Stratford area of East London began to take shape, a new postcode was created within the E15 area: E20, previously only a fictional postcode used in the British soap *EastEnders* and its internet spin-off *E20*.[3] The consolidation of a newly defined space within London emphasized the importance of this relatively small geographical area on the edges of the city as the place which would be responsible for presenting London to the world. Furthermore, the creation of E20 highlighted the centrality of *place* as a historically significant constituent in the formation and consolidation of national identity: as Ian Baucom writes, Englishness in particular 'has consistently been defined through appeals to the identity-endowing properties of place [...] *generally* understood to reside within some type of imaginary, abstract, or actual locale, and to mark itself upon that locale's familiars'.[4] In 2012, traces of celebration were inscribed throughout London, investing the city with markers of its national history and heritage: the Queen's Diamond Jubilee in June 2012 gave rise to a multitude of Union Jack flags throughout the city, a 100-metre-wide picture of the Royal Family towered over the banks of the Thames, and the Thames Diamond Jubilee Pageant that marked the culmination of the weekend reinstated (albeit fleetingly) the river, so central in the city and nation's history, as a prominent and meaningful site (for other reflections on the 'spectacular city', see Stuart Hampton-Reeves's chapter in this volume).

The creation of E20 consolidated these resonances into a specific locale, forging a place that became newly assimilated into Britain's national geography. The cultural rejuvenation of Stratford worked, to borrow Susan Bennett's description of the revitalization of the South Bank, 'to show the city to itself and to inspire its occupants and its visitors to become actors in a reconfigured landscape, to forge emotional connections to a neighbourhood not so long ago more dead than alive'.[5] Significantly, what the reconfigured landscape of E20 represented and inspired was a new vision of the city, and of Britain: it created a place where new modes of national identity formation befitting the contemporary moment could be performed. 'Britishness' was continually reimagined

FIGURE 12 *A building-sized display of the Royal Family at the Queen's Silver Jubilee in 1977 along the River Thames during the 2012 Diamond Jubilee. Photograph by Charlotte Mathieson.*

throughout 2012: if the monarchical celebrations of the Jubilee were met with ambivalence from those disdainful of the pomp and circumstance surrounding this problematized aspect of Britain's history, Danny Boyle's 'Isles of Wonder' Ceremony that launched the Olympic Games was widely and hyperbolically lauded as a defining moment of a new national culture.[6] Demonstrating an inclusive, left-wing politics that shied away from vindications of an imperial past and instead celebrated Britain for its idiosyncrasies, national social institutions and diverse cultural spectrum, 'Isles of Wonder', as Jonathan Freedland wrote, 'had barely finished before it had become a byword for a new approach, not only to British culture but to Britishness itself', providing the nation 'with a new, unfamiliarly positive view of itself'.[7]

The nation's history and (particularly literary) culture was central to the Ceremony, through which the performance created its own form of cultural canonization – at times inevitable, but diverse and often unexpected. The most high-profile manifestation of this was the deployment of Shakespeare in the Opening Ceremony, where the Northern Irish actor Kenneth Branagh, playing Isambard Kingdom Brunel, recited Caliban's speech from *The Tempest*. Little has been said so far about the visual context in which this aural tribute to Shakespeare was performed. Erin Sullivan's description of the appearance of the great Shakespearean as the great Victorian is illuminating:

> [...] a nineteenth-century stagecoach approached a recreation of England's grassy Glastonbury Tor [...] From the stagecoach emerged Sir Kenneth Branagh, dressed as a Victorian industrialist (Isambard Kingdom Brunel, to be exact), looking excitedly, expectantly and triumphantly at the expansive bucolic stage set before him.[8]

Although this was not the start of the Ceremony, Branagh's Brunel acted as the catalyst for the initiation of catastrophic change, the tearing apart of the pastoral set and the initiation of 'modern' Britain, out of which were forged the Olympic rings. The visual aesthetic of the moment drew on recognizably Victorian tropes, with stagecoaches, smokestacks and top hats presenting an image of industrial upheaval.

In this, the Ceremony demonstrably resonated with the 1951 Festival of Britain, which took place as Britain attempted to heal its postwar wounds and consolidate its identity following a particularly scarring period of international engagement: the Festival, as Herbert Morrison wrote, was 'the British showing themselves to themselves – and the world'.[9] Key to this was a strategic deployment of Shakespeare as 'an unarguable figure of achievement, recognized nationally and internationally', who could contribute to forming 'a new de-imperialized history to drive Britain into the future'.[10] So too was the use of a Victorian aesthetic important, with a stagecoach featuring prominently in the Festival literature and a Dickensian feast forming one of the many events (see for instance Figure 13).[11] The Festival's instatement of the Victorians as an integral feature was appropriate in its marking the centenary of the Great Exhibition of 1851, and it also initiated the resurgence of interest in the Victorians that has continued to develop into the neo-Victorian fascination of recent years: as Ann Heilmann and Mark Llewellyn note, the 'very instability and insecurity relating to the recent memories of the twentieth century, from the Second World War through to a post-9/11 landscape' lies beneath this 'reassuringly nostalgic attraction to the nineteenth century' demonstrated in the Festival of Britain, and again visible in 2012.[12]

With the great number of Dickensian celebrations of 2012, this was arguably the year of 'neo-Victorianism *par excellence*', and it was thus fitting to see Victorian symbols take visual prominence in the aesthetics of the Opening Ceremony.[13] Yet amid this spectacle, Dickens himself was nowhere to be seen, his presence and texts curiously absent from the stage which instead saw a turn to Shakespeare's words spoken through the figure of Brunel. Again, though, this was in some respects a suitably neo-Victorian moment: it was,

FIGURE 13 *'Dickens Festival Pageant' poster from the Festival of Britain (1951). Reproduced with the permission of the National Archives, London, ref. WORK 25/243.*

after all, the Victorians who solidified Shakespeare's status as national symbol through the consolidation of Bardolatry and the founding of Shakespeare societies in the context of a simultaneous strengthening of national cultural identity.[14] The use of Shakespeare within a Victorian aesthetic was thus representative of, and resonant with, the Victorians' own acts of cultural formulation: in this setting Shakespeare's voice emerged, not from the collaborative and chaotic milieu of a representation of Elizabethan or Jacobean London, but from the organized and powerfully authoritarian society inculcated by a great Victorian.

In the Closing Ceremony of the Games, performed on 12 August 2012, Shakespeare and Dickens again came into contact as prominent among the quotations disguised as newspaper cuttings that decorated the stage.[15] This too is perhaps also a Victorian feature. Gary Taylor argues that

> Nineteenth-century Britain realized, more clearly than any previous society, that goods can be manufactured, and information can be processed, more efficiently when broken down into components. Shakespeare's writings were accordingly broken down into so many systematically arranged components of word usage, grammatical usage, metrical usage. Sometimes the books themselves were literally broken down into fragments; some of the early material collected for the *New English Dictionary* consisted of passages torn out of rare sixteenth-century books and pasted onto slips.[16]

The practice of excerption and quotation is, inevitably, a nostalgic process, a process that draws on memory and recognition for its effects. Margreta de Grazia points out that one of the most enduring compilations of Shakespearean quotations, William Dodd's 1752 *Beauties of Shakespear*, appeared in the same period as the 1769 Shakespeare Jubilee in Stratford-upon-Avon, 'the event that is often taken to mark the beginning of Shakespeare bardolatry'.[17] Tied into the 'new longing for writing in Shakespeare's own person [that] emerged in the later eighteenth century',[18] de Grazia's observation links moments of anniversary with strategies of remembrance and appropriation that resonate usefully with an Olympic year in which Shakespeare, Dickens, Brunel and Churchill were all evoked bodily and in quotation (all, not coincidentally, entrants in the 100 Greatest Britons poll conducted by the

BBC in 2002).[19] Nostalgia and quotation militate against unified interpretation, however: 'The disruptive intertextual effect of citation enfolded within performance can summon up for individual spectators independent and unpredictable memories of past performances and past texts', as Margaret Jane Kidnie notes.[20] As commentators on Twitter debated the appropriateness of Caliban's words, it became clear that the borrowing of the author did not necessarily lead to a unified national moment of collective remembrance.[21] Internationally, this was even less the case, as some American commentators wondered what Abraham Lincoln was doing in this green English field.[22]

What took place at E20 was an attempt to define and perform an iconic representation of the nation in a specifically located place, aligning historical figures with such local-born celebrities as Dizzee Rascal and David Beckham. Yet we can and should question the extent to which the emotional connections to a city are, indeed, grounded in the local. At the Opening Ceremony, Branagh's Brunel spoke Caliban's 'Be not afeard' speech while presiding over Glastonbury Tor, while nationally significant songs were sung by children's choirs from all around the British Isles. At the Closing Ceremony, on the other hand, Timothy Spall offered a pastiche of Branagh's performance, addressing the audience from the top of Big Ben in a microcosmic London, situated in the centre of the same stadium in an event that insisted on a metropolitan rather than national narrative. The shift from Britain to London between the two ceremonies bespoke the anxiety felt about the role of the Olympics in juxtaposing a city's identity and a nation's, particularly given that one of that nation's constituent members, Scotland, would soon (in 2014) be undergoing a referendum about its continued membership. The Shakespeare and Dickens Festivals further iterated this tension between city and nation and, through their insistence on the location of authors, served to suggest a renewed statement of the prevalent pull towards London, as the next sections of this chapter explore.

Locating Dickens in the bicentenary year

Running throughout the year, but focused particularly around the bicentenary itself on 7 February, Dickens 2012 was emphatically marketed as an 'international' celebration, incorporating global partners to develop projects specific to individual countries, and utilizing digital technologies to connect international audiences in pan-global activities.[23] At the same time, a frequent return to 'local Dickens' was suggestive of a demonstrable impulse to (literally) locate Dickens in the spaces of national culture. To signal the contrasting forces that situated Dickens as local and/or global writer is not to suggest that these elements were in direct competition with one another: Dickens 2012 operated across a broad cultural spectrum that enabled a multitude of perspectives on his life and works to come into play. Yet at the same time, the London activities of Dickens 2012 opened up an indicative set of questions about the cultural placing of 'national' authors and the ways in which national identities are enacted and performed through cultural celebrations.

'Local Dickens' was a prominent theme throughout 2012, taking multiple forms in various celebratory events and activities. An exhibition at the Museum of London aimed to 'evok[e] the atmosphere of the streets of Victorian London and the river Thames' allowing visitors to 'follow in Dickens's footsteps and be taken on a memorable and haunting journey', while Southwark's Cuming Museum aimed to 'uncover the places, people and living conditions' of Dickens's time in the area.[24] Numerous walking tours traversed 'Dickens's London', whether by guided group tours or downloadable podcast recordings;[25] and interactive maps plotted out the places of Dickens's novels, whilst mobile apps such as 'Dickens: Dark London' promised to take the user on 'a journey through the darker side of Charles Dickens' London'.[26] Films such as the resources produced by the

British Council explored 'the relationship between the writer and the city he lived in'.[27]

It was of little surprise that in a bicentenary year emphasis should be placed on the life, times and locations of Dickens, or that London in particular should highlight Dickens's city roots: the appeal of 'Dickens's London' has a strong tradition both in academic criticism and in popular culture. Literary tourism – 'the interconnected practices of visiting and marketing sites associated with writers and their work', as Nicola Watson defines it[28] – has a long history in reference to Dickens: Dickens-themed cycle and walking routes became a popular form of leisure pursuit as early as the 1880s, and the places associated with Dickens's life and works have subsequently generated a variety of forms of tourism that constitute a significant section of the heritage industry.[29] Dickens's texts invite such practices, rich as they are with locatable details of literary places, and because of the ways in which they manufacture what Juliet John terms a 'heritage aesthetic', commodifying an evocative and definable idea of 'Victorian London' that creates a conflated concept of 'Dickensian-Victorian-London' that has become 'embedded in the British cultural consciousness and in the image of England abroad', both a source of intra-national identity and a national cultural export.[30]

The recourse to place was evident at the time of the centenary of Dickens's birth: as Karen Laird discusses, the film adaptation of *David Copperfield* produced in 1913 emphasized its ties to the English landscape, creating 'a timely form of virtual literary tourism for an international audience'.[31] One hundred years later, the marketability of locating Dickens in London was much more stringently capitalized on, not least because the broader ongoing popularity of heritage tourism intersects with the current surge of interest in neo-Victoriana in fiction, film and TV.[32] Furthermore, a key appeal of heritage and literary tourism is the experience of feeling an affiliation with the past: heritage involves 'an emotional attitude to the past' and an 'almost spiritual investment' in the value of places, which offer 'a sense of organic and emotional connection to our ancestors, a sense of roots and of belonging'.[33] Quoting one literary tourist from 1910, Watson reiterates the point that the association is not just a nearness to the descriptions found in Dickens's writing but the feeling of 'treading in Dickens's footsteps': 'It isn't so much because Dickens has described these places [...] It's because I know he went over every inch of the ground himself. And that being so, when I see these places, they seem to bring me near *him*.'[34]

In a year that placed particular emphasis on the interconnections of life and literature, it was fitting that the value of 'treading in Dickens's footsteps' should become prominent. Indeed, it is notable that in the discourses surrounding 2012 activities a particular emphasis was placed on *experiencing* Dickens's London, not simply asserting the importance of London in Dickens's works but offering up location itself as a means of accessing and understanding Dickensian places today. Interestingly, this was the case both in place-specific activities (walking tours, museums) and in forms of new media (maps, apps and podcasts) that, despite their global reach, frequently focused upon the association between Dickens and London as a core context. 'Dickens and London' thus constituted an intra-national and globally exported form of understanding Dickens, but always returned to the importance of London as the centre-point. These experiences were not so much about 'treading in the footsteps' of Dickens as a means of seeking individual emotional connectivity with the author himself: instead it was place, and particularly London, that became privileged as a means of authenticating the locality of the written word. Laird writes of the 1913 *David Copperfield* that its recourse to the English landscape served to 'crystalliz[e] the writer's reputation as a national treasure'[35] and created a claim that, Joss Marsh adds, 'only a *British* [film] company could make'.[36] A similar claim might be made about 2012 literary tourism: in a globally accessible touristic landscape, the value of national place as *the* site of access was repeatedly reiterated.

The various formulations of 'Dickens and London' constituted an unofficial history that similarly worked to co-opt

Dickens as firmly situated within the nation. Literary tourism has its roots in cultural nationalism: the rise of the practice in the nineteenth century was coterminous with the rise of cultural nationalism and, as Watson writes, 'the emerging national literary canon [was] seized upon in order to effect a sort of interiorised national mapping'.[37] The literary tourisms of 2012 effected a similar form of 'national mapping'. In a city marked by Union Jack flags, images of the Royal Family and Olympic Celebrations, walking 'Dickens's London' in 2012 was implicitly walking Dickens in Britain: walking a route that confirmed Dickens's place within, and contribution to, the national narrative of the city. If the city is a 'tourist stage', as Susan Bennett writes, then the tourists are its players, performing and thus mapping out the relationship between place, nation and author.[38] If 2012 was a year that performed 'the simultaneous feat of returning us to the Victorian past through Dickens's bicentenary and of propelling us into a very modern twenty-first century with the London Olympics',[39] then touristic traversals of Dickens's London provided a site where this apparent dichotomy was negotiated, inscribing the (national) past as part of the contemporary narrative of the city.[40]

Yet this national narrative – privileging London's right to Dickens and suggesting that the essence of understanding his works lies in experiencing his London, in grounding his works within their national origins – was seemingly at odds with the broader discourses of Dickens 2012 as an international celebration. The global reworkings of 'Dickens and London' via digital technologies insisted on (national) place as a requisite to accessing Dickens wherever one was in the world, implicitly confirming Dickens as a national cultural export. At the same time, many of the forms through which these walks and tours were presented – podcasts and apps, online media – meant that the idea of Dickens's London *could* be anywhere, anytime. They invoked but did not necessitate the requirement that one be in Dickens's London oneself, all existing primarily in the non-space of the internet and entirely portable in their forms. While connected to a discourse of 'Dickens's London' residing in the emotional, direct experience of place, these modes created 'Dickens's London' as something portable, dis-placed and detachable from the sites themselves, something to be experienced anywhere/nowhere. This both indicated the persistent attraction of privileging places as sites of meaning and highlighted the intrinsic instability of spatial centres, drawing attention to the notion of 'Dickens's London' as a cultural construct that can be transported from London itself to new sites of meaning.

Further indicative of these impulses, a number of global refractions of Dickens in 2012 took the idea of 'local Dickens' into new national contexts. The British Council's 'Sketches by Boz; Sketching the City' and 'The Uncommercial Traveller' projects took Dickensian modes of urban observation and literary tourism to the streets of cities including Karachi, Beijing, Shanghai, Buenos Aires and New York.[41] In these projects, cities around the world became contact zones that generated new versions of 'local Dickens' via the reworking of Dickensian modes of representing locality. These projects offered new perspectives on the idea of locality and nation, encouraging us to be attentive to the ways in which locality interacts with and can be detached from national narratives, and the ways in which author celebrations are experienced in different national contexts – something that became more apparent in the World Shakespeare Festival.

Encountering London in the Globe to Globe Festival

One production in the WSF explicitly confronted the meeting of local/global experiences in an act of staged tourism that visited and mark(et)ed a site of cultural significance. At the opening of Two Gents Productions' *Vakomana Vaviri Ve Zimbabwe* (*The Two Gentlemen of Verona*), one of the Globe to Globe productions during the Festival year, the empty silence of the Globe stage was disturbed by a trapdoor being pushed open. A head appeared, looked around nervously, then retreated. A moment later, the trapdoor re-opened with a crash, silencing the audience, and two Zimbabwean men wearing Elizabethan costume climbed through it and onto the stage, looking about in wonder and carrying a huge travelling trunk. Denton Chikura and Tonderai Munyevu then proceeded to a prologue, delivered in English and translated live into Shona, beginning 'Two gentlemen, both alike in friendship'.

The complexities of this moment of staged tourism, 'blown temporarily onto the Thames Bankside', run deeply.[42] The two African men arriving on the Globe stage with travelling gear foreshadowed the moment in the 'Isles of Wonder' Olympic Opening Ceremony that conflated the arrival of West Indian immigrants to the UK on the SS *Empire Windrush* with the Industrial Revolution (one of the few moments of the Ceremony in which the colour-blind casting policy was ignored), and mirrored it in costuming the arrivals in the perceived uniform of the destination: suits for the West Indian arrivals to London, doublet and hose for arrival at the Globe. This was deliberately mischievous, however. The Globe itself is a representation of an Elizabethan theatre, the majority of whose visitors are dressed in twenty-first century clothes. The 'irredeemably contemporary' audience, in Paul Prescott's terms, was acknowledged by the performance of arrival by the actors: in a reversal of the Globe's usual dynamic which invites a visiting audience to step back into the world created by the playhouse, here we saw Elizabethan actors arriving into a contemporary world for which they were clearly inappropriately dressed.[43] As the actors broke open their trunk and began putting on more trans-historical clothes to represent their various characters, the initial acknowledgement of the Elizabethan was forgotten, replaced by a performance style reliant on Shona storytelling and a form of *gestus* that contrasted with the Globe's usual house style.

The company's introduction into the space was greeted with laughter, suggesting the perceived incongruity of two African men in Elizabethan costume tiptoeing onto the Globe stage, unsure of whether or not they were meeting the correct conventions. In some ways, this was a deliberate strategy of Two Gents Productions, which is a British-based company (see Colette Gordon's chapter in this volume). This performance was the first time the play, which had been touring for several years, had been translated into Shona from its usual English text.[44] In explicitly drawing attention to the conventions of the Globe space, they then enacted an imposition of a Zimbabwean language and performance culture, evoking and then rejecting Elizabethan performance traditions. Yet it spoke to the power structures of a space of cultural tourism, making explicit the status of the company as 'visitors' to the 'home' Shakespeare audience, while also drawing attention to the playing of an act of tourism.

Returning to Juliet John's notion of the 'almost spiritual investment' in the value of places, which offer 'a sense of organic and emotional connection to our ancestors, a sense of roots and of belonging', we can use the example of *Vakomana Vaviri ve Zimbabwe* as paradigmatic of the inversion of cultural tourism in the World Shakespeare Festival. While the *Year of Shakespeare* website featured a map indicating the 'home' locations of the productions staged throughout the year, the global scale elided the *performance* map that was much more narrowly focused. Performances during the Festival took place almost entirely in London and Stratford-upon-Avon, sites of local significance connected to authorial biography and geographical footprint, with scattered other locations throughout the United Kingdom showcasing a handful of further productions.[45] The literary tourism that characterized Dickens 2012 involved the mobilization of audiences, inviting app users and visitors to experience the spaces of Dickens's London. For the World Shakespeare Festival, it was performers who were mobilized, brought in from around the globe to share London stages.

The slippage between local and national identities thus becomes more obvious in the place of performance, as the BBC Four documentary *Shakespeare from Kabul* (broadcast 21 July 2012) made clear.[46] Following the journey of the Afghan production of *The Comedy of Errors* from initial inception to final performances at the Globe to Globe Festival, the documentary concentrates on the local contexts of production, the political and social pressures on the company, the struggles to find appropriate modes of rehearsal and the fears of ongoing stigmatization. London, spoken of in reverential terms, is a distant goal. As the documentary moves to London, revealed in panoramic aerial shots capturing the glistening Thames, the sunlit landmarks and the resplendent Globe, the focus of the documentary moves to the wonder of the actors visiting for the first time, the joy of reception in Shakespeare's home theatre and the role of London in consolidating personal achievements.

The significance of this in an Olympic year cannot be lost: as with the sporting festival, personal achievement can only be fully realized on a London stage. Yet even if this is not the documentary's intention, it reveals a hierarchy of experienced place. London is both the site of original production of Shakespeare's texts and the place of the performed 2012 Festival, and it is within this site that the productions devised, rehearsed and perfected overseas were received. Against the shared backdrop of the facsimile Elizabethan stage, ghosts of Africa, Asia, Europe, America and Australasia were fleetingly seen. The Globe as the Shakespearean heritage site was the fixed point, and several companies made this explicit by kissing the stage or acknowledging their delight in arriving for their holiday, often bringing their camera-phones onto the stage during the curtain call to enact an explicit act of London tourism as soon as the performers were out of character.

The more complex foregrounding of the tourist experience by Two Gents Productions was suggestive of anxieties over what it means for Shakespeare to be 'the world's dramatist'.

The ownership and appropriation of Dickens in places all around the world, appropriating modes of city-writing for locations other than London, saw Dickens 2012 spread internationally. The World Shakespeare Festival, however, instead seemed to offer Shakespeare bound to his historical places of operation, a home member of Team GB. While many of the productions of the Festival had been and would continue to be experienced around the world, the role of the Festival was to concentrate these interpretations of Shakespeare in a relatively confined geographical area – to borrow Stephen Purcell's reading of the Globe to Globe Festival, in some cases within a concentric circle even smaller than E20.[47]

The principle of the Globe stage has always been to foreground the fictional production of space, from the first time the Chorus of *Henry V* acknowledged the insufficiency of place and invited its audience to engage in the production of a space of European conflict. The World Shakespeare Festival continued this ethos of delocalization even as it hosted productions that had begun locally in their places of origin. At Stratford-upon-Avon, the Courtyard and Royal Shakespeare Theatres played host to representations of 'India' (Iqbal Khan's *Much Ado about Nothing*) and 'Africa' (Gregory Doran's *Julius Caesar*) populated by companies of British-Indian and British-African actors. Both productions went to great lengths to create something of the atmosphere of those locales – *Caesar* through onstage music and a recruited cast of extras who joined the stage for crowd scenes, *Much Ado* through extensive pre-show entertainments, inviting audience members on stage for the wedding and so on (these productions are discussed in detail by Purcell and Gordon in this volume). These strategies in turn transformed theatregoers into tourists, most noticeably in *Much Ado* as a shady man in sunglasses accosted audience members before the play started, offering them cut-price rates in his nearby hotel. In both productions, the divorce from the place of representation was made complete, ensuring that the relationship between audience and fictional world was always considered from the tourist perspective, the temporary and detached visitor to a socially constructed imaginative space.

At the Globe, the site-specificity of the place of reception conflated the permanent significance of the faux-Elizabethan tiring house and pillars with the fluidity of a stage that allows for complete geographical and temporal variation of imagined place. To borrow the title of the British Museum's exhibition curated as part of the Festival, the Globe itself was involved in 'Staging the world'. The fixed place of the stage, however, makes the world itself mobile. If the appropriations of Dickens's London were delocalized in order to be staged any/everywhere, the international appropriations of Shakespeare's works were similarly detached from their local contexts in order to be performed in London, picking up on the ideas of embodied mobility that characterize the Dickens walking tours. Places of personal origin are collapsed in favour of a shared experientiality at the point of reception, participating in the production of an Elizabethan literary tourism even when the words being spoken are not Shakespeare's. Both Festivals prioritized the relatively homogeneous site of encounter over the broader networks of cultural heritage staged within.

London calling

Both Festivals therefore played a prominent role in articulating London as the centre-point of the production of national capital, taking advantage of the profiles of the city's major writers as well as London itself as tourist destination to create a located literary tourism. Despite attempts to involve the whole country in the London Olympic Games, the branding of the Games repeatedly suggested otherwise, that 2012 was not so much Britain's year but the capital's: 'London 2012' became a byword for this consolidation of the capital's pre-eminence on the national, and global, stage. London 2012 involved a performance of London to the world and to itself, in a manner not dissimilar to that in which it once welcomed the newly crowned King James I, formerly James VI of Scotland. Thomas Dekker, Stephen Harrison, Ben Jonson and Thomas Middleton's *Magnificent Entertainment* of 1604 created an event in which 'the civic community, headed by its chief officers, became the King's host, as if London was a great country house and the mayor its lord'.[48] As Janette Dillon remarks of this extraordinarily opulent event,

> In the very act of gracious deferral to the king, the city seeks to present its own best face not only to the king and queen and the royal court but also to London citizens themselves, to foreigners living and working in London and to visitors to London for the occasion. There is no clear distinction to be made between spectators and participants.[49]

The city performs the role of host, and simultaneously re-performs this spectacle for the benefit of its constituent members. Likewise in 2012, everyone in London, native or visitor, became an actor on the city stage.

For Dickens, London was 'the "magic lantern" which filled his imagination with the glimpse of strange dramas and sudden spectacles'.[50] The 'strangeness' of the city stage is most apparent in the self-awareness of mobile tourism, whether inviting walkers to experience the city streets through the lens of a Dickensian topography or staging the arrival of Shakespearean tourists on the city's literal stages. In all cases, however, the city itself creates the conditions for the performances of its actors. Even as James's entry collapsed the division between spectators and participants and 'Dickens's London' turned the walking tourist into a participant in the city environment, so too did the Shakespeare and Dickens Festivals turn the populace of London into actors by insisting on the role of London itself as a stage for the world.

The tension between London and the rest of Great Britain and Northern Ireland (the full name of Team GB, reminding us of the abbreviation's elision of a significant constituent member) was felt deeply during the relay of the Olympic Torch around the country, taking in literary tourist destinations such as Stratford-upon-Avon, where it was photographed in front of the Birthplace (see p. 40), and Higham, where the Torch changed hands in front of Gad's Hill Place, the site of Falstaff's humiliation and Dickens's writing of *Great Expectations* and *A Tale of Two Cities*. Philip Hensher, writing in the *Guardian*, traced problems surrounding the torch back to the 2008 Games:

> [F]our years ago the Chinese sent the flame abroad, followed by security staff whose job it was to beat up protesters against the Chinese human rights record. In the wake of some appropriately violent scenes in London, the then Chinese ambassador distinguished herself by quoting a correspondent who had said they could not believe this was the land that created Shakespeare and Dickens. What Dickens would have thought of massively expensive and over-policed festivals of minor sport, not to mention what the Chinese government did to its blind dissidents, might not have been quite what the ambassador believed.[51]

The show of unity offered by the Olympic Flame was undercut at points of protest during both the 2008 and 2012 relays, and it is interesting to note that Dickens and Shakespeare were evoked as representative of unified, peaceful, national conservatism. Yet as Hensher goes on to say, 'on the occasion of the Bearing of the Torch Through Exeter, I've stayed safely in south London, so I can't tell you what it was like at all'. Once the flame had arrived in London, of course, and the 'Isles of Wonder' Opening Ceremony had offered a united, neo-Victorian and Shakespeare-quoting vision of the country, far less dissent was heard. As David Beckham's speedboat docked in E20 and the torch was passed to Sir Steve Redgrave to be carried into the stadium, the nation-building exercises that led up to the sporting competition were united. The implications of being 'safely in London', away from the problems posed by a greater nation that may not always be in line with the cultural centre, are unpacked in Adam Hansen and Monika Smialkowska's chapter in this volume, but despite gestures towards the cultural activity happening around the country, all roads ultimately led to London E20, at the heart of which were situated Shakespeare and Dickens.

Notes

1 Charles Dickens, *The Letters of Charles Dickens* Mamie Dickens and Georgina Hogarth (eds) (London: Macmillan, 1893), p. 17.

2 'About Dickens 2012', *Dickens 2012*, http://www.dickens2012.org/about-dickens-2012 [accessed 1 October 2013].

3 'Olympic Park to Share EastEnders' Walford E20 postcode', *BBC News*, 19 March 2011, http://www.bbc.co.uk/news/uk-england-london-12789694 [accessed 1 October 2013].

4 Ian Baucom, *Out of Place: Englishness, Empire and the Locations of Identity* (Princeton: Princeton University Press, 1999), p. 4.

5 Susan Bennett, 'Universal Experience: The City as Tourist Stage', in *The Cambridge Companion to Performance Studies*, ed. Tracy C. Davis (Cambridge: Cambridge University Press, 2008), pp. 76–90 (p. 84).

6 'Isles of Wonder', dir. by Danny Boyle, performed on 27 July 2012 at the Olympic Stadium, London.

7 Jonathan Freedland, 'Danny Boyle: Champion of the people', *Guardian*, 9 March 2013, http://www.guardian.co.uk/film/2013/mar/09/danny-boyle-queen-olympics-film?CMP=twt_gu [accessed 1 October 2013].

8 Erin Sullivan, 'Olympic Performance in the Year of Shakespeare', in *A Year of Shakespeare: Re-living the World Shakespeare Festival,* Paul Edmondson, Paul Prescott and Erin Sullivan (eds) (London: Bloomsbury, 2013), pp. 3–11 (p. 3).

9 Quote by Herbert Morrison in 'Festival of Britain 1951',

Exploring 20th Century London, http://www.20thcentury
london.org.uk/festival-britain-1951 [accessed 1 October 2013].

10 Stuart Hampton-Reeves, 'Shakespeare, *Henry VI* and the
Festival of Britain', in *A Companion to Shakespeare and
Performance*, Barbara Hodgdon and W. B. Worthen (eds)
(Oxford: Blackwell, 2005), pp. 285–96 (p. 295).

11 See 'Festival of Britain', Museum of London, http://collections.
museumoflondon.org.uk/Online/group.aspx?g=group-18135
[accessed 1 October 2013].

12 Ann Heilmann and Mark Llewellyn, *Neo-Victorianism:
The Victorians in the Twenty-First Century, 1999–2009*
(Basingstoke: Palgrave Macmillan, 2010), pp. 225–6.

13 Charlotte Boyce and Elodie Rousselot, 'The Other Dickens:
Neo-Victorian Appropriation and Adaptation', *Neo-Victorian
Studies*, 5:2 (2012), pp. 1–11 (p. 2).

14 Howard Felperin, 'Bardolatry Then and Now', in
*The Appropriation of Shakespeare: Post-Renaissance
Reconstructions of the Works and the Myth*, ed. Jean I.
Marsden (Hemel Hempstead: Harvester Wheatsheaf, 1991),
pp. 129–44 (pp. 131–3).

15 As well as quotes from *Hamlet, Richard III* and *The Tempest*
and the opening lines of *A Tale of Two Cities*, the stage
featured lines by Samuel Johnson, John Keats, Lord Byron,
T. S. Eliot and John Osborne.

16 Gary Taylor, *Reinventing Shakespeare* (New York: Weidenfeld
& Nicolson, 1989), p. 193.

17 Margreta de Grazia, 'Shakespeare in Quotation Marks', in *The
Appropriation of Shakespeare*, ed. Jean I. Marsden, pp. 57–71
(p. 61).

18 Ibid., p. 57.

19 For the 2002 poll, see 'BBC Reveals 100 Great British Heroes',
22 August 2002, *BBC News*, http://news.bbc.co.uk/1/hi/
entertainment/tv_and_radio/2208532.stm [accessed 1 October
2013].

20 Margaret Jane Kidnie, 'Citing Shakespeare', in *Shakespeare,
Memory and Performance*, ed. Peter Holland (Cambridge:
Cambridge University Press, 2006), pp. 117–32 (p. 132).

21 See the Storify page 'Shakespeare and the 2012 Olympics Opening Ceremony' compiled by 'shakesinstitute', http://storify.com/shakesinstitute/shakespeare-and-the-2012-olympics-opening-ceremony [accessed 1 October 2013].

22 See Maria Vultaggio, 'Kenneth Branagh at 2012 Olympic Opening Ceremony', *International Business Times*, 27 July 2012, http://www.ibtimes.com/kenneth-branagh-2012-olympic-opening-ceremony-was-branagh-dressed-abe-lincoln-734180 [accessed 1 October 2013].

23 For the full list of global projects see *Dickens 2012*, http://www.dickens2012.org [accessed 1 October 2013]; and the British Council 'Dickens 2012' pages, http://literature.britishcouncil.org/projects/2011/dickens-2012 [accessed 1 October 2013]. On the academic contexts and interpretations of 'global Dickens', see Regenia Gagnier, 'The Global Circulation of Charles Dickens's Novels', *Literature Compass*, 10.1 (2013), http://onlinelibrary.wiley.com/doi/10.1111/lic3.12021/abstract [accessed 1 October 2013].

24 'A tale of one man and his city', Museum of London, 7 December 2011, http://www.museumoflondon.org.uk/corporate/press-media/press-releases/dickens-and-london/ [accessed 1 October 2013]; 'Fact into Fiction', Southwark Cuming Museum, http://www.southwark.gov.uk/news/article/1005/explore_southwarks_charles_dickens_exhibition_this_half_term [accessed 1 October 2013].

25 See for example the *Guardian*'s series of Dickens audio walks, which consisted of podcasts and mapped walking tours around London and neighbouring locations, 'The Guardian Dickens Audio Walk: Heart of the City', *Guardian*, http://www.guardian.co.uk/books/interactive/2012/jan/02/dickens-walk-heart-of-the-city; *Charles Dickens London*, http://www.charlesdickenslondon.net; 'Tour of Dickens's London locations', Dickens 2012, http://www.dickens2012.org/event/tour-dickens-london-locations-sandra-shevey and 'Tour of Dickens's Film Locations', Dickens 2012, http://www.dickens2012.org/event/charles-dickens-film-locations-london-walk; and 'The Dickens connection' graveyard walks, http://www.dickens2012.org/event/dickens-connection [all accessed 1 October 2013].

26 See 'Dickens: Dark London', Museum of London, http://www.museumoflondon.org.uk/Resources/app/Dickens_webpage/index.html [accessed 1 October 2013]. Interactive maps include the 'Celebrating Dickens' mobile app produced by the University of Warwick, http://www.warwick.ac.uk/dickens [accessed 1 October 2013].

27 'Dickens and London', British Council, http://www.teachingenglish.org.uk/dickens/dickens-london [accessed 1 October 2013].

28 Nicola Watson, 'Introduction', in *Literary Tourism and Nineteenth-Century Culture*, ed. Nicola Watson (Basingstoke: Palgrave Macmillan, 2009), pp. 1–12 (p. 2).

29 Nicola Watson, *The Literary Tourist* (Basingstoke: Palgrave Macmillan, 2006), pp. 10, 172–5.

30 Juliet John, *Dickens and Mass Culture* (Oxford: Oxford University Press, 2011), pp. 267–8.

31 Karen Laird, 'The Posthumous Dickens: Commemorative Adaptations, 1870–2012', *Neo-Victorian Studies* 5:2 (2012), pp. 12–34 (pp. 20–1).

32 Literary and cultural engagement with the Victorians can be traced throughout the nineteenth century but the last 20 years have seen a rapid growth in the genre of neo-Victorian fiction, amidst what Louisa Hadley identifies as 'a wider cultural fascination with the Victorians' that spans across TV and film adaptations, heritage culture and political discourse; Louisa Hadley, *Neo-Victorian Fiction and Historical Narrative: The Victorians and Us* (Basingstoke: Palgrave Macmillan, 2010).

33 John, *Dickens and Mass Culture*, p. 253.

34 Quoted in Watson, *The Literary Tourist*, p. 174.

35 Laird, 'The Posthumous Dickens', p. 20.

36 Joss Marsh quoted in Laird, 'The Posthumous Dickens', p. 20.

37 Watson, *The Literary Tourist*, p. 14.

38 Bennett, 'The City as Tourist Stage', p. 76.

39 Boyce and Rousselot, 'The Other Dickens', p. 2.

40 The British Library's 'Writing Britain: Wastelands to Wonderlands' exhibition in summer 2012 further articulated

these connections between nation, authors and place: see http://www.bl.uk/whatson/exhibitions/writingbritain [accessed 1 October 2013].

41 'Sketching the City', British Council, http://literature.britishcouncil.org/projects/2011/dickens-2012/sketches-by-boz-sketching-the-city [accessed 1 October 2013]; 'The Uncommercial Traveller', British Council, http://literature.britishcouncil.org/projects/2011/dickens-2012/punchdrunk-the-uncommercial-traveller [accessed 1 October 2013].

42 Penelope Woods, '*The Two Gentlemen of Verona*', in *A Year of Shakespeare*, p. 224.

43 Paul Prescott, 'Inheriting the Globe: The Reception of Shakespearean Space and Audience in Contemporary Reviewing', in *A Companion to Shakespeare and Performance*, ed. Barbara Hodgdon and W. B. Worthen (eds), pp. 359–75 (p. 362).

44 See Sonia Massai, '*Two Gentlemen of Verona* For/By Zimbabwean Diasporic Communities', in *Shakespeare Beyond English*, ed. Susan Bennett and Christie Carson (Cambridge: Cambridge University Press, 2013), pp. 157–60 (p. 158).

45 See Hansen and Smialkowska's chapter in this volume.

46 *Shakespeare from Kabul*, dir. Harriet Shawcross, BBC Four, 21 July 2012.

47 Steve Purcell, 'Circles, Centres, and the Globe to Globe Festival', *Year of Shakespeare*, 22 June 2012, http://bloggingshakespeare.com/year-of-shakespeare-circles-centres-and-the-globe-to-globe-festival [accessed 1 October 2013].

48 R. Malcolm Smuts, '*The Whole Royal and Magnificent Entertainment*', in *Thomas Middleton: Collected Works*, Gary Taylor and John Lavagnino (eds) (Oxford: Oxford University Press, 2007), pp. 219–23 (p. 220).

49 Janette Dillon, *Theatre, Court and City, 1559–1610: Drama and Social Space in London* (Cambridge: Cambridge University Press, 2000), p. 140.

50 Quoted in Peter Ackroyd, *London: The Biography* (London: Chatto & Windus, 2000), p. 152.

51 Philip Hensher, 'Olympic Torch Route, Day 3: A Conscientious Objector Writes', *Guardian,* 21 May 2012, http://www.guardian.co.uk/sport/2012/may/21/olympic-torch-route-day-3 [accessed 1 October 2013].

10

1948/2012: Building Nations

Tony Howard

Playing history

Elderly readers might have found the media build-up to the 2012 London Olympics familiar. Similar anxieties and grudges were expressed in 1948 before London's postwar 'Austerity' Games:

> *Are the Olympic Games worthwhile?*
>
> *Are they an unnecessary expense to an impoverished Britain?*[1]
>
> *The average range of British enthusiasm for the Games stretches from lukewarm to dislike. It is not too late for invitations to be politely withdrawn.*[2]

But equally, in the wake of the 38 Shakespeare productions of the Globe to Globe Festival, another press story from 1948 also looks familiar – 'Players from Abroad':

Almost we might fancy ourselves living in a golden age of theatrical hospitality with all the traditional styles of acting offering themselves one by one for our instruction and delight.[3]

Both London Games were unexpectedly successful; however there was no equivalent in 1948 to 2012's Cultural Olympiad programme, at whose centre the British organizers (perhaps in desperation) put Shakespeare. In 1948, the range of international theatre that took place in London had less to do with systematic or Olympic-themed planning, more to do with a wider postwar dynamic of rebuilding Europe through culture. In the archives it sometimes seems that during the summer of 1948 events in sport and the arts happened in different universes, and indeed a *Times* leader that May warned: 'By now any other nation would have called in the best stage managers, the best costume designers, the best architects, typographers and sculptors to help and advise. With only a few weeks left there is little evidence that Britain is grasping this opportunity.'[4] The nearest the sports-packed *Pathé Newsreel Review of the Year* came to discussing culture was a mention of the hurdler Maureen Gardner who was also 'a young Oxford ballet mistress'; and in the opposite direction even the British Council's survey of *The Year's Work in the Theatre* never mentioned the Olympics at all.[5] It would be very different in 1952 at Helsinki when the Soviet Union proclaimed the unity of sport and culture, body and mind, by taking the Bolshoi to entertain the team and help in training. Where, then, did 1948's 'golden age of theatrical hospitality' come from, and was Shakespeare part of it?

A letter to the *Manchester Guardian* (July 1948) praised the memory of Demetrius Bikelas, the first President of the International Olympic Committee, for whom the kinship of sport and art was fundamental. 'Bikelas also made Shakespeare known to modern Greeks in their own language. He translated *Hamlet, Romeo and Juliet, King Lear, Macbeth* and *Othello*, and I think he achieved something resembling

Schlegel's triumph'.[6] But the 'Austerity' Games were actually the last to award medals to competing artists, a tradition dating back to 1912. By 1948 it had shrunk to a *Sport in Art* exhibition displaying undistinguished sculptures, medallions, paintings and graphics alongside architects' models of arenas and ski jumps. Several prominent British artists were asked to submit work and declined; judges in several categories refused to award prizes. A small literary component did remain, though there were no drama finalists that year, and the lyric poetry gold medal went to a Finnish translator of Shakespeare, Aale Tynne.[7] The reasons for the Artistic Olympics' decline were complex – dislike of the competitive principle, boredom at the banality of the compulsory 'sport' subjects, and a deep reaction against Goebbels's expansion of the 1936 Berlin Games into a Wagnerian *Gesamtkunstwerk*. It would not be until 1972 and Munich that a truly impressive non-competitive theatre festival stood alongside the Games, involving as it did Peter Brook's *Dream* and a host of experimental companies staging pieces inspired by Olympic history (Berlin 1936 was not a permitted topic). Then terrorism and the deaths of 11 Israeli athletes trivialized both sport and art.[8]

J. B. Priestley wrote in 1947 that the Nazis' manipulation of crowd psychology had instilled a proper suspicion of 'the heightened collective response'. Yet there was a growing belief in postwar Britain that the essence of both sport and theatre – '*this sharing of experience*' as he put it – was fundamental to democratic life.[9] Partly at Priestley's instigation, a British Theatre Conference was held in February 1948 to discuss reorganizing the industry. Most theatre managers boycotted it, but Labour's Chancellor of the Exchequer Stafford Cripps attended and offered moral and financial support (local authorities would be permitted to levy a sixpenny entertainment rate). In Priestley's opinion 'the collective personality of the audience' could counter social disunity and psychological 'isolation', and Shakespeare was a symbol of this: 'Our theatre, from Shakespeare's day onwards, except during a few short periods, has always been a Popular Theatre'.[10] Both the

1948 Games and the theatrical events that overlapped with them were unique because of war and the Reconstruction. As a July 1948 Government press advertisement headline announced, 'This Day Makes History':

> Insurance and assistance to help in all the changes and chances of life, a free national health service for all – these are the great landmarks in British social progress which we have reached this month.[11]

Danny Boyle's hospital beds in his 2012 Opening Ceremony commemorated the fact that the last London Olympics coincided with the creation of the Welfare State. 1948's theatrical activities also registered a sense that a battered world must change.

Rapier and dagger

On 20 August 1948, six days after the Games ended, a Shakespearean Olympiad began. Or it did for Kenneth Tynan. The young critic described two *Hamlet*s – Olivier's new film and Jean-Louis Barrault's stage production, both showing at the Second Edinburgh International Festival. For Tynan, the victor was obvious. He pitted Olivier's 'dead-marching, middle-of-the-road, metronomically monotonous, definitive Denham Hamlet' against the brilliance of Barrault – 'a *chameleon*, practising cadenzas of mercurial transitions […] With total abandon Barrault will switch from the gestures of farce to the poses of genuine agony […] He acknowledges no periods of *becoming*: he brusquely is, or is not, this or that kind of man.'[12] In a Festival lecture Barrault considered *Hamlet* in relation to national identity.[13] 'For England', he argued, Shakespeare 'is universal, no doubt, but he is British born'. In other words:

> The English people try with all their might to hold him back in the midst of their chivalry and to prevent him

crossing the water; we on the other hand try to draw him to us. Can we be blamed for that?

The French, he said, instinctively 'denationalize' Shakespeare, which in practical terms meant that whereas the English were still preoccupied with historical realism ('chivalry', 'blood', 'crenelated walls') Parisian Shakespeare offered abstraction. Barrault's *Hamlet* used experiments in sound, music created by Honegger and Boulez, and minimal 'significant objects' – the skull, a throne like twin headstones. For Barrault himself, a great mime, emotions were *actions*: 'We all like to pull Shakespeare to ourselves'. The terms Barrault and Tynan used to categorize approaches – *'denationalize'*, *'national'*, *'universal'*, *'definitive'* – resonated after the war, and would have done so still more powerfully had Orson Welles also come to Edinburgh as planned, with the American National Theatre and Academy in *Othello*.

The Edinburgh International Festival and the London Olympics were both conceived towards the end of the war and, ideologically and temperamentally, were closely linked. *The People Next Door*, a 1948 film from the Council of Europe, made the connections explicit. It called London's Games a supreme example of 'competition and co-operation' while the Festival proved 'art has no boundaries [...] Things of beauty rise above the barriers of language'. Both showed 'we can't stay remote on our island any longer [...] Today the barriers of space and time are dissolving'. Barrault hinted that the British vision of Shakespeare was touched by insularity, but Edinburgh's Lord Provost, again anticipating Danny Boyle, evoked Prospero's isle. A visitor from South America, he reported, quoted the play to him and said the Festival was 'an island where life was real and meant something'.[14]

General de Gaulle advocated 'intellectual nationalism'. Even during the Occupation he had insisted that France's 'cultural influence can spread for the good of all'; and now art became a means, in his words, 'to maintain abroad the presence of her genius'.[15] Strikingly, however, although the

Compagnie Renault-Barrault had Molière and other French classics in their repertoire, Barrault stated that Shakespeare in 1948 meant much more to him: Shakespeare 'was, as we are now, struggling in a vale where murders and catastrophes were parts of life, and where all human values were again questioned'. His plays spoke directly to everyone who had survived the war only to confront 'anxieties caused by the behaviour of the two world powers which are holding peace in their hands'.[16] For some, the idealism of the Games and the Festival was overshadowed by politics. In 1948 South Africa imposed apartheid, Gandhi was assassinated, and on 29 July Reuters stated that the Israeli provisional government refused to permit 'the return of Arab refugees to Palestine before a final settlement was reached', because 'humanitarian considerations could not be separated from the political and military issues'.[17] Some of those events reflect a world we have left behind, others – as the Globe to Globe productions of *Richard II* and *The Merchant of Venice* proved – remain intractable. As the Austerity Games began, so did the Berlin Blockade, and Barrault quoted *3 Henry VI*: 'Oh pity, God, this miserable age!' (2.5.88):

> To us, who have still present in our minds the memory of Buchenwald and Auschwitz, the retreat of Dunkirk or the horrors endured by Coventry and Hiroshima, these cries of despair easily find an echo in our souls.[18]

His was a Sartrean Hamlet transfixed by 'the equilibrium of life [...] as unstable as the mechanism of a clock'.[19] He must finally pass the future to Fortinbras (cut by Olivier) to ensure 'the restoration of ordered justice' in 'a world of death and suicide'.[20] Apologizing for prewar French attempts to make *Coriolanus* an apology for Fascism, he described Shakespeare as 'the patron of the artist who is committed'.

The Archbishop of Westminster prayed the Games would make 'a tremendous contribution to the peaceful solution of the problems confronting the world'.[21] Ironically, viewed as performance, the Opening Ceremony was dominated by the armed services. It was only three years since the war; the new road into Wembley was laid by German POWs as 'reparation'; Germany and Japan were excluded (Italy, having surrendered in 1943, was welcomed); and the USSR chose not to attend. The 6 August was the third anniversary of Hiroshima. Seven thousand pigeons were freed as a symbol of peace during the Opening Ceremony but before that, and on a more belligerent note, a British destroyer brought the Olympic flame to the White Cliffs of Dover; a 21-gun salute welcomed the torchbearer into the stadium; the Household Cavalry played fanfares; the massed bands of the Brigade of Guards joined a choir of 1,200 in Handel's 'Hallelujah Chorus'; and the 'Olympic Hymn' composed by Richard Strauss for Berlin was replaced by Rudyard Kipling.[22] The *Times* correspondent liked 'the sudden and dramatic release of the pigeons' but thought the arrival of the torch to the sound of guns 'perhaps the most dramatic event of all'.[23]

But if the Games ceremonies seemed frozen in the mindset of the war years, there were concerted attempts elsewhere to make 1948 a turning-point in cultural history and global relations.

Shakespeare into the world

Four days before the Olympics began, the International Theatre Institute (ITI) published the report of its first Congress, held in Prague a month earlier.[24] The United Nations Educational, Scientific and Cultural Organization organized it, hoping 'the exchange of plays and performing companies' might promote 'international understanding'. It was a further drive for reconciliation and reconstruction, echoing the Labour minister Hugh Dalton's recent warning that without cooperation at all levels 'economic collapse and social dissolution' threatened: 'We are all members one of another'.[25] J. B. Priestley was

Chair of the ITI's Provisional Executive Committee and conceded that a theatrical assembly might seem trivial 'in a world threatened by gigantic conflicts' – but 'any international organization crossing frontiers was at least one thread in the fabric of a world society'. Theatre as a form, Priestley argued, makes us 'deal with real human beings concretely and intimately', showing 'how others were living, thinking and feeling'. Theatre replaced the 'monsters' of propaganda with 'knowledge of common human nature' – creating 'faith in it'. The message was reaffirmed by Jindřich Honzl, head of the Czech host delegation: 'Our Theatres are developing into living centres of information and mutual understanding [and] seek everywhere that real and noble humanity which the artistic efforts of all nations are endeavouring to bring into existence'. For example 'the theatres of Prague threw open their doors to companies from abroad' when peace came, including 'the Arts Theatre Company from London with its repertory of Shakespeare and Shaw'.[26] Indeed, according to the ITI report, Honzl stressed that '[t]he Czech theatre had originally been inspired by Shakespeare, to whose genius and knowledge of man tribute had been paid in the festivals of 1864 and 1906'. 'In Shakespeare's day', Priestley wrote, 'we sent plays and players all over Europe. We are still sending them.'[27]

'What country, friends, is this?'

The British Government had been 'sending them' for some time. In summer 1945, as hostilities ended, an Old Vic troupe led by Laurence Olivier, Ralph Richardson and Sybil Thorndike in uniform had toured Europe with ENSA (the Entertainments National Service Association), and mapped the foundations for a postwar programme of ambassadorial theatre. The Old Vic took *Richard III* and *Arms and the Man* – a portrait of a tyrant and a lampoon on militarism, with Shakespeare and Shaw embodying Britain Past and Present.[28]

They visited Brussels, Antwerp, Ghent and 'advanced stations' of the British Liberation Army including Hamburg, where to quote Peter Copley (Hastings in *Richard III*), 'There was half a theatre left. The rest of the city was a devastation of such horror [...] people just lived among stones and rubble and ruin.'[29] The tour was closed to the local population. Sybil Thorndike: 'We were met by the Army of Occupation, and were given orders never to speak to a German – not a single word [...] when we demurred we were told we should be sent back to England.' They visited Belsen. 'We did one matinee for the staff. This was an unforgettable horror [...] The camp was still smouldering and the children were still there. The sight of these little distorted creatures nearly paralysed us.'[30] Thorndike insisted on comforting the child victims of typhoid. En route to home, a two-week season in Paris (May–June 1945) was organized by the new French Government and the British Council. The Old Vic was the first foreign company invited to play at the Comédie-Française and reported that 'Parisians' reactions [...] were very different from the indignation aroused by the German company which commandeered the theatre in 1941'.[31] In exchange their hosts visited London in July '45 with a season marking 'the French theatre's deliverance from a dark threat'.[32]

The Old Vic returned to Paris in 1946 with Olivier's *King Lear* and the British Council sent the Arts Theatre to tour Europe (1946–7), again with Shakespeare and Shaw: *Hamlet, Othello, Candida* and *Don Juan in Hell*. Alec Clunes played Hamlet and Jack Hawkins Othello and for diplomatic reasons performances began in Prague. This involved a long train journey through Germany, and when Clunes queried some details the British Council's Walter Humphreys wrote, 'I think that a little more missionary spirit, cooperation, and a preparation of your company's minds to meet a certain amount of hardship on this tour would be more helpful than the anticipation of a very easy passage everywhere, with priority over everything and everybody else'.[33] During the tour the cast received letters and cards from teachers, military staff, fellow-performers and a teenager who shared her own recent pain with 'her Hamlet': 'The Shakespeare on the tour was having a profound effect on some of its audience'.³⁴ *Richard III, King Lear, Hamlet, Othello*: Britain thought those who had endured the Nazi years should be shown Shakespeare's grasp of suffering. Barrault in Edinburgh agreed, quoting Stendhal: Shakespeare gave 'our contemporaries the kind of tragedy which they need but which they dare not ask for'.³⁵

But despite Priestley's faith in theatre as the antidote to political rhetoric, there are always less disinterested aspects to cultural diplomacy. In 1947 a secret Anglo-Czech Cultural Convention had been signed as part of Whitehall's policy of 'recruiting culture as a means of wrestling Czechoslovakians' minds away from the Soviet Union'.³⁶ The Communists gained control of the Czech Government early in 1948 and Sovietization tightened through the year. As a small sign of this, in November the Czechs insisted that an 'Additional Statement' be added to the ITI report of Honzl's speech, inserting warm, less Anglophile, references to Schiller, Lorca and the theatres of Russia, Poland, Yugoslavia, Sweden and France. In 1950 the Prague and Budapest governments shut down the British Council's offices.

Nonetheless British theatres of the Left still saw the situation in Eastern Europe as rich in promise. Theatre Workshop toured 16 towns in Czechoslovakia in autumn '48 – and although they were about to stage *Twelfth Night* and *As You Like It* at home for schoolchildren, the work they took abroad was internationalist (Moliere's *The Flying Doctor*, Lorca, Chekhov) and radical (two new plays by Ewan MacColl). No Shakespeare. In an article for *Reynold's News*, Gerry Raffles explained how Czechoslovakia's Art for the People movement arranged their tour, alongside Louis Jouvet, Moscow's Vakhtangov Theatre and many others: 'This international exchange [...] must result in a great broadening of the outlook of all the artists there'.³⁷ But Raffles's piece was rejected, and as far as the British Foreign Office was concerned Art for the People was a suspect organization. So too was the Anglo–Soviet Friendship Society, yet while the Berlin crisis hardened, contradictory cultural messages were being sent to our former allies. In 1948 the Society and the Arts Council created an important exhibition on the history of Shakespearean production, which went to Moscow itself. It would not be followed by live performers till 1955.[38]

Beginnings

Some acts of theatrical diplomacy were more strategic. Tyrone Guthrie had headed the Old Vic organization on and off from 1932–45 and would do so again. In 1947–9 he went abroad to help organize, adjudicate and direct drama in four diversely 'new' nations: Australia, Finland, Palestine and Poland. Australia had a progressive Labour government; Finland, Guthrie said, was still 'reeling' after its war with the USSR; in Palestine 'it was the beginning of the end of the British mandate'; and Poland was under tightening Soviet control. Elements in each country wished to create national theatres as part of their construction of a new society, and were encouraged to turn to Britain for advice.[39]

There would be clear analogues in 2012, when Shakespeare's Globe and the RSC invited theatre artists from Palestine, South Sudan, Afghanistan, the Balkans and Iraq to explore Shakespearean texts – companies who had experienced or witnessed recent political traumas, and were imagining or building the fabric of a democratic culture. 'Globe to Globe Shakespeare' emerged as a symbol, potentially even an agent, of nation-building. Yet it was an ambiguous and controversial process, with this London management suggesting plays and in some cases fostering collaborations with 'expert' British directors [see Colette Gordon's chapter in this volume]. The difference was that in the late 1940s Tyrone Guthrie at first decided not to take Shakespeare with him.

Asked to direct at the Habima Theatre in Tel Aviv – under the suspicious eyes of British soldiers – Guthrie suggested a classic. But it 'should be as foreign to me as to Habimah'.[40] Declining to impose the English canon during the Jewish struggle for independence, Guthrie preferred a work 'of universal significance', 'to transcend the geographical and racial differences'. He chose *Oedipus the King*. In 1948 he directed it again in Helsinki – which had been scheduled to host the 1940 Olympics before the Soviet invasion but was too war-damaged to stage them until 1952. In Australia, Guthrie visited six cities to investigate the practicalities of creating a subsidized theatre network, but he sensed that the priority must be to encourage local 'talent' and 'taste' – 'the human material of a national theatre' – and at that point it seemed Shakespeare had to enter the calculations. So in 1948 Olivier in *Richard III* led an Old Vic company on an extraordinary seven-month Australasian tour.[41] In 1949 Guthrie returned to Finland – 'There was more food, more money, a sensation of life returning'[42] – and he staged a (controversially) populist and celebratory production of *The Taming of the Shrew*. Much later, in 1959, he directed a modern-dress *Merchant of Venice* at the Habima (the play this company would bring to Globe to Globe in 2012). But Poland was where Guthrie himself was confronted by Shakespeare's role in nation-building and reconstruction. For the Polish Shakespeare Festival (1947), state-run theatres all across the country mounted productions of his plays, with finalists competing in Warsaw. Guthrie attended as an expert observer.

He was unimpressed by their 'old-fashioned' work: 'The grand actors ranted and spouted, the comic characters were red-nosed burlesques from vaudeville. It was none of it in what we were conditioned to regard as good taste'.[43] Guthrie seemed unheeding that hundreds of Polish actors had been killed in the war. But he was appalled by the physical devastation of the Warsaw Ghetto and astonished by the rebuilding of the National Theatre in a wasteland. Guthrie told BBC listeners what he had seen: 'Here were ambitious

Shakespeare productions in provincial cathedral cities, in remote railway junctions, in small coal-mining towns [...] serious interpretations of masterworks which were being seen, and evidently enjoyed, by large and essentially "popular" audiences'. The first volume of *Shakespeare Survey* (1948), which significantly included an international news section, observed that Shakespeare's 'genius seems most to be appreciated when men's minds are stirred and life is uneasy. Poland's Shakespeare festival may stand as a symbol of this.'[44] And Tyrone Guthrie added, 'We thought ruefully of the low priority in which the British theatre had been regarded in the postwar reconstruction'.[45]

Decades later, the émigré Polish director Kazimirz Braun dismissed this festival as a 'ploy', a propagandist distraction from the fact that while the regime was boosting 'universal' Shakespeare, Poland's own classics – poetic, epic and often bitterly anti-Russian – were being suppressed.[46] Yet some of the productions emerged as landmarks of East European theatre, especially *The Tempest* directed by Leon Schiller, an Auschwitz survivor and friend of Gordon Craig. He made it a *faux-naïf* morality play, with weird folk-art creatures fusing fauna and flora. A Shakespeare-like scientist-artist Prospero, in a set dominated by his giant easel, showed how to fabricate a strange new world.

Stakhanovite reconstruction encouraged comedy after the war. The Warsaw festival did include *Hamlet* and *Othello,* but here also were *The Winter's Tale, Twelfth Night,* the *Dream, Merry Wives, The Tempest, As You Like It, Two Gentlemen of Verona* and *Much Ado*. Snapshots from elsewhere in Europe were similar: in 1948 Theatre Workshop encountered *Twelfth Night* in Czechoslovakia and *As You Like It* in Sweden, and though Joan Littlewood was even blunter than Guthrie (at the National Theatre of Moravia: 'The tattiest, dreariest production of *Twelfth Night* I have ever seen'[47]) she testified to the power of drama as exchange, across borderlines of language, ideology and taste. One Swedish management 'brought out their most prized possession in our honour, the décor for the first production of *As You Like It* in their theatre – gauzes, cut cloths scattered with red-gold leaves; branches high up on the scrims, mossy rocks on the stage itself. It was magical.'[48] A London reviewer of the Comédie-Française's choice of plays to open their 1945 visit (*The Barber of Seville* and *The Versailles Impromptu*) made a significant judgement: 'From comedy we seek the reassurance we know it can give of the reality of civilized values, and so, more aptly than tragedy, it graces an occasion which joyously celebrates the survival of those values'.[49]

1948: Europe into London

In 2012, as the Globe to Globe visitors arrived, some common tendencies emerged. Some presented themselves metatheatrically as neo-Elizabethan travelling players, whether ebullient (the Greek *Pericles*) or sardonic (the National Academic Theatre of Armenia dragged their suitcases to a sullen assignation with the endless power-games of *King John*). Some groups' creative use of the Globe space revolutionized our understanding of its potential, and of the play, like the Maori *Troilus and Cressida* which gave the vaunting of the Greeks and Trojans unprecedented physical life. Some productions transferred awkwardly onto the thrust stage; some casts seized the opportunities for carnival, like the South Korean *Dream* actors who ended the night in the foyer being photographed with the audience. Every company adopted its own solution to the language barrier, whether sprinkling in English jokes or keeping sternly to their texts. Meanwhile the Arts Council experiment of putting the productions online in The Space (www.TheSpace.org) suggested important possibilities for theatre's relationship with new media; this became radicalized in 2013 when the return of the Belarus Free Theatre's *King Lear* was live-streamed to Belarus and the Globe audience was asked to shout out in support of the dictatorship's opponents. And as London's enclaves of Turks, Russians,

Nigerians, Pakistanis, Poles, Israelis, Palestinians, etc., altered the chemistry of the audience nightly, it also became obvious that one significance of a theatrical exchange is the effect on the host community's perception of itself (see the chapters by Rose Elfman and Steven Purcell in this volume). In 1948 all the details were different, but the stories ran parallel.

'A golden age of theatrical hospitality'

In that postwar Olympic year too London saw a wealth of international drama. An ambitious Italian Theatre Festival included the Piccolo Teatro di Milano in Gozzi's *Il Corvo*; *Six Characters in Search of an Author* with the Accademia Nazionale d'Arte; and Sophocles's 'universal' *Oedipus*. A striking number of European plays were produced commercially. *Medea* (via New York and the Edinburgh Festival) starred Eileen Herlie (Olivier's Gertrude). Mai Zetterling and Anton Walbrook appeared in *The Wild Duck*. Michael Redgrave was *The Father*, and there were two *Cherry Orchards* (from Liverpool Playhouse and the Old Vic). Crucially, the French postwar influence was obvious with a modern-dress *Tartuffe* at the Arts; Armand Salacrou's *The Unknown Woman of Arras;* Sartre's *Crime Passionel* ('Some resemblance to the theme of *Hamlet*' according to *The Times*[50]); Emanuel Roblè's *Montserrat*; a version of George Neveux's *Pleinte Contre Inconnu*; and the farce *Don't Listen Ladies* 'from the French of Sacha Guitry'. The Old Vic rehearsed Jean Anouilh's *Antigone* and *The Miser* which both opened in January '49. *The Glass Menagerie* arrived to increase the growing American presence in the West End, and *The Times* praised its professionalism ('slow and sure in a very American way') and the breeding techniques of the US Olympic equestrian team in almost the same words. Olsen and Johnson's *Hellzapoppin'* played at the Casino Theatre; Mae West was *Diamond Lil'* at the Prince of Wales; and Danny Kaye played the Royal Variety Show and was mobbed.

Unfortunately there was also a crisis in London's theatrical life which Kenneth Tynan diagnosed as complacency. The war had led to the creation of CEMA (the Council for the Encouragement of Music and the Arts) and its successor the Arts Council. This was transformational. As Guthrie said, 'The British Treasury, for the first time since the Tudors, had made manifest a belief that the theatre in particular is a necessity to a nation which wishes to consider itself civilized'.[51] As a result the Old Vic could begin to build a Shakespearean and international programme, performed 'in rotation after the manner of a Continental repertoire'.[52] The Labour government was preparing a Bill (passed January 1949) to establish a future National Theatre with the Old Vic at its heart. But now, ironically, the company was overstretched. With Olivier in Australia and Ralph Richardson filming in America, it seemed leaderless. Harcourt Williams, a former Artistic Director (and the Player King in Olivier's *Hamlet*), believed the Vic was failing in its most basic duty – there were no 'important' Shakespeare productions, and 'It is not good enough'.[53] Alec Guinness's Richard II and John Clements's Coriolanus were both rigid, unemotional figures – Austerity personified – isolated in dull underpopulated sets. E. Martin Browne, T. S. Eliot's favourite director, made the Roman people oafs and their tribunes grotesque. *Twelfth Night*, directed by Guinness, was dark and unpopular; he made Feste omniscient but tragic, in love with Olivia and death. A hunt for box-office celebrities ended in the disastrous miscasting of the Shavian Sir Cedric Hardwicke as Marlowe's Faustus. Money was lost, a US tour cancelled, and the London company disbanded prematurely.

In that situation, the return of the Comédie-Française was embarrassing. In October 1948 they brought *Le Misanthrope*, *Andromache* and *Le Malade Imaginaire* along with curtain-raisers by Henri Becque, de Musset and Labiche for a three-week season; and if Kenneth Tynan had contrasted Olivier and Barrault playfully that summer, now the critics' comparisons were brutal. The *Spectator* spoke for many: the French company through 'its sense of purpose and in its general level of competence' exposed the Old Vic's 'failure', 'the poor diction', and 'the unevenness of the company as a whole'. Lessons 'taught by the Moscow Arts Theatre, by the Comédie-Française', had been ignored: 'The strength of a repertory company is not in its stars'.[54] Some of the criticism actually came from the Old Vic's friends: the contrast with French theatre helpfully underlined the need for changes in policy, financing and structure which had been in development for some years – and especially since 9 July, when Olivier in Sydney and Richardson in Hollywood were sent a 'Private and Confidential Memorandum on Future Administration', stating their contracts would not be renewed by the Old Vic Board.

Priestley had called for the Vic to become 'a completely self-contained theatrical unit, as the great continental theatres are'.[55] Plans were now announced to achieve this, involving classical and 'experimental' work in two theatres, drama training, plays for young audiences and creative links with civic theatres across the country, and at the heart of this vision was the Frenchman Michel Saint-Denis. He had founded La Compagnie des Quinze and the London Theatre Studio in the 1930s, was a key figure in Free French radio, and had rejected offers to run the Comédie-Française when the war ended, in order to create the Old Vic Centre. There could be no better proof of the new internationalism. The school trained actors, directors and designers in techniques developed in Paris and Moscow; the Young Vic played Shakespeare, Jonson, Goldoni and André Obey at home and abroad. Meanwhile the Arts Council was developing a network of repertory theatres across Britain: in summer 1948 a new London festival showcased regional repertory productions including *Hamlet* and Chekhov from Bristol and Liverpool. But the economic situation was worsening. With hopes raised, London's theatre community was dismayed by rumours that the Comédie-Française grant equalled half Britain's total spending on the arts.[56]

There were ferocious debates about the role of Shakespeare in a democratic culture. The *Spectator* insisted that 'a National Theatre must be not only a memorial to Shakespeare and a repository of tradition, but a living force in the country's dramatic life'.[57] Harcourt Williams worried that Shakespeare had become a refuge for escapists who 'wanted colour, costumes, romance, something they could love, the drama of an earlier age, and were not interested in a modern problem'.[58] And elsewhere there was patrician distaste for new audiences like those Olivier had attracted, especially Americanized young 'film-fans' and 'bobbysoxers' replacing 'knowledge and judgment' with 'sex and hysteria' (Harold Hobson).[59] Perhaps the undereducated masses were unready for theatre. Perhaps Britain needed a 'school for audiences'.[60]

Actually it already had one: BBC radio. And it was here that the strands of the Olympic year – sporting, artistic and political – came together.

The globe in the corner of the room

Across three stations – the Light Programme, Home Service, and the new elite Third Programme (in 1948 virtually the Oxbridge of the Air) – the BBC developed an integrated policy to make great drama accessible and attractive to all. Its historic importance can't be overstressed.

For UK listeners, Olympic year drama was cosmopolitan. A Third Programme series called *International Drama: Comment and Action* offered extracts and analysis, and the BBC transmitted plays by for example Bjørnstjerne Bjørnson (*Love and Geography*), Karl Zuckmayer (*The Devil's General*), Jean-Jacques Bernard (*National 6*), Anouilh (*Medea*), Sartre (*Crime Passionnel*), Zola (*Thérèse Raquin*), Ibsen (*The Master Builder)*, Chekhov (*The Cherry Orchard, The Seagull*) and Strindberg (*Easter, Miss Julie* and *The Dream Play*). The output was deliberately intensive: on 26 March, *Easter* was broadcast on the Home Service at the same time as Goldoni's *Servant of Two Masters* on the Third *and* a 'radio version' of the Anna Neagle film *Spring in Park Lane* on the Light

Programme, whose screen adaptations also included Powell and Pressburger's dreamlike exploration of the love-hate relationship between England, America and Europe – *A Matter of Life and Death*. As in the film, Maurius Goring (one of Saint-Denis's key collaborators) played the English hero's French guide to Heaven.

The postwar *Radio Times* printed wavelength details of foreign stations. In 1948 it recommended programmes 'From the Continent' such as a French 'lyrical drama' about Gaugin and an Italian-language *Jekyll and Hyde*. For those who had served in Europe the interest was obvious, and the climax of this internationalism came when the Third Programme broadcast 90 minutes of scenes in French from the Comédie-Française season. From one angle minority programming, it was educational and political too: 'Our young people will be more than British', *The People Next Door* predicted: 'They'll be European'. Guthrie and the BBC discussed how best to popularize drama. One result was a Light Programme fortnightly magazine, *Theatre Programme*: that summer it featured Saint-Denis and his Old Vic students discussing Europe's 'Theatres of the Future'.

Shakespeare's place in this public service mission was central. Besides the obvious wish to popularize the plays, the BBC debated their social role. In 1947 *Theatre Programme* presented *A Plain Man's Guide to Shakespeare* featuring mixed 'methods of appreciating Shakespeare', including some satire, discussions and Peter Powell exploring scenes from his production of *Othello* with Jack Hawkins (*Theatre Programme* had already covered his Czechoslovakian tour). Summer 1948 offered multi-disciplinary perspectives: a survey of recent scholarship, the director Michael MacOwan on *Producing Shakespeare* and Roger Manvell asking Olivier's script editor *Can Shakespeare be Filmed*? In some ways the most revealing were two Third Programme talks on Salvador de Madariaga's new book *On Hamlet*. The historian C.V. Wedgwood reviewed it, Henry Reed responded ('*Hamlet*' *Once More*) and its British impact was intense. It inspired

Alec Guinness to direct the tragedy and play Hamlet again because 'I was thrilled', 'appalled' and 'completely convinced by his assumption that the Elizabethan world was as much influenced by Spain as we are today by America'.[61]

De Madariaga had translated the play into Spanish and found himself rejecting Romantic preconceptions and stage traditions: 'For a translator must retrace every mental step of the author, without skipping a single shade of meaning'.[62] Peter Conrad found both his method and his downbeat historicist reading (Hamlet was a Revenger; Ophelia, a Court lady, was his mistress) 'irrefutable'[63]. In Edinburgh Jean-Louis Barrault took a more jaundiced view of translation:

> Shakespeare's entry on the French stage begins with a crime [...] The poetic atmosphere of his art [...] is cruelly dispelled by the cold light of our severely rationalized language [...] which destroys rhythm and music, and seeks to pierce the most shaded and mysterious recesses.

With an eye on Voltaire and perhaps de Madariaga, Barrault added: 'When he is shorn of his poetic appearance, there are people who only see in him the representative of a barbarous age, dealing in ghosts, female pimps, murderers, and plotters'.[64] But the investigations into translatability at the heart of the 2012 Globe to Globe Festival were anticipated by the postwar BBC. The 1947 programmes included de Madariaga reading from his Spanish *Hamlet*, extracts from Schlegel's *Hamlet* and *Macbeth,* and André Gide, Barrault's translator, with his *Antoine et Cléopâtre*. They returned to the topic by producing the Closet Scene in English, French and Spanish, with three casts including Guinness and Barrault. Two weeks later, Tyrone Guthrie reported to British listeners on the Polish Shakespeare Festival. In 1948 de Madariaga – an activist at the League of Nations, a minister in Republican Spain and co-founder of the College of Europe – made a speech calling for a future that would honour national histories and cultures, yet transcend and share them: 'This Europe must be born.

And she will when Spaniards say "Our Chartres", Englishmen "Our Krakow", Italians "Our Copenhagen" and Germans "Our Bruges", and step back horror-stricken at the idea of laying a murderous hand upon it.'[65]

The London Olympics became 'The Biggest Outside Broadcast Operation in History'.[66] The BBC relayed it in 40 languages to its 'European and overseas listeners'. And the sports coverage was supported, explained Laurence Gilliam (Head of Features), by programmes on the lives of 'ordinary men and women' in other countries and continents: 'There is no surer foundation for world peace [...] Radio is awake now to its international obligation.'[67]

It was also a defining moment in the history of television, and when the Games were over BBC TV applied its new technical confidence to Shakespeare: on 22 and 29 August, William Devlin as King Lear journeyed through two studios and 17 sets to reach Dover.[68] Yet the intellectual ambition of the radio projects was even more remarkable. If this was a time to think of Shakespeare globally, the BBC also used the plays to consider British identity. Shakespeare was, E. M. W. Tillyard told the *Radio Times*, the creator of '[o]ur nearest approach to a national epic'.[69] In October 1947 the Third Programme broadcast all the Histories from *Richard II* to *Richard III* in a single week.[70] *Henry VI* was compressed into one play, but as if in compensation the Reithean Corporation also broadcast *Macbeth* (Home Service) on the same night as *Henry IV, Part 1*. In 1948 the BBC announced another project that would build on the achievement: 'Five Great Tragedies'. *Hamlet, Othello, Lear, Romeo and Juliet* and *Macbeth* would be broadcast in scholarly 'definitive' versions. This series launched on Boxing Day with a full-text *Hamlet* starring John Gielgud. Its four-hour duration was a reproof to Olivier's heavily cut film, and so the Olympic year closed with one last Shakespearean duel across the media. The Gielgud *Hamlet* was released on vinyl, pioneering, it was hoped, the creation of home audio libraries of Shakespeare's plays. *National, universal, definitive, scholarly, popular, personal* – the postwar BBC explored all these perspectives on the plays. However the real legacy of 'The Chronicles' was that it defined the unique role the Histories were to play in British broadcasting and theatre from that day to this – from Stratford's *Richard II–Henry V* season (1951) to BBC TV's *An Age of Kings* (1960), the RSC's *Wars of the Roses* (1963) and so many bloodstained cycles since, including the Globe's *Henry VI* (2013) performed on historic battlefields.

Crossover and legacy: The audience

In 1948 the BBC celebrated diversity within Britain. It broadcast the opening of the National Eisteddfod live ('the Welsh Olympiad') and launched *Curtain Up!*, a season introducing Light Programme listeners to recent regional stage plays. It also addressed the question of the audience in a democracy. In the build-up to the Austerity Games, Tyrone Guthrie travelled across England. He began a series of radio talks called *Public Pleasures* with Orwellian observations on the condition of the working class. He described lines of taciturn men queuing for a midweek match between Manchester City and United, 'sucking the mental dope provided by the press barons – *Russia, Czechoslovakia, Blue baby in Oxygen Tent; Russia, Margaret Lockwood, Bantu Minstrel Wins Again; Russia, Czechoslovakia, A New Way with Hake Fritters; Russia...*'. Fed an alienating diet of poverty, film stars and Cold War anxiety, in the stadium they became 'a colossal oblong of pink sago pudding – each grain of sago being a human face'. But then the whistle blew.[71]

Guthrie visited a diverse set of popular events – soccer, boxing, a brass band heat, dog racing and a scouting jamboree watched by the King – to investigate, as a theatre director, the nature of mass entertainment. He was appalled by the shrivelling of sport into commerce at the dog track – a 'loveless' betting evening with no sense of community, excitement or release. However he found the Manchester match 'a very fine spectacle'; admired the audience's expert knowledge of brass band music (he borrowed its 'Ruritanian' imagery for his 1956 production of *Troilus and Cressida*); and his account of boxing in the Albert Hall, a spotlit stage enveloped by murmurs and darkness, is haunting. Above all, Guthrie became fascinated by his own self-immersion in the crowd, by the psychology of the stadium where 'the separate identity of each one of us – with his private impulses, private impressions, his own individual standards of propriety and conventions of good behaviour', clashed yet merged with a 'great uninhibited, unintellectual' collective self.[72] Although he began by saying, 'One of the dangers in a society that is trying, as ours is, to be egalitarian, is that activities tend to be thought of as important simply because they are popular', Tyrone Guthrie's pre-Olympic encounters with English sport had personal consequences that helped him reshape the nature of Shakespearean production on two continents.[73] In September 1948 he staged David Lindsay's *The Thrie Estates* at the Edinburgh Festival and adapted the General Assembly Hall of the Church of Scotland to evoke the dynamics of the Elizabethan playhouse – and 'I now felt convinced that for plays written before about 1640, the open stage was the answer'.[74] 'There will be no radical improvement in the production of Shakespeare's plays', he insisted, 'until we get back to an architectural form which relates the player to the audience in the manner that prevailed in Shakespeare's time'. For Shakespeare was 'a popular, not a coterie dramatist'.

Guthrie argued that Shakespeare requires 'a large, excited, and not necessarily sophisticated audience', and he could speak from experience: 'An audience feels excitement in proportion as it is crowded […], the tighter it is squeezed, the more receptive it is to the infection of mass-excitement':

And if anyone dares to maintain that an audience will prefer comfort to excitement, there are innumerable instances and statistics to confute him. Let him consider the crowds at sporting events...[75]

Class is a foreign country: they do things differently there. Consciously crossing a social and cultural line, Guthrie gained insights that would colour his career: 'The spark which links audience to performers in a living relationship is most often evident in spectacles and sports which have nothing to do with theatre' – 'Interesting things are happening elsewhere'. He and his designer Tanya Moiseiwitsch went on to create open stages for Shakespeare in Canada and the USA where every spectator would be aware of the rest, and his speeches to businessmen, politicians and volunteers restated the message which closed those radio talks in 1948: 'Don't let us be merely passive spectators, or money-makers on the side. Let us be participants.'[76]

On 22 June 1948 the *Empire Windrush* docked from Jamaica. British identity was developing in ways Guthrie missed as he scanned those Manchester faces, and the postcolonial meeting of cultures was changing Shakespeare already. In 1947 the Trinidadian Robert Adams became the first black actor to play Shakespeare on television (Morocco in the *Merchant* for the BBC). In February 1948 the Jamaican-born American actor Frank Silvera wrote in the British magazine *New Theatre*:

> Let us have a Negro production of *Hamlet*. Then let us have productions of *King Lear*, *Romeo and Juliet*, *Ghosts*, or a *St. Joan* done at the highest level.[77]

The hopes of 1948, internationalist and domestic, were not all realized. The Old Vic School closed in 1952. Michel Saint-Denis returned to France. From 1953–8 the company presented nothing but Shakespeare. Sixty-four years after Silvera's article and with great publicity, the RSC staged its 'African' *Julius Caesar,* and the *Empire Windrush* and its passengers became an element in Danny Boyle's Opening

Ceremony in the Olympic arena; they were onscreen in the global TV relay for a few brief seconds. 'The process of development is slow and exacting', Silvera had written, 'but this should not be discouraging.'

Notes

1 'Focus on the Olympic Games', *Radio Times*, 6 August 1948.
2 *Evening Standard*, September 1947. Quoted in Janie Hampton, *The Austerity Olympics* (London: Aurum Press, 2008), p. 23.
3 *The Times,* 11 October 1948.
4 *The Times*, 8 May 1948.
5 See *The Year's Work in the Theatre: 1948–1949* (London: published for the British Council by Longmans Green & Co., 1949).
6 *Manchester Guardian*, 24 July 1948.
7 See Richard Stanton, *The Forgotten Olympic Art Competitions* (London: Trafford Publishing, 2002).
8 At the Exhibition, 'the book of the last Olympics' was on display, featuring Hitler's signature.
9 J. B. Priestley, *Theatre Outlook* (London: Nicholson and Watson, 1947), p. 73. Italics mine. His book concluded: Britain must 'give the Theatre, which we can all share, its proper place in our new democratic society' (p. 76).
10 Ibid., p. 15.
11 Government press advertisement, here cited from *Radio Times*, 5 July 1948.
12 Kenneth Tynan, *He That Plays the King* (London: Longmans, Green and Co., 1950), pp. 134, 132.
13 Jean-Louis Barrault, *The Theatre of Jean-Louis Barrault*, trans. Joseph Chiari (London: Barrie Books, 1961), p. 100. From his Edinburgh lecture, 'Shakespeare and the French', delivered 8 September 1948.

14 Andrew H. A. Morley, 'Edinburgh International Festival 1948', *Radio Times*, 20 August 1948.

15 De Gaulle speaking in Algeria on the future of the Alliance Française, October 1943. Quoted in Philippe Lane, *French Scientific and Cultural Diplomacy* (Liverpool: Liverpool University Press, 2013), p. 131. 'Intellectual nationalism' should not however become 'outrageous', said de Gaulle: it should aspire to elevate moral standards through language and education.

16 Barrault, *The Theatre of Jean-Louis Barrault*, p. 94.

17 *The Times*, 30 July 1948.

18 Barrault, *The Theatre of Jean-Louis Barrault*, p. 94.

19 Ibid., p. 96.

20 'The restoration of ordered justice' is Tynan's phrase, reporting on Barrault's lecture. *He That Plays the King*, p. 128.

21 'Sermon Preached by His Eminence Cardinal Griffin in Westminster Cathedral', *Bulletin du Comité International Olympique*, 11 (1948), p. 31.

22 Rudyard Kipling, '*Non Nobis Domine*'; composer, Roger Quilter.

23 *The Times*, 30 July 1948. The Games ran from 29 July to 4 August.

24 The Congress ran from 28 June to 3 July in Prague; the report was published in Paris on 25 July.

25 Hugh Dalton opening the International Monetary Conference, London, 11 September 1947. He was pointing to a coming crisis caused by price rises and inadequate financial reserves – 'Events have overrun all our calculations.' For video footage of the Conference, see here: http://www.britishpathe.com/video/international-monetary-conference-1/query/ [accessed 12 February 2014].

26 *Report on the First Congress of the International Theatre Institute* (Paris: 1948), Corrigendum 2.

27 Priestley, *Theatre Outlook*, p. 16.

28 The company also performed *Peer Gynt* directed by Tyrone Guthrie in Paris.

29 Peter Copley speaking to the European *Memory 2000* project: http://www.memory2000.net/int_uk_1.asp [accessed 12 February 2014].

30 Elizabeth Sprigge, *Sybil Thorndike Casson* (London: Gollancz, 1971), p. 253.

31 *Five Seasons of the Old Vic Theatre Company: A Scrapbook Record of Production for 1944–49* (London: Saturn Press, 1949), p. 14.

32 *The Times*, 3 July 1945.

33 Letter quoted in sale catalogue: *Materials from the Career of Alec Clunes* (2008), http://www.callumjamesbooks.com/Clunes.pdf [accessed 12 February 2014].

34 Ibid. Bookseller's commentary.

35 Stendhal quoted by Barrault, *The Theatre of Jean-Louis Barrault*, p. 94.

36 Aiko Watanabe, 'Cultural Drives by the Periphery: Britain's Experiences', *History in Focus* 10 (2006), http://www.history.ac.uk/ihr/Focus/cold/articles/watanabe.html [accessed 12 February 2014].

37 First printed in Joan Littlewood, *Joan's Book* (London: Methuen, 1994), p. 768.

38 The Peter Brook/Paul Scofield *Hamlet* premiered there – shortly before Khrushchev's speech denouncing Stalin's crimes. 'Scofield was the first Western artist who satisfied the hunger that the Moscow public felt for foreign art [...] His amazing performance was a breakthrough in the country's cultural history during the Cold War isolation.' See Assary Messener, 'Gifts Exchanged with Paul Scofield', http://www.stosvet.net/12/messerer/index_print.html [accessed 12 February 2014]. The Shakespearean stage history exhibition became part of the British Theatre Festival in Birmingham in 1949, as did a replica of the Globe in which extracts from the plays were performed by the Midland Theatre Company. It was, incidentally, in 1949 that Sam Wanamaker conceived his quest to build the Globe.

39 See Tyrone Guthrie, *A Life in the Theatre* (London: Hamish Hamilton and Readers Union, 1961), pp. 233–57. In Tel Aviv 'almost every night there would be outrages committed either

by British troops or by the members of Irgun Zwai Leumi, or as the British newspapers phrased it, "terrorists"' (p. 236). Guthrie declined to leave the country as requested by the British Army, and was afterwards accompanied by an armed local bodyguard.

40 Ibid., p. 233.

41 Guthrie followed and surveyed the country's theatrical life in April 1949. The plan for an Australian National Theatre was soon discarded by the new Conservative government led by Robert Menzies.

42 Guthrie, *A Life in the Theatre,* p. 244.

43 Ibid., p. 255.

44 Allardyce Nicoll, 'International News', *Shakespeare Survey 1* (1948), pp. 113, 116. In 1947 the British Council helped organize an international conference of Shakespeare scholars in Stratford-upon-Avon, an event which laid foundations for the creation of the Shakespeare Institute.

45 Guthrie, *A Life in the Theatre,* p. 253.

46 Kazimierz Braun, A *History of Polish Theater, 1939–1989: Spheres of Captivity and Freedom* (Westport: Greenwood Press, 1996), p. 32.

47 Littlewood, *Joan's Book,* pp. 349–50.

48 Ibid., p. 364.

49 *The Times,* 3 July 1945. The season also included *Tartuffe* and Barrault's production of *Phèdre.*

50 *The Times,* 5 August 1948.

51 Guthrie quoted in Harcourt Williams, *Old Vic Saga* (London: Winchester Publications, 1949), p. 167.

52 Ibid., p. 170.

53 Ibid., p. 21.

54 *Spectator,* 17 December 1948.

55 Priestley, *Theatre Outlook,* p. 33.

56 Charles Landstone, *Off-Stage* (London and New York: Elek, 1953), p. 178. In 1951 the Old Vic's plans collapsed, six months before the Conservatives' return to power – and

incidentally one of Churchill's first acts was to order the demolition of the site of the Festival of Britain, which he called 'three-dimensional socialist propaganda'.

57 *Spectator*, 17 December 1948.
58 Williams, *Old Vic Saga,* p. 197.
59 Quoted in *Spectator*, 17 December 1948.
60 Williams, *Old Vic Saga,* p. 203.
61 Alec Guinness, 'My Idea of Hamlet', *Spectator*, 5 July 1951.
62 Quoted in *Spectator*, 6 May 1948.
63 *Spectator*, 6 May 1948. See Tom Cornford, 'The English Theatre Studios of Michael Chekhov and Michel Saint-Denis, 1935–1965' (unpublished PhD thesis, University of Warwick, 2012).
64 Barrault, *The Theatre of Jean-Louis Barrault*, p. 89.
65 Anthony Sampson, *The New Europeans* (London: Panther Books, 1971), p. 26.
66 *Radio Times,* 9 July 1948.
67 Ibid.
68 *Radio Times*, 3 August 1948.
69 *Radio Times*, 3 October 1948.
70 The cycle ran 5–10 October 1948.
71 Tyrone Guthrie, *In Various Directions: A View of Theatre* (London: Michael Joseph, 1965), p. 201. Like *A Life in the Theatre*, this book reworks some of Guthrie's radio talks.
72 Ibid., p. 204.
73 Ibid., p. 210.
74 Ibid., p. 67.
75 Tyrone Guthrie, 'Shakespearean Production', *Year's Work in the Theatre 1949–1950* (London and Toronto: New York: Published for the British Council by Longmans Green & Co., 1950), pp. 39–40.
76 Guthrie, *In Various Directions*, p. 221.
77 *New Theatre*, February 1948, pp. 18–19.

11

Olympic Shakespeare and the Idea of Legacy: Culture, Capital and the Global Future

Erin Sullivan

Every party has a morning after. And when the party is as big as a 'mega-event' like the Olympics, the 'what-happens-next' can be as important, and as symbolic, as the celebrations themselves. In the case of the London 2012 Olympics, the morning after was always known as its 'legacy', even years before the Games had actually begun. In its 2005 presentation to the Olympic Selection Committee, the London planning team pledged legacy as one of its three core ambitions, assuring members that a London Games would result not only in a rich sporting, cultural and environmental legacy for Britain, but also in 'a far-reaching legacy for the Olympic Movement' itself.[1] After the bid was secured, Lord Coe, Chairman of the newly formed London Organizing Committee of the Olympic and Paralympic Games, described legacy once again as 'absolutely epicentral' to London 2012's aims, adding that '[l]egacy is probably nine-tenths of what this process is about, not just 16 days of Olympic sport'.[2]

This chapter explores the idea of legacy as produced by the political and public discussion surrounding the London 2012 Games, paying attention to the visions of cultural legacy imagined and in some cases achieved through the promotion and performance of Shakespeare. Thinking through legacy as a form of inheritance, and by extension as a kind of capital to be spent, the chapter considers how the World Shakespeare Festival and Cultural Olympiad at once consolidated investment in widely recognized forms of British culture, achieving maximum visibility and coherence through an established icon like Shakespeare, while at the same time speculating more daringly on new and less familiar ways of approaching this well-known figure – most notably through the use of non-English languages and performance traditions. The result, I suggest, was a reaffirmation of Shakespeare as one of the UK's chief cultural assets, but in a markedly new guise. With Shakespeare as a figure of British triumphalism no longer feasible on a global scale, Shakespeare as the representative of cultural equality and exchange predominated, although the extent to which this paradigm will continue to be valued outside of high profile, nationally appointed festive times remains an open question. In the long aftermath of the Games, London 2012's Olympic legacy seems poised to prove more symbolic than systematic in the way that it affects British cultural life, shaping the articulation of cultural values if not the lived experience of them.

Imagining legacy

One of the most immediate legacies of the Olympic year was an awareness of, and perhaps even obsession with, the idea of legacy itself. A year before the Games even began, British news outlets were already dubbing legacy 'the buzzword of the London 2012 Olympics', and in his interview for this book, Tom Bird, the Director of the Globe to Globe Festival, has called it 'the most overused word in the city' in 2012 (p. 57).[3] The potential vapidity of legacy-speak became a running joke on BBC 2's TV series *Twenty-twelve*, a mockumentary that aired in the UK in 2011–12 and depicted the travails of the fictional 'Olympic Deliverance Committee' as they attempted to organize the London Games. In several episodes characters from the committee struggled to articulate the difference between 'legacy' agendas and those of the equally woolly 'sustainability' department, resulting in a running gag that poked fun at the interchangeability of these indisputably worthy, but suspiciously opaque political ideals. By the end of the Olympic and Paralympic Games in August 2012, 'legacy' had become the word of choice for discussions about the collective value of the Olympic celebrations and their longer-term influence on British public life, a refrain that continued to draw critical attention to the concept of legacy itself and the expectations bound up in it.[4] In a playful deflation of the idea of the Olympics as a remedy for a wide range of social problems, Jonathan Liew of *The Telegraph* predicted that the phrase 'Olympic legacy' would eventually 'suffer the same fate as "political correctness": a nobly-conceived phraseology contorted and corrupted to such an extent that it is ultimately drained of all meaning'.[5]

While the language of legacy very likely reached its peak during the London Olympics, it's worth noting that it didn't actually originate there. In a 2008 article on 'legacy discourse', the Olympic historian John J. MacAloon argues that legacy-speak emerged in the early 2000s within the International Olympic Committee itself. Such language grew out of a need to accommodate but also conceal the growing emphasis within the IOC on the idea of an 'Olympic Brand', and the consumerist ideology that came with it:

[W]hile brand speech both evidenced and instrumentally furthered the penetration of managerial rationality in

Olympic institutions through the 1990s, its ineradicable association with a commercial base left it unable to spread across all functional areas and organizational networks in the Olympic system. That was to be the rather magical accomplishment of legacy discourse in the present decade.[6]

According to MacAloon, 'legacy discourse' is 'brand discourse' in a more palatable guise; it avoids the potential crassness of the language of marketing and commercialization while still encompassing its core principles – that the value of a product or experience does not derive solely from the thing itself, but also from the idea and story that surrounds it. As part of his critique of the power of legacy within IOC thinking, MacAloon tells the story of a consultant he met in Lausanne while he was working in the Olympic archives. The consultant was on a fact-finding mission for a prospective Olympic host country, and MacAloon was charged with giving him an introduction to the history of the modern Olympics and its underlying philosophy of 'Olympism' [outlined by Paul Prescott in his opening chapter for this volume]. What quickly became clear, however, was that the consultant was not in search of Olympic ideals, but of what he called the IOC's 'bottom line'. And much to MacAloon's dismay, it wasn't long before the consultant sniffed it out: '"Legacy," he reported back to his superiors, "the IOC is going to want to know about our legacy plan more than anything. Everyone says so".'[7]

In London, Olympic organizers seem to have learned to speak the crucial language of legacy in time for their 2005 bid – like Calibans to the IOC's Prospero, they mastered the prevailing discourse, and certainly profited on't. But whether or not this idiolect managed to retain its 'magical', panaceaic properties over the course of the 2012 Games is less certain. Its repeated use in political and public discourse, and the subsequent sending-up it received in the media and beyond, no doubt punctured its imaginative appeal – to indulge in a bit more PR and marketing-speak, we might say that legacy became overexposed. At the same time, it would be wrong to suggest that legacy as a concept and process was completely ineffectual, or devoid of any consequence. In the creation of legacy agendas, the pursuit of legacy targets, and the post-Games analysis of legacy impacts, we can see how the generation of a future Olympic inheritance was anything but spontaneous. As Vassil Girginov, another historian of the Olympics, has asserted, legacy is not 'a retrospective but a prospective concept', which must be anticipated and very often governed.[8] Legacies in this sense are designed, managed and ideally achieved. They are a set of aspirational and at times instrumental targets, wrapped in the language of promise.

If we want to understand 2012 Olympic legacies, then, we would do well to think of them in more practical and temporal terms, and to look more deeply into the processes underpinning them. MacAloon has pointed out that in the IOC's communications in French, its other official language, the favoured equivalent for legacy is *héritage*, a word that he describes as 'more encompassing and more weighted [...] toward the accumulated capital of the past arriving in the present'. The English 'legacy', on the other hand, is 'more narrowly specified – e.g. through its legal referents – and tilted toward the present's contribution to the future'.[9] This narrower, more legalistic side of legacy is also its explicitly economic side; in such contexts the word shifts from an abstract sense of inheritance (not just financial, but also cultural, spiritual or ideological) to a 'sum of money, or a specified article, given to another by will'.[10] Within the UK, this financially bound understanding of legacy coheres remarkably well with another favoured national and political discourse, that of 'value for money', which Louse Phillips has argued emerged in the 1980s as part of Thatcherism's 'spread of market principles into the public sector', and was in turn perpetuated by New Labour in the 1990s.[11]

Twenty years on, the powerful appeal of the language of investment and economy has not waned – if anything, decades of neoliberal politics and thinking have fully naturalized it – and the financial echoes underpinning legacy-talk help explain at least in part its ready take-up and proliferation during the 2012 Olympic period. The London Olympics eventually cost the state about £9 billion, and from beginning to end questions about their worth, specifically understood in economic terms, dominated public discussion. (A typical media headline from the run-up to the Games – 'London 2012: Taxpayers have "paid too much" for Olympics'.)[12] Legacy from this perspective becomes a way of explaining and justifying cost, both in terms of what organizers call 'hard' legacies, such as new buildings and facilities, and 'soft' ones, such as increased volunteerism and participation in sport. The UK's Prime Minister, David Cameron, even equated legacy with the economy itself, claiming that the London Games brought £9.9 billion into the UK in the form of increased trade and investment, resulting in a 'lasting business legacy [...] that will help make Britain a winner in the global race'. Such assertions were not without their critics, of course, and economist Tony Travers described Cameron's legacy claim as 'clearly a stylised interpretation' of a particular data set.[13] In doing so he drew attention to the role that narrative construction – that is, the 'anticipation of retrospection' – plays in any attempt to identify and articulate legacy dividends.[14]

But what, we might ask, does any of this have to do with Shakespeare? In some ways the playwright's prominence in London's Olympic festivities complicated the distinction MacAloon makes between past-oriented *héritage* and future-looking legacy. There's no doubt, for instance, that Shakespeare is deeply embedded in the UK's 'accumulated historical, cultural, and moral capital', an entity MacAloon imagines is valued by genteel *héritage*, but largely ignored by the instrumental demands of brash legacy. Such an observation might lead us to posit that Shakespeare managed to defy the worst of prescriptive legacy-construction, and by association brand-creation, by maintaining a connection to British cultural heritage, identity and the past. But bearing in mind Kate Rumbold's critique of the so-called 'Shakespeare brand', a concept that she suggests relies on the perpetuation of a perceived division between culture and commodity, we might likewise pause to consider how fixed the dichotomies of *héritage* and legacy, past and present, intrinsic value and created value truly are, especially for an entity as wide-ranging and unpredictable as what we might call Olympic Shakespeare.[15] MacAloon's own language suggests a way forward; in his use of the word 'capital' to describe the accumulated cultural and even moral wealth of an Olympic nation – its *héritage* – he returns us to the language of economics and its indelible presence in the way we understand cultural and social power.

In the remainder of this chapter I want to think about the legacy of Olympic Shakespeare along these lines, framing it within the temporally and economically oriented concepts of inheritance, investment, consolidation, speculation and pay-offs. In my use of such language I do not mean to suggest that events such as those staged as part of the Olympic Shakespeare celebrations, or indeed the Olympic Games more generally, are reducible to a bottom line – any public event involving thousands of people giving their time and commitment is always more than a financial exercise. At the same time, I do want to suggest that the cultural and communal festivities involved in an event the size of the Olympics are never fully separable from the financial and political imperatives that frame them. According to Theodor Adorno, 'Whoever speaks of culture speaks of administration as well, whether this is his intention or not', and we might also consider how speaking of culture and administration always involves speaking of money too.[16] Indeed, in her deconstruction of 'The Commercial Bard', Kathleen McLuskie has argued that the 'assimilation of Shakespeare and the valued arts of the past into the cultural logic of late capitalism requires a more complex account of competing values than the simple opposition between culture and commerce, or the more or less cynical or defiant rejection of one in favour of the other'.[17] In the discussion that follows I want to consider how both the metaphor and reality of economic thinking offers us a powerful way of working through the processes involved in the management and creation of the London Olympics' cultural legacy, particularly concerning Shakespeare, as well as what the future implications of such a legacy might be.

Consolidating culture

In a panel discussion with Shakespeare scholar Michael Dobson in June 2012, Deborah Shaw, the Artistic Director of the World Shakespeare Festival, explained how this strand of the Cultural Olympiad evolved alongside the London Games themselves:

> The genesis of this, of the World Shakespeare Festival, actually goes right back to the bid, the Olympic bid by London, and lots of excited people talking about what the cultural content might be, and someone saying, 'Of course Shakespeare's got to be in it!', and then someone talking to Michael Boyd – 'Would you be interested?' – and him saying, 'Yes! Of course we are!', and being totally thrilled about it because he didn't think it would ever happen.[18]

Of course, we know now that in 2005 the bid did prove successful (to the surprise of many – Paris had been the favourite), and with it began the long process of developing a Shakespeare-focused set of Olympic events. While it is significant that the playwright was in the minds of what would become LOCOG from the outset, it is perhaps not entirely surprising. As several chapters in this volume have shown, Shakespeare has long been the favourite author and artist when it comes to celebrating British achievement, and Dobson himself has explored the early history of this phenomenon in *The Making of the National Poet*. Since the time of Voltaire and Dr Johnson, he argues,

> Shakespeare has been as normatively constitutive of British national identity as the drinking of afternoon tea [...] This analogy may be less trivializing than it appears: the national habit of Shakespeare, after all, and the national habit of tea have their origins in exactly the same period of expanding trade abroad and vigorous nationalism at home [...] That Shakespeare was declared to rule world literature at the same time that Britannia was declared to rule the waves may, indeed, be more than a coincidence.[19]

That Shakespeare became the most consistently prominent cultural figure in London 2012's Olympic celebrations may well be, once again, more than just a coincidence. Though it took a little while for the World Shakespeare Festival to get off the ground, by 2008 it was officially one of the eight 'major projects' making up the Cultural Olympiad, and the only one to focus on a single, named artist.[20] Five years later, when the final budgets for the LOCOG-funded cultural activities had all been tallied, Shakespeare again came first. In a table of 88 events and programmes funded by LOCOG, only eight entries exceeded £1 million and only two surpassed £2 million. Of these two, the highest was the amount allocated to the RSC – £3,365,697 – and when this is combined with the £514,040 allocated separately to the Globe, as well as further funding secured by each institution, the total cost of the World Shakespeare and Globe to Globe Festivals came to £5.996 million. It was the highest expenditure across the entire Cultural Olympiad, demonstrating in fairly clear financial terms the size of the investment made in Shakespeare during the Olympic year.[21]

Still, the biggest and most visible of all of Shakespeare's Olympic contributions would be the presence of *The Tempest* in three of the four ceremonies that opened and closed the Olympic and Paralympic Games.[22] With their own budget of £80 million, and with by far the greatest viewing audiences worldwide (the figure for the Olympics Opening Ceremony alone has been estimated at 900 million), these ceremonies really did represent, in the words of the London 2012 slogan, a 'once in a lifetime' opportunity for the UK to say something important about itself to the world.[23] Jenny Sealey, the director of the Paralympic Opening Ceremony, suggested in an interview that the mutual attraction among the ceremony directors to Shakespeare and *The Tempest* was a sort of magical kismet: 'All of us went to the Tempest [sic] for inspiration. It is also my favourite play. There's a theme of the Tempest [sic] going through all the ceremonies, which was a coincidence.'[24] But even if the directors were indeed independently drawn to *The Tempest* as they planned their respective events (and it does seem hard to believe), the fact that Shakespeare appeared so frequently and so deliberately across the cultural programming for the Olympics, so much so that he made the crucial crossover into the sporting arena via the ceremonies, also suggests an inevitability of inclusion that few, if any, other British cultural figures enjoy (the possible co-candidates being the Beatles, Winston Churchill and, for the present moment at least, Harry Potter).

Within the context of large but potentially diffuse events such as the Cultural Olympiad, this kind of inevitability, and the weightiness that comes with it, can play an important role in helping to consolidate cultural festivities. Much of the existing literature on the role of arts and culture within Olympic celebrations focuses on their limited visibility – rather understandably, people associate the Olympics with sports, with very few even realizing that a cultural component is present.[25] Organizing a concurrent cultural programme has been a mandatory part of the modern Olympic Games since their inception in 1896, with founder Pierre de Coubertin seeing 'sport, culture and education' as the three essential elements making up Olympism's focus on 'harmonious balance between body, will and mind'.[26] Nevertheless, researchers working on the Olympics have consistently identified a lack of awareness among the wider public concerning the existence of an Olympic cultural programme, at least one that extends beyond the extremely high-profile ceremonies and torch relay (the latter having had its origins in the 1936 Berlin Olympics, discussed by both Stuart Hampton-Reeves and Tony Howard in this volume).[27] In his account of 'the curious history of the relations between arts, culture and sports at the Olympics', David Inglis has drawn attention to the 'strange paradox' of the Cultural Olympiad: while 'the cultural dimension of Olympiads has expanded greatly in the last two decades, the media and public presence of this dimension has become ever more fragmented'.[28] Such fragmentation, he suggests, also means low visibility and low impact, a point seconded by Beatriz García: 'the more dispersed an activity is, the more difficult it is to ensure that the programme is widely visible, recognized and impacting on a large scale'.[29]

One way to bring greater coherence and attention to cultural programming is to consolidate events both geographically and temporally – something the four-year Cultural Olympiad did end up doing with its London 2012 Festival, which was the London-based finale that ran just before and then during the Olympic Games.[30] But to consolidate too much in this way would be to pull against other London Olympic priorities, including staging a set of celebrations that was accessible to UK citizens across the entire country and that helped make the Olympics into something greater, and longer, than one explosive summer of fun. Another tack, then, and one much commented upon by Cultural Olympiad researchers and programmers, was through the use of concerted branding practices across events, including in particular the use of the official Olympic logo. Historically this has been more difficult than it sounds, due to the heavy restrictions placed on the use of the Olympic rings by non-commercial sponsors. As a result, most recent Cultural Olympiads have had a separate logo to identify them, but the London Games worked to circumvent this by developing a shared logo that included the rings within it without being fundamentally dependent on them. Instead, the logo was based on the numbers '2012', with the space in the '0' able to be filled by the rings, the Paralympic 'agitos' (rather incredibly, the London Games were the first to allow the Paralympics to have essentially the same logo as the Olympics), or, in the case of the cultural arm, left empty and accompanied by the word 'Festival' along the logo's right side (see Figure 14).[31] In her role as cultural advisor to the 2012 Olympics, García pointed to the creation of this 'One Logo Family' as a key step in the quest to put 'culture at the heart of the Games': 'This was the first time in a Games edition

FIGURE 14 *The London 2012 Olympic, Paralympic and Festival logos. Reproduced courtesy of the International Olympic Committee, the International Paralympic Committee and the Arts Council England.*

that the Cultural Olympiad visual identity was exclusively a variation on the main Games logo rather than a different pictogram. The concept of culture at the heart of the Games was therefore reinforced through integrated and highly visible branding'.[32]

Logo use was the most explicit attempt towards brand consolidation during the Olympics, but the use of other highly recognizable assets or 'brands', including Shakespeare, became another important way of injecting coherence and thus visibility into the cultural festivities. By anchoring a major strand of Olympiad programming in the celebration of Shakespeare, as well as creating a Shakespearean refrain that ran throughout the majority of the ceremonies (including kicking everything off by ringing a *Tempest*-inscribed Olympic Bell), organizers assembled more Olympic attention around Shakespeare than any other cultural figure. It is perhaps understandable, then, that in the arts magazine *The Stage*'s special issue on the London 2012 Festival (published 7 June 2012, and thus well before the content of the Olympic ceremonies had been revealed), Shakespeare featured front and centre. On the cover, Harry Venning's cartoon illustration showed five cultural figures – a mime, a clown, a ventriloquist, a ballerina and Shakespeare – taking their marks on an Olympic racetrack as thousands of anonymous spectators looked on from the surrounding stadium (Figure 15). Slightly smirking at the centre of the otherwise nervous group was Shakespeare, as if he had already won the race, and inside the magazine he certainly proved dominant. Five headlined articles discussed the London 2012 Festival's Shakespearean offerings, with one of them, a two-page spread featuring an interview with Festival Director Ruth Mackenzie, beginning with the line, 'There's no doubt that Shakespeare is the jewel in the crown of the London 2012 Festival'. Two paragraphs later, the sentiment was reiterated, this time with a greater sense of inevitability: 'The truth is that, unavoidably for many reasons, Shakespeare is the core of the London 2012 Festival's drama programming'.[33]

FIGURE 15 *Harry Venning's cover image for* The Stage's *special issue on the London 2012 Festival, published 7 June 2012. Reproduced with the permission of Harry Venning.*

In the end, this drama programming also made up the bulk of the Festival itself, constituting 32 per cent of the summer's cultural Olympic offerings. (Music came next at 21 per cent, and visual arts at 17 per cent.)[34] And Shakespeare was indeed the most prominent player, especially once his extended role in the ceremonies became apparent. In *The Civic Culture*, Gabriel

A. Almond and Sidney Verba argue that in order for a nation 'to create a civic culture', it must have 'a symbolic event, or a symbolic, charismatic leader' around which to gather.[35] What Shakespeare seems to have offered programmers across the Cultural Olympiad was the opportunity to represent, in a single, highly recognizable figure, a vision of Britain that transcended temporal boundaries, seamlessly uniting the value of past *héritage* with the future prospects of legacy. Speaking to the *Guardian*, Stephen Daldry, the overarching Creative Director for the four Olympic and Paralympic Ceremonies, characterized the significance of Shakespeare and *The Tempest* in such atemporal terms: 'It is a journey that will celebrate who we are, who we were and indeed who we wish to be'.[36] Though a different form of timelessness than that invoked by Ben Jonson in the First Folio ('not of an age, but for all time'), this idea of Shakespeare being able to bring together Britain's past, present and future in a single moment presented organizers with a unique opportunity to harness the value of the appeal of a merrie England past, while still locating British identity and culture resolutely in the present.

Shakespearean speculation

Such acts of consolidation – whether in terms of British cultural and economic capital, festival programming or British identity itself – were a key part of the legacy-making process in the Olympic year. They reflected a drawing together of the UK's existing cultural inheritance, and a determination not to lose any of this wealth through a potentially fragmentary and dispersed series of celebrations. But capital isn't created through consolidation, only protected. In order to generate new cultural wealth, and to produce legacy bequests arising specifically from the Olympic celebrations, programmers also had to speculate. The main way this speculation manifested itself was through the decision to present London first and foremost as a diverse, energetic and global capital, made strong by its past but not defined by it. In their analysis of the London Olympic bid, John and Margaret Gold have shown how this future-oriented, and we might also say speculative, approach to the presentation of the UK's capital city had already taken shape by 2004–5:

> The bid strove hard to offer a rebranding of London away from being identified by its historic heritage to that of a diverse city with a vibrancy based on its multiculturalism. Much was made of London's diverse ethnic identities and the multicultural character of the five 'Olympic boroughs' in the East End [...] The theme of the world coming to London to meet the world was carefully fostered in marketing the notion of 2012 and, indeed, was tellingly picked up in the presentation made at the IOC's final selection meeting [...][37]

Such a theme was also picked up in the subsequent development of several strands of Olympic programming, including much of the Cultural Olympiad. It is not hard to see how the slogans for the World Shakespeare and Globe to Globe Festivals echoed this message, describing themselves respectively as 'a celebration of Shakespeare as the world's playwright', and a celebration in which 'Shakespeare's coming home'. Consciously or not, these taglines played directly upon and bettered the earlier positioning of him as 'the national poet', releasing him into a geographically unbounded space and, ideally, taking the UK with him. In this way Shakespeare – described by Boris Johnson, Mayor of London, as the country's 'greatest cultural export', representative of a time 'when this country was a boom nation leading trade around the globe and setting the foundations for modern England' – could be celebrated not just as a heritage treasure from the past, but as a form of usable currency that was still existing and thriving in the global marketplace today.[38]

I am calling this process a kind of cultural 'speculation',

but we might also describe it as 'innovation', a concept that Emily Linnemann has shown has particular traction within the world of cultural economics: 'The process of innovation is assumed to be radical and risky, but, most importantly, value-generative. It is thus part of an idealized process of production which ensures both aesthetic excellence and cultural value creation.'[39] Such acts of innovation, Linnemann writes, do not involve departing entirely from existing cultural wealth, but rather 'rework[ing] and redefin[ing]' it by 'embrac[ing] new technologies and new working methods'.[40] And chief among such new and value-creating methods for Shakespeare was the incorporation of intercultural art forms and languages. While Linnemann's 2011 analysis focuses largely on the foreign-language offerings in the RSC's 2006–7 Complete Works Festival, the insights she offers there apply just as well, if not even better, to the 2012 Olympic Shakespeare celebrations. Of the 73 stage and television productions created for the Olympic year, 47 of them were performed either entirely or largely in languages other than English. This means that, in the end, roughly 65 per cent of the Olympic Shakespeare offerings were non-Anglophone – a significant departure from Shakespeare's usual presentation in the UK, to say the least.[41]

Such an achievement, and indeed risk, should not be underestimated. While other UK-based theatre festivals have included international and non-English Shakespeare productions, they have remained a distinct minority. The RSC's Complete Works Festival included eight foreign-language productions among 37 Anglophone ones, and Elinor Parsons has argued that on the whole these non-English offerings 'suffered [...] from somewhat apologetic publicity and cursory evaluation. Responses fluctuated between wary suspicion of what was alien and enthusiastic acclaim for what seemed new.'[42] This is not to say that the organizers of the Complete Works Festival weren't enthusiastic about producing Shakespeare in languages beyond English; in an interview for the journal *Cahiers Élisabéthains*, then RSC Artistic Director Michael Boyd picked Luk Perceval and Münchner Kammerspiele's German reworking of *Othello* as one of his Festival favourites, noting that RSC collaborations with Perceval were set to continue.[43] But while theatre organizers may have been supportive of these more innovative, and speculative, productions, the wider audience reception was less affirming. Perceval's *Othello*, for instance, received a four-star, glowing review from the *Guardian* newspaper's Michael Billington, but reports of audience walk-outs plagued the production's short, four-night run. Indeed, in his own (very positive) review of the production, Peter Kirwan included a comment overheard from an audience member sitting nearby: 'Where do we queue to get our money back for THAT rubbish?'[44]

Of course, each production, foreign or otherwise, must be taken in part on its own terms, and it is certainly the case that questions of translation were compounded with questions of adaptation in the critical response to Perceval's *Othello*. Featuring a new, expletive-ridden translation by Turkish-German writer Feridun Zaimoglu, a white actor (Thomas Thieme) playing Othello, and a highly conceptual set and jazz soundscape, the production challenged traditional expectations of Shakespeare in ways that went beyond its language.[45] But it is worth noting that, six years later, several of the foreign-language productions in the 2012 Globe to Globe and World Shakespeare Festivals also blurred the uncertain distinction between translation and adaptation, or 'straight' Shakespeare and Shakespeare 'reworked': the Italian *Julius Caesar* removed the character of Caesar and represented him symbolically as an empty chair, the Nigerian *Winter's Tale* started the story in Bohemia and replaced the kings and queens with gods and goddesses, the Iraqi *Romeo and Juliet in Baghdad* had the lovers die from a suicide bomber's blast, and the Chinese *Richard III* included a trio of witches more familiar to productions of *Macbeth*.[46] Charles Spencer's complaint in 2006 that Perceval and the Complete Works Festival organizers were 'buggering about with the Bard' could have easily been levelled at these 2012 productions as well.[47]

So the question we are left with is why did the 2012

speculation on foreign Shakespeare work in a way that the 2006 did not? One answer comes from the context of the Festival and its performances. As has already been mentioned, the global emphasis of the Festival very much matched that of the wider Olympic celebrations, resulting in an overarching concept that framed how these productions might be situated and understood. Within the context of the Olympics, an international, multilingual celebration of Shakespeare seems to have made more sense to many audience members than it would have done at any other time. This did not, of course, completely silence potential critiques; in a response to a preview article on the Globe to Globe Festival featured in the *Guardian*, one commenter wrote, 'So much of Shakespeare depends on the language and the blank verse that I have some doubts on the advantages of presenting it to English speaking audiences in foreign languages'.[48]

But this emphasis on audiences offers further insights; more so than in the Complete Works Festival, many of the World Shakespeare and Globe to Globe Festivals' non-English performances took place in parts of the UK where the performance language was actually spoken, meaning that what was supposedly foreign proved quite the opposite for many audience members – and perhaps nowhere more so than in the National Eisteddfod and North Wales performances of *Y Storm / The Tempest*. This was also frequently the case for the Globe to Globe Festival's performances in south London, where organizers sought to match performance languages with existing language communities in the city. While we will likely never know the exact demographics of these audiences, Rose Elfman and Stephen Purcell's research on the Festival, as well as the anecdotal evidence offered in production reviews and the *Year of Shakespeare* project's collection of audience responses, shows that people able to understand the performance languages were attending these productions in noticeable numbers and finding the artistic experience on offer anything but alienating. As one woman who attended the Nigerian *Winter's Tale* at the Globe wrote: 'It was an amazing night. As an early thirties Yoruba girl, it was glorious to see so many of my contemporaries in the audience and loving the interaction between so many different generations.'[49]

Of course, the presence of audience members who speak the performance language doesn't mean that those who aren't fluent in it magically start to understand what is being said, and it's clear that non-speakers of the performance language also attended these productions in significant numbers. But both Elfman and Purcell have shown in their chapters how language speakers' reactions to moments in performance repeatedly helped guide, focus and inform the perceptions of non-speakers, reshaping the kind of theatrical experience ultimately produced. This is perhaps nowhere more the case than in a theatre like the Globe, where the audience is not only audible but also visible to one another, and where close to half of those in attendance may be standing and indeed moving. The result is something more akin to the performance dynamics of a music gig or festival than a typical night at the theatre in the UK. Being able to see how others were responding to the performance event, especially if that response was different from one's own, almost certainly influenced the reception of the non-speaking audience members, not least in the case of the theatre critics. It is telling that all but one of the productions in the Globe to Globe Festival received at least three stars from reviewers at the *Guardian* (the only major British newspaper to cover almost all of the Festival), with many receiving four and even five stars – a critical reception that few seasons of Shakespeare in English might hope to enjoy. Some might read this as indicative of the inherently high quality of the productions, others as a sign of the reviewers' anxious rush towards political correctness, and others still as an attempt on the newspaper's part to show some kind of return on the time and energy they speculated in covering the productions – and each of these interpretations was voiced freely in the online comments under many of the paper's reviews. But I would suggest that it was most centrally a result of the reviewers responding not just to the performance on stage, but also to its reception among audience members, and in particular language speakers, whose very presence and cultural knowledge unsettled traditional assumptions about expertise and authority in the theatre space.

In addition to the context of the 2012 Festival's speculation on global Shakespeare was the size of its investment. The sheer amount of foreign Shakespeare on offer meant that attention focused not just on the particular, but also the aggregate. In the case of Globe to Globe, which included 36 productions in languages other than English, those productions that were not as warmly received in the press or by audiences could blend into the more generally positive reception of the Festival as a whole. More conceptually abstract productions, such as the Italian *Julius Caesar*, the Japanese *Coriolanus* or the German *Timon of Athens*, received mixed and often befuddled responses from critics and audience members alike, including one non-German speaker at *Timon* who remarked that 'the surtitles were really unhelpful and I missed out on most of the ad-libs as I was completely unable to understand the language [...] The Gloria Gaynor, the Trampoline, the skateboard; without an understudying of the language they felt a bit like empty props.'[50] In her response she further noted that she left at the interval, with the hope that she'd get more from the English-language production of *Timon* playing at the National Theatre later in the summer (also part of the 2012 Festival). Such a response was not at all dissimilar to those elicited by Perceval's *Othello* in 2006 at the RSC; the crucial difference, however, was that the scale of foreign Shakespeare within the Globe to Globe Festival and its positive overall reception meant that such critiques became less audible and less influential in the combined narrative, and legacy, of what the Festival achieved. The fact that the Globe went on to win a special Critics' Circle Award in 2013 for the Festival as a whole – despite the fact that comparatively few critics actually went to its productions – reinforced the sense that the dominant unit of evaluation for the project was the entire Festival, as opposed to its constituent parts.[51] This was less the case for the RSC's 2012 foreign-language shows, whose performances were geographically and temporally more spread out, meaning that the productions more often had to stand (or fall) on their own, and for audiences that were less likely to include language speakers. The critical reception of these productions was accordingly more diffuse, and their speculative efforts arguably less effective.

But beyond these infrastructural, institutional and geographical factors that helped make the overall 2012 speculation on foreign Shakespeare pay off, there is the wider and seemingly inevitable fact that in almost all facets of life 'the global' has become an increasingly pressing reality in the past several years. Most influential in the daily experience of the global, I would suggest, has been the dramatic proliferation of smartphones and their associated technologies since the introduction of the iPhone in June 2007 – just two months after the close of the Complete Works Festival. Academic engagement with the global as a cultural force has also accelerated over the past decade, and a quick search in the World Shakespeare Bibliography catalogue offers a rough illustration of it within the field of Shakespeare studies: from 1990–9 the word 'global' comes up as a keyword for 26 publications, but from 2000–9 it nearly quintuples to 127 hits, the majority of which are concentrated in the latter part of the decade.[52] The emergence of digital archives of foreign-language Shakespeare performance, such as Global Shakespeares (globalshakespeares.mit.edu) and the Asian Shakespeare Intercultural Archive [A|S|I|A] (a-s-i-a-web.org), which include full-length video recordings of non-English Shakespeare productions, has made access to global Shakespeare increasingly immediate and indeed familiar. For academics, at least, the 2012 Festivals came at a time in which thinking about Shakespeare beyond his native language had already gained considerable momentum, helping encourage receptivity to and interest in such a project. The timing, context and level of investment in foreign Shakespeare in 2012 were all more conducive for greater pay-offs and more significant legacies than those produced by previous celebrations of his works' global dispersal.

The dividends

I started this chapter by drawing attention to the prescriptive nature of legacy-formation, both in terms of its bureaucratic planning and its reliance on narrative interpretation. And having come close to its end, I am now faced with the prospect of participating in this act of projection myself. As is the case for the Olympics more generally, identifying the hard legacies is easier than the soft ones. The most obvious of these come again from the Globe, which launched follow-on Globe to Globe seasons in 2013 and 2014 featuring return performances from four of the 2012 foreign-language productions (the Georgian *As You Like It*, Belarusian *King Lear*, South African *Venus and Adonis* and Gujarati *All's Well that Ends Well*), as well as three new ones (a French-Indian *Tempest*, a British Sign Language *Dream* and a Spanish production of Lope de Vega's *Punishment without Revenge*).[53] Several other visiting companies involved in the Festival have also toured their productions in their home countries and beyond, a point that applies to both the Globe's Festival offerings and those produced by the RSC.[54]

The Globe has also continued working with the digital arts broadcaster, The Space (www.TheSpace.org), a free, online 'pop-up' channel which began during the London 2012 Festival period and included high-quality recordings of most of the Globe to Globe productions (but not, controversially, the Globe's own *Henry V*, presumably due to more restrictive UK rights issues). Of all the theatres involved in the 2012 Shakespeare festivities, the Globe was the only one to broadcast full-length recordings regularly on The Space (re-launched in an enhanced, more permanent form in 2014), and it was also the only one to do so again after the close of the Olympic celebrations.[55] Perhaps most ambitious of all has been the theatre's Globe to Globe *Hamlet* project, which involves taking a touring production of the play to every country in the world between April 2014 and April 2016 – an enterprise that has once again attracted considerable political debate, this time for the theatre's commitment to touring even in countries such as North Korea.[56] Of all the institutions involved in the Olympic Shakespeare celebrations, the Globe both ventured and gained the most, and it is possible that 2012 will prove the year in which its cultural status shifted from an important player in the UK classical theatre scene to one of its leaders. Mark Shenton, chair of the 2013 Critics' Circle drama committee and a London-based theatre critic, certainly said as much: 'The Globe to Globe season was a one-off, once-in-a-lifetime event that changed the cultural landscape of London theatreland in every sense [...] Together with the Stage's naming of it as the London theatre of the year in its own Stage 100 awards, the Globe is now the leading place to celebrate our greatest playwright'.[57]

Beyond the UK, and more in the Olympic vein, the Instituto Gandarela in Brazil has also announced plans to construct a 1599 Globe theatre near the city of Belo Horizonte, about 200 miles from Rio de Janeiro, host of the 2016 summer Olympics. Plans are afoot not only for the building of the theatre itself but also for the organization of a Globe to Globe-style season of Shakespeare, ideally timed to complement the 2016 Olympic celebrations. (As with so many Olympic ventures, however, there are questions as to whether or not the building works will be completed in time.) No doubt organizers there will have their own way of articulating the playwright's relevance and significance in twenty-first-century Brazilian society. Early publicity materials have stressed the value not of Shakespeare in and of himself, but rather the importance of using him and his theatre to meet the needs of communities dominated by mining industries, and to create new 'socio-educational and employment opportunities' for the region more generally. 'Do not search here [... for] the theater's greatest playwright in the world', the English version of the Instituto's website warned in 2013. Instead, look for 'a cultural development [... that] allows a close encounter with the audience [... and] a rapport that leads to numerous cultural opportunities to rethink artistic and educational innovation'.[58]

These forms of 'innovation' will continue to be of interest to Shakespeare scholars in the coming years, and perhaps also to government policy makers. In May 2013, Professor Alex Huang addressed the US Congress on the topic of funding for the humanities, focusing specifically on how the translation, performance and study of Shakespeare across cultures might be used as a way of 'addressing national security and other global challenges through cultural understanding'.[59] Around the same time, the universities of Queen Mary and Warwick announced plans for a global Shakespeare research centre, which likewise aims to consider how 'Shakespeare in non-traditional contexts' might be used to address political issues such as 'social cohesion, literacy, leadership and intercultural understandings'.[60] As with global history, global economics, global media and global culture, the study of global Shakespeare is now enjoying a surge in interest that looks set to continue for at least the coming decade.[61]

But what about the UK and its culture? What might the wider, and softer, cultural legacies be for this country, particularly as it moves squarely into the morning after phase of its Olympic festivities? There's little doubt that the 2012 celebrations reaffirmed Shakespeare's status as a metonym for Britishness, although what that metonym signals seems to have shifted. The triumphalism of Rule Britannia has faded – even the BBC's Shakespeare Unlocked season of history plays shied away from shows of British might – and has been replaced with a less colonial, though equally political, message of equality and diversity. In this sense Shakespeare continues to play an important part in the production of British 'soft power', an entity the political scientist Joseph Nye has defined as the 'attractiveness of a country's culture, political ideals, and policies', and the international power and influence that comes with it.[62] Indeed, a few months after the close of the Olympics, the UK won top position in the magazine the *Monocle*'s annual 'Global Soft Power' survey, a historic first in a contest consistently dominated by the US. And in the spring of 2013 the House of Lords established a select committee headed by Lord Howell of Guildford (Director of Shakespeare's Globe from 1999–2010) intended to 'examine the use of soft power in furthering the United Kingdom's global influence and interests'.[63]

Still, whether or not Britain's soft power message of multicultural acceptance and celebration will survive beyond the festive time of the Olympics remains very much an open question. In January 2013 Steve Bell, cartoonist for the *Guardian*, resurrected the most prominent Olympic Shakespeare set piece – Caliban's 'The isle is full of noises' speech – to send up MEP Nigel Farage, the current leader of the right-wing, Eurosceptic UK Independence Party (UKIP). In this staging of Farage's 'Caliban moment', Bell's absurdist style drew attention to the delusive patriotism of the anti-immigration and arguably anti-diversity UKIP party, as it stood stridently abreast the 'horseless carriage' that was David Cameron's Britain (Figure 16).[64] In choosing Caliban's Olympic speech, recited as a mindless pledge by Farage amid the idle honking of nearby geese, Bell also raised the question of the significance and indeed legacy of the ideals celebrated during the Olympic period, chief among them cultural diversity and toleration.

The fact that UKIP policymaking might not embrace such ideals probably wouldn't strike many *Guardian* readers in the UK as particularly surprising. Although the party has worked hard in recent years to present itself as a more moderately conservative political force, its history and public image are still very much linked to a protectionist and traditionalist stance that borders on racism (exemplified by MEP Godfrey Bloom's comments about foreign aid being wastefully sent to 'Bongo Bongo Land' in the summer of 2013).[65] More surprising, however, was the increasingly hostile stance the ruling Conservative party took on immigration over the

OLYMPIC SHAKESPEARE AND THE IDEA OF LEGACY 309

FIGURE 16 'Nigel Farage's Caliban Moment' by Steve Bell, published in the Guardian on 30 January 2013. Reproduced with the permission of Steve Bell and Belltoons.

course of 2013 and into 2014. A few months after the close of the London Olympics, the thinktank British Future published a report indicating that one in three Britons saw tensions between native Britons and immigrants as the most significant cause of social division in the country.[66] While the survey did not indicate that those questioned thought stricter policing of immigration was necessarily the solution, the governing party certainly seemed to interpret it as such. Timed almost perfectly to coincide with the one-year anniversary of the Olympics, and thus an especially concentrated period of media coverage concerning the question of legacy, officials at the UK Home Office intensified efforts to eliminate so-called immigration loopholes and round up visa over-stayers across the country. Such measures included spot checks at public transport stations where immigration officers requested the identity papers of select travellers, seemingly based on ethnicity; the use of an advertising van driven throughout London that targeted illegal immigrants and featured the phrase 'GO HOME OR FACE ARREST' (Figure 17); and running Twitter updates on 1 August detailing raids on alleged illegal immigrants with links to photos of suspects being rounded up into police vans. (Two examples among many from the @ukhomeoffice feed: 'A total of 139 suspected #immigrationoffenders have been arrested in raids across the UK today bit.ly/13y0CvT', 'A suspected visa overstayer arrested at Swansea nail bar – 94 suspected #immigrationoffenders arrested across UK pic.twitter.com/aoBAXAHVJB'.)[67]

Such acts were widely condemned by UK citizens, journalists and human rights organizations, many of which argued that undercurrents of racism motivated the initiatives. And in a rather surprising volte-face, Farage himself spoke out against the use of the 'go home' vans, describing them as 'Big Brother, nasty [... and] unpleasant'.[68] The Equality and Human Rights Commission accordingly opened up an enquiry into the legality of immigration spot checks, and the labour union Unite sought similar guidance about the immigration vans.[69] Just a year after the close of the Games, cultural

FIGURE 17 *The UK Home Office's 'Go Home' van driving through the streets of London. Photograph by Alain Tolhurst and reproduced with his permission.*

and political attitudes towards immigration, integration and cultural diversity in the UK appeared to be at their lowest point in a decade.

Within the narrower world of Shakespeare and the arts, questions of ethnic diversity and immigration have been less polemically volatile, but the practical realities of cultural integration have nevertheless remained fraught. In a recent article on the status of colourblind casting in Shakespeare productions, Jami Rogers has called into question the openness of UK theatres to employing black, Asian and other non-white actors in both regional and major West End London productions, and directly after the close of the World Shakespeare Festival the RSC itself attracted considerable public and media scrutiny for its staging of the Chinese play *The Orphan of Zhao* with only a small proportion of East Asian actors, none of whom played a major role. (Others pointed out that the RSC had a few months earlier staged productions of *Much Ado about Nothing* and *Julius Caesar* with entirely British South Asian and black casts, showing a commitment to inclusive casting.)[70] While it would be wrong to suggest that the British theatre industry has been more troubled by questions of racial access and equality than other UK professional sectors (including higher education), these recent events and analyses have demonstrated that it is not immune from such issues either.

Taken together, such findings offer a rather mixed view of what the sum total of the Olympic Shakespeare inheritance is proving to be. On the one hand, it is highly likely that we will continue to see a growth in global Shakespeare, not just in the context of intercultural celebration, but also increasingly in mainstream theatre seasons, academic curricula and political discourse. The individual, idiosyncratic and long-term effects of such initiatives may indeed be rich; Globe to Globe Director Tom Bird is in a sense himself a legacy of the RSC's historic tenure at Newcastle, which as he suggests in his interview for this volume helped shape his eventual career path. We will have to wait and see what personal passions and legacies the celebration of global Shakespeare in the Olympic year may have inspired, and how they may repay British culture and society in the future. But on a wider, more collective level, it seems less likely that 2012's ideological, artistic and economic investment in an inclusive and diverse Britain will eventually translate – or, to pursue the financial metaphors of this chapter, convert – into a more everyday, integrated and accepted presence of actors, audiences and citizens from a wide variety of cultural backgrounds. Legacy cannot live on language, rhetoric and symbolism alone – it actually needs long-term financing, and practical policymaking, to thrive. And while the UK did indeed manage to sustain a cultural budget within the Olympics that has historically been cannibalized by sporting and infrastructural spending, it has not been able to maintain the cash flow or ideological goodwill needed to continue to support many of its legacy ideals in the aftermath of the Games.[71] What's left, the morning after, is the memory of the legacy that was planned, articulated and celebrated during the party itself – admittedly fabulous – and the hope that such memories have their own value and power in the absence of hard cash.

Notes

1 'Singapore Presentation – 6 July 2005', London 2012 documents archive, http://www.london2012.com/mm/Document/aboutus/General/01/22/85/87/singapore-presentation-speeches.pdf [accessed 21 June 2013].

2 Andrew Culf, 'Legacy is central to 2012, says Coe', *Guardian*, 6 May 2006, http://www.guardian.co.uk/sport/2006/may/04/Olympics2012.politics [accessed 23 July 2013].

3 Simon Hunter, 'London 2012: Where is Northern Ireland's legacy?', *BBC News*, 27 July 2011, http://www.bbc.co.uk/news/uk-northern-ireland-14310859 [accessed 21 June 2013].

4 See for instance David Conn, 'London 2012 euphoria has died, but will the Olympic legacy live on?', *Guardian*, 12 August 2012, http://www.guardian.co.uk/uk/2012/aug/14/london-2012-olympic-legacy [accessed 21 June 2013].

5 Jonathan Liew, 'Tom Daley's ITV1 reality show Splash! Is an undignified leap in the right direction for London 2012 Olympic legacy', *Telegraph*, 14 January 2013, http://www.telegraph.co.uk/sport/olympics/diving/9799166/Tom-Daleys-ITV1-reality-show-Splash-is-an-undignified-leap-in-the-right-direction-for-London-2012-Olympic-legacy.html [accessed 21 June 2013].

6 John J. MacAloon, '"Legacy" as Managerial/Magical Discourse in Contemporary Olympic Affairs', *International Journal of the History of Sport*, 25:14 (2008), pp. 2060–71 (p. 2062).

7 Ibid., pp. 2063–4. See also John R. Gold and Margaret M. Gold, 'Introduction', in *Olympic Cities: City Agendas, Planning and the World's Games*, Gold and Gold (eds) (Abingdon: Routledge, 2008), pp. 1–16 (pp. 2–7).

8   Vassil Girginov, 'Governance of the London 2012 Olympic Games Legacy', *International Review for the Sociology of Sport*, 47:5 (2012), pp. 543–58 (pp. 543–4).

9   MacAloon, '"Legacy" as Managerial/Magical Discourse', p. 2067.

10 'legacy, n, 5a', *Oxford English Dictionary*, http://www.oed.com [accessed 21 June 2013].

11 Louse Phillips, 'Hegemony and Political Discourse: The Lasting Impact of Thatcherism', *Sociology*, 32:4 (1998), pp. 847–67 (p. 855). Several sociologists have suggested that the language of neoliberalism is also directly connected to the modern practice of 'nation branding', of which the Olympics is no doubt a major part. See Somogy Varga, 'The Politics of Nation Branding: Collective Identity and Public Sphere in the Neoliberal State', *Philosophy and Social Criticism*, 39:8 (2013), pp. 825–45; Zala Volcic and Mark Andrejevic, 'Nation branding in the era of commercial nationalism', *International Journal of Communication*, 5 (2011), pp. 598–618 (pp. 600–3).

12 *BBC Sport*, 18 April 2012, http://www.bbc.co.uk/sport/0/olympics/17753800 [accessed 21 June 2013].

13 Both quoted in Roger Blitz, 'Olympics 2012: Cameron's claims over economic legacy questioned', *Financial Times*, 21 July 2013, http://www.ft.com/cms/s/0/009f532a-f207-11e2-8e04-00144feabdc0.html#axzz2ZtyhvQR3 [accessed 23 July 2013].

14 Peter Brooks, *Reading for the Plot: Design and Intention in Narrative* (Cambridge: Harvard University Press, 1992), p. 23. My great thanks to Richard Meek for reminding me of this description.

15 Kate Rumbold, 'Brand Shakespeare?', *Shakespeare Survey 64* (2011), pp. 25–37.

16 Theodor Adorno, *The Culture Industry: Selected Essays on Mass Culture* (London: Routledge, 2001), p. 107.

17 Kathleen McLuskie, 'The Commercial Bard: Business Models for the Twenty-First Century', *Shakespeare Survey 64* (2011), pp. 1–12 (p. 12).

18 Deborah Shaw in conversation with Michael Dobson, plenary

at the British Graduate Shakespeare Conference, Shakespeare
Institute, Stratford-upon-Avon, 15 June 2012, audio recording
available at http://backdoorbroadcasting.net/2012/06/the-2012-
british-graduate-shakespeare-conference/ [accessed 21 June
2013].

19 Michael Dobson, *The Making of the National Poet:
Shakespeare, Adaptation and Authorship* (Oxford: Oxford
University Press, 1992), p. 7.

20 'Reflections on the Cultural Olympiad and London 2012
Festival', Arts Council England, 25 April 2013, http://www.
artscouncil.org.uk/media/uploads/pdf/Reflections_on_the_
Cultural_Olympiad_and_London_2012_Festival_pdf.pdf,
pp. 20–1 [accessed 23 July 2013].

21 'Cultural Olympiad Board, 12th March 2013, Finance Report',
obtained through a Freedom of Information request to the
UK's Department of Culture, Media and Sport (15 October
2013). These figures come from 'Appendix 1: Expenditure
managed direct by LOCOG', p. 8, and 'Appendix 3: Activities
receiving some or all of funding through LOCOG', p. 10.
Three other major Cultural Olympiad strands were close to the
WSF total – Film Nation (£5.722), Discovering Places (£5.308)
and River of Music (£5.05m) – though their expenditures were
spread more broadly across multiple projects and institutions.

22 For a more detailed account of Shakespeare's presence in these
ceremonies, see Erin Sullivan, 'Olympic Performance in the
Year of Shakespeare', in *A Year of Shakespeare: Re-living the
World Shakespeare Festival*, Paul Edmondson, Paul Prescott
and Erin Sullivan (eds) (London: Bloomsbury, 2013), pp. 3–11
(pp. 3–7).

23 'London 2012 Olympic ceremonies budget doubled', *BBC
News*, 5 December 2011, http://www.bbc.co.uk/news/
uk-16030785 [accessed 23 July 2013]; Avril Ormsby, 'London
2012 opening ceremony draws 900 million viewers', *Reuters*, 7
August 2012, http://uk.reuters.com/article/2012/08/07/uk-oly-
ratings-day-idUKBRE8760V820120807 [accessed 23 July
2013].

24 Jenny Sealey, 'London 2012: Shakespeare influences
Paralympics opening ceremony', *BBC News*, 24 February

2012, www.bbc.co.uk/news/uk-england-17151869 [accessed 23 July 2013]. In his interview for this volume Frank Cottrell Boyce also indicates that for the most part the groups working on the different ceremonies did not communicate directly with one another and did not know about their shared use of *The Tempest* (see p. 48–9).

25 In particular see Beatriz García, 'One hundred years of cultural programming within the Olympic Games (1912–2012): Origins, Evolution And Projections', *International Journal of Cultural Policy*, 14:4 (2008), pp. 361–76 (pp. 373–5).

26 'The Olympic Movement', *The Olympic Museum*, www.olympic.org/Documents/Reports/EN/en_report_670.pdf, p. 2 [accessed 25 July 2013].

27 For more on culture within the Olympics see García, 'One Hundred Years', pp. 368–70; David Inglis, 'Culture Agonistes: Social Differentiation, Cultural Policy and Cultural Olympiads', *International Journal of Cultural Policy*, 14:4 (2008), pp. 463–77 (pp. 465–8); Margaret M. Gold and George Revill, 'The Cultural Olympiads: Reviving the Panegyris', in *Olympic Cities*, pp. 80–107.

28 Inglis, 'Culture Agonistes', p. 468.

29 García, 'One Hundred Years', p. 373.

30 'Reflections on the Cultural Olympiad', p. 5.

31 'London unveils logo of 2012 Games', *BBC News*, 4 June 2007, www.news.bbc.co.uk/sport1/hi/other_sports/olympics_2012/6718243.stm' [accessed 25 July 2013]. For more on the history of the Paralympic logo, see John R. Gold and Margaret M. Gold, 'Access for All: The Rise of the Paralympic Games', *The Journal of the Royal Society for the Promotion of Health*, 127:3 (2007), pp. 133–41 (pp. 138–9).

32 Beatriz García, with Tamsin Cox, 'London 2012 Cultural Olympiad Evaluation: Final Report', Arts Council England, 2013, www.artscouncil.org.uk/media/uploads/pdf/london_2012_report/London_2012_Cultural_Olympiad_Evaluation_ICC_updated.pdf, p. 168 [accessed 25 July 2013]. Regional Creative Programmers Debbi Lander and Richard Crowe have likewise argued that branding across regional

events, most significantly through the Olympic logo, is central to the Cultural Olympiad's visibility; see 'Vancouver 2010 Meets London 2012', *Culture @ the Olympics*, 12:7 (2010), pp. 35–46 (pp. 35–7).

33 Simon Tait, 'Drama on display', *The Stage*, 7 June 2012, p. 18.

34 'Reflections on the Cultural Olympiad', p. 24.

35 Gabriel A. Almond and Sidney Verba, *The Civic Culture: Political Attitudes and Democracy in Five Nations*, 3rd edn (Newbury Park: Sage, 1989), p. 372. My great thanks to Tobias Döring for introducing this book to me.

36 Owen Gibson, 'London 2012 Olympics opening ceremony to reflect "people's Games"', *Guardian*, 27 January 2012, http://www.guardian.co.uk/sport/2012/jan/27/london-olympics-2012-opening-ceremony [accessed 21 August 2013].

37 John R. Gold and Margaret M. Gold, 'Olympic cities: regeneration, city rebranding and changing urban agendas', *Geography Compass*, 2:1 (2008), pp. 300–18 (pp. 310–11).

38 'The World Shakespeare Festival is Launched', Royal Shakespeare Company press release, 6 September 2011, http://www.rsc.org.uk/about-us/press/releases/the-world-shakespeare-festival-is-launched.aspx [accessed 16 August 2013].

39 Emily Linnemann, 'International innovation? Shakespeare as intercultural catalyst', *Shakespeare Survey 64* (2011), pp. 13–24 (p. 13).

40 Ibid., pp. 13–14.

41 See Appendix 1 in *A Year of Shakespeare*, pp. 271–4.

42 Elinor Parsons, '"This wide and universal theatre": Shakespeare in different voices', *Cahiers Élisabéthains*, Special Issue (2007), pp. 7–12 (p. 7).

43 'Michael Boyd speaks to Peter J. Smith', *Cahiers Élisabéthains*, Special Issue (2007), pp. 13–18 (p. 17).

44 Michael Billington, 'Othello', *Guardian*, 28 April 2006, http://www.theguardian.com/stage/2006/apr/28/theatre.rsc [accessed 16 August 2013]; Peter Kirwan, 'Othello (Munchner Kammerspiele) @ The Royal Shakespeare Theatre', *The Bardathon*, 29 April 2006, http://blogs.nottingham.ac.uk/

bardathon/2006/04/29/othello-the-royal-shakespeare-theatre/ [accessed 16 August 2013].

45 For a more detailed account of the production see Peter Malin, 'Othello', *Cahiers Élisabéthains* (2007), pp. 32–4.

46 For accounts of each of these productions see the reviews by Emily Oliver, Susan Bennett and Christie Carson, and Peter J. Smith in *A Year of Shakespeare*, as well as the online reviews by Julie Sanders and Sonia Massai for the *Year of Shakespeare* blog at www.yearofshakespeare.com.

47 Charles Spencer, 'Mucking around with Shakespeare', *Daily Telegraph*, 29 April 2006 (Shakespeare Institute Newspaper Cuttings Collection, 2006, 20 Mar.–30 Apr.).

48 Comment from 'usini' on Andrew Dickson, 'World Shakespeare festival: around the Globe in 37 plays', *Guardian*, 20 April 2012, http://www.theguardian.com/stage/2012/apr/20/world-shakespeare-festival-globe-theatre-rsc [accessed 21 August 2013].

49 Comment from 'Oloja' on Julie Sanders, '*The Winter's Tale*', *Year of Shakespeare*, 28 May 2012, http://bloggingshakespeare.com/year-of-shakespeare-the-winters-tale [accessed 21 August 2013].

50 Comment from 'Katie' on Emily Oliver, '*Timon of Athens*', *Year of Shakespeare*, 3 June 2012, http://bloggingshakespeare.com/year-of-shakespeare-timon-of-athens [accessed 21 August 2013].

51 Matt Trueman, 'Shakespeare's Globe reaps "rare" reward at Critics' Circle awards', *Guardian*, 15 January 2013, http://www.theguardian.com/stage/2013/jan/15/globe-critics-circle-awards [accessed 21 August 2013]. Paul Prescott shows that beyond the coverage offered in the *Guardian* and the *Financial Times*, the British national press published just 15 reviews for the 37 foreign productions in the Globe to Globe Festival (he discounts the Globe's own *Henry V*, due to the fact that it was part of the Globe's more traditional summer season). By way of comparison he notes that 17 national critics attended the press night on 22 May 2012 for *Chariots of Fire*. See Paul Prescott, *Reviewing Shakespeare: Journalism and Performance from the Eighteenth Century to the Present* (Cambridge: Cambridge University Press, 2013), p. 180.

52 Of course, there is a long history of very important globally focused Shakespeare criticism from scholars such as Dennis Kennedy, Inga-Stina Ewbank, and many others. But in terms of wider disciplinary trends the global has undoubtably gained momentum over the past decade.

53 'Globe to Globe', Shakespeare's Globe, http://www.shakespearesglobe.com/theatre/whats-on/globe-theatre/globe-to-globe [accessed 28 February 2014].

54 For a very helpful account of such tours through 2013, see Kimberly Richards, 'Performance calendar', in *Shakespeare Beyond English: A Global Experiment*, Susan Bennett and Christie Carson (eds) (Cambridge: Cambridge University Press, 2013), pp. 19–28.

55 Maggie Brown, 'The Space: click here for culture', 8 October 2012, http://www.theguardian.com/culture/2012/oct/08/the-space-click-for-culture [accessed 24 August 2013].

56 'Hamlet Globe to Globe', Shakespeare's Globe, http://globetoglobe.shakespearesglobe.com [accessed 28 February 2014]; Maev Kennedy, 'Amnesty criticises Globe theatre's North Korea visit on Hamlet world tour', *Guardian*, 10 March 2014, http://www.theguardian.com/stage/2014/mar/10/globe-theatre-amnesty-hamlet-tour-north-korea [accessed 10 March 2014].

57 Quoted in Trueman, 'Shakespeare's Globe'.

58 'Brazilian Globe Shakespeare – Rationale', Instituto Gandarela, http://www.gandarela.com.br/site/en/brazilian-globe/ [last accessed 23 August 2013; no longer available].

59 'Alex Huang addressing the U.S. Congress on the humanities', YouTube, 17 May 2013, http://www.youtube.com/watch?v=ILMLjDVKNO4 [accessed 23 August 2013].

60 'Launch of Global Shakespeare', Queen Mary, University of London, http://www.qmul.ac.uk/globalshakespeare/ [accessed 23 August 2013].

61 Indeed, not long after this Congressional address, Huang published an article arguing that 'global Shakespeares' had finally arrived as a core area in Shakespeare studies; see 'Global Shakespeares as Methodology', *Shakespeare*, 9:3 (2013), pp. 273–90.

62 Joseph Nye, *Soft Power: The Means to Success in World Politics* (New York: PublicAffairs, 2004), p. x.

63 Kenneth Rapoza, 'The empire strikes back: U.K. beats U.S. in "soft power", survey says', *Forbes*, 18 November 2012, http://www.forbes.com/sites/kenrapoza/2012/11/18/the-empire-strikes-back-u-k-beats-u-s-in-soft-power-survey-says/ [accessed 9 September 2013]; 'The Committee on Soft Power and the UK's Influence', UK Parliament, http://www.parliament.uk/business/committees/committees-a-z/lords-select/soft-power-and-the-uks-influence/ [accessed 28 February 2014].

64 Steve Bell, 'Steve Bell's If... on Nigel Farage's Caliban moment', *Guardian*, 30 January 2013, http://www.theguardian.com/commentisfree/cartoon/2013/jan/30/nigel-farage-ukip-europe-caliban [accessed 24 August 2013]. My great thanks to Charlie Morton for telling me about this wonderful cartoon.

65 'Godfrey Bloom on "bongo bongo land" and UK foreign aid', *BBC News*, 7 August 2013, http://www.bbc.co.uk/news/uk-23599140 [accessed 24 August 2013].

66 Daniel Boffrey, 'Immigration is British society's biggest problem, shows survey of public', *Guardian*, 13 January 2013, http://www.theguardian.com/uk/2013/jan/13/immigration-british-society-biggest-problem [accessed 24 August 2013].

67 The UK Home Office Twitter feed, 1 August 2013, https://twitter.com/ukhomeoffice/status/362976862282063872 and https://twitter.com/ukhomeoffice/status/363032876373114881 [accessed 1 August 2013].

68 'Farage attacks "nasty" immigration posters', *BBC News*, 25 July 2013, http://www.bbc.co.uk/news/uk-politics-23450438 [accessed 24 August 2013].

69 'Immigration spot checks: Equality watchdog investigates', *BBC News*, 3 August 2013, http://www.bbc.co.uk/news/uk-23552088 [accessed 24 August 2013]; 'Home Office vans: Unite union in "race hatred" query', *BBC News*, 2 August 2013, http://www.bbc.co.uk/news/uk-politics-23545955 [accessed 24 August 2013].

70 Jami Rogers, 'The Shakespearean Glass Ceiling: The State of Colorblind Casting in Contemporary British Theater',

Shakespeare Bulletin, 31:3 (2013), pp. 405–30 (pp. 421–2); Matt Trueman, 'East Asian actors seek RSC apology over Orphan of Zhao casting', *Guardian*, 31 October 2012, http://www.theguardian.com/stage/2012/oct/31/east-asian-actors-rsc-apology [accessed 24 August 2013].

71 This drying up of funding applies to sport as well as culture (not to mention social services); for a few telling examples see Ben Rumsby, 'British Basketball stripped of all Olympic funding by UK Sport a year after winning it back', *Telegraph*, 4 February 2014, http://www.telegraph.co.uk/sport/othersports/basketball/10617091/British-Basketball-stripped-of-all-Olympic-funding-by-UK-Sport-a-year-after-winning-it-back.html [accessed 4 March 2014]; 'British Swimming to appeal cut in funding for Olympic sports', *Guardian*, 11 February 2014, http://www.theguardian.com/sport/2014/feb/11/british-swimming-appeal-funding-cut [accessed 4 March 2014]; 'Hockey chief shocked by narrow escape from Olympic cull', *BBC Sport*, 13 February 2013, http://www.bbc.co.uk/sport/0/hockey/21447760 [accessed 4 March 2014].

AFTERWORD

Kathleen McLuskie

In the 1988 afterword to Graham Holderness's *The Shakespeare Myth*, Terry Eagleton described Shakespeare as 'the quintessential commodity, at once ever new and consolingly recognisable, always different and eternally the same, a magnificent feat of self-identity persisting through the most bizarre diversions and variations'.[1] Like many of the gestures of late-century iconoclasm, Eagleton's comment now seems curiously essentialist, attributing to 'Shakespeare' the very qualities of protean adaptability equally admired by the most ardent of bardolaters. His quality was being described as a universal essence that could transcend its local and contingent manifestations and though Eagleton's analysis linked this quality of Shakespeare to the complex economic and social relations of the commodity form, it proved surprisingly easy in later discussions to sever that link and to revert to the generalized admiration of the universal bard.

The adaptive qualities found in the formal constituents of Shakespeare's plays – the familiarity of the narratives, the recurring address to family dynamics in history, comedy and tragedy and the resonance of a metaphorical poetics – indeed lend the plays a diverse functionality that is evident in the multiple adaptations that began with their seventeenth-century revival from the back-list of the pre-civil war repertory. Yet

Shakespearean innovation depends less upon the intrinsic formal qualities of the plays than on the contingent work of artistic choices and organizational conditions that give each and every re-production its form. Speaking from the midst of late-century academic politics of culture, for example, Alan Sinfield had insisted that adaptation would involve 'reworking the authoritative text so that it is forced to yield against the grain explicitly oppositional kinds of understanding'.[2] A quarter of a century later, Dominic Dromgoole, director of Shakespeare's Globe, announcing 'the next stage' in the Globe's development, took a rather different view. While acknowledging the 'transforming insights of feminist, Marxist, queer and post-colonial theorists over the last few decades', he deplored what he called the 'weird closed conversation between directors, critics and academics, a conversation that short-circuited the central heart of any theatrical presentation, the audience'.[3] Both Sinfield and Dromgoole were dealing with the elusive connection between text, performance and audience. However where Sinfield in 1988 deployed the language of authority and resistance, Dromgoole imagined his organization's work as an open road to Shakespeare: 'The productions aren't cluttered by concepts, they don't play any tricks, they aren't trying too hard to be clever. They just are what they are.'[4]

The shift of attention from production to audience retained a sense of the cultural politics of performance. Dromgoole claimed that the new 'wooden O' 'housed a small revolution in which, night after night, benign dictatorship was swept away and democracy – some might say anarchy – was installed in its place'.[5] The politics, however, were not those of institutions or actually existing social relations. Instead they were a politics of the communal imaginary in which the arts could serve to remind their audience 'that the greatest playwright who ever lived wrote for an audience capable of great joy and irreverence and sensuality, for a society in which different strata were constantly and publicly challenging each other, and for a space in which there was nowhere to hide'.

For Dromgoole, the continuity between early modern performances and contemporary ones was more than a matter of performance style, or textual consistency: it was assured by a commitment to values located in a new, more enlightened, more liberal version of 'Englishness', an Englishness that lay in both the repudiation and the embrace of history:

> [T]he English – to speak in generalisations – were not simply the tortured inheritors of Victorian repression and Edwardian good manners: before that we were a robust and raucous people, happy to welcome outsiders, eager to embrace the new in any form, who would cheerfully congregate in all weathers to hear stories and to celebrate stories.[6]

There is no need to dwell on the historical lacunae and ideological assertions of Dromgoole's statements: they were written to launch the Sam Wanamaker Playhouse, to create a narrative for the Globe's larger aspirations, not to provide an analysis of contemporary or early modern social relations. The vision he offers of the connection between Shakespeare and his audience is less to do with contested textual hermeneutics (the oppositional reading that Sinfield imagined might be 'forced' out of the text and onto an audience) and more a matter of the pleasant somatic connectivity of 'sensuality', 'irreverence' and 'joy'.

In its presentation of an immediate and spontaneous embrace between Shakespeare and his audience, Dromgoole's statement demonstrates how the twenty-first century has developed – and the festivals of the Cultural Olympiad especially have consolidated and re-launched – the Shakespeare of utopian modernism.[7] Today we see a revival of the modernist efforts to use the arts as a way of 'preserving and containing utopian counter memories hostile to the dynamics of instrumental reason and capitalist economics'.[8] However, where the modernists between the world wars were dealing with an explicitly hostile and authoritarian political system, the 'utopian counter memories' marshalled for the re-launch projected a much softer public discourse in which Shakespeare is presented as a democratic, international, universally available, free good that takes its place in and for an imagined community. Such a community consists of social beings untrammelled by inequality or social conflict, taking pleasure in universal narratives that affirm the desired continuity of love and courage as a means to a happier world. Perhaps paradoxically, this vision continues to be held in place by a public education curriculum with Shakespeare at its centre and public funding for the arts that identifies the Royal Shakespeare Company as a Regularly Funded Organization (RFO) with priority claims on an Arts Council budget committed to widening access to the arts.[9]

Shakespeare's role in both the material and discursive realms of the arts was thus mutually reinforcing, but though academic discussion often acknowledged their connection, the two were, for the most part, kept distinct. The discourse of Shakespeare as commodity, begun by Eagleton and his fellow cultural materialists, addressed his deformation in the tourist industry or the expropriation of cultural goods by commercial culture industries, while Shakespeare the universal bard appeared more frequently in the advocacy for particular productions or accounts of the efficacy of his plays in education or projects of social amelioration.[10] The distinction between the two manifestations of Shakespeare was not one that could be resolved by recourse to argument or evidence. Rather, it represented the continuity of two distinct strands in English intellectual life: between a romantic, utopian, communal egalitarianism that imagines the possibility of social change through creative encounters and a pessimistic materialism that identifies the barriers to social progress in a generalized distrust of both 'capitalism' and the state. The fact that, in the UK, the state had been largely responsible for the postwar growth in arts provision and education and that capitalism had created the surpluses that made investment in the arts a social as well as a financial imperative was rarely acknowledged by the materialists, while intellectual reservations about the difficulty of identifying precise connections between the content of the plays and their social impact did not often trammel romantic enthusiasm.

Laura Marcus has described the distinction between these two ways of thinking as the tension between 'critical negativity' and 'a politics of identity in which literature has a crucial affirmative function'.[11] Seamus Perry has also tracked a longer-term strand of romantic utopianism across English literary culture whose 'proponents form a continuous line with Blake and several other Romantics at the far end, going through some aspects of Arnold and Ruskin, to Pater, Yeats and Lawrence, Graves, elements of Eliot and Woolf, and down to Leavis, Dylan Thomas and then, coming towards the nearer end of the line, the dark, odd and uncouth figure of Ted Hughes'.[12] While one might dissent from the detail of such broad sweeps of literary history, it is possible to recognize the outlines of a similar anti-materialist trend in twenty-first-century culture. It is found in objections to the commercialization of culture, in the resistance to new forms of bureaucracy, and as Perry notes among his students, in 'a pervasive distaste for the spiritual blight of materialism and rationalism and experimental science, even as a MacBook Air purrs away beneath their fingertips'.

This metaphorical 'faultline' between materialism and romanticism also divides advocacy from analysis, creativity from critique, optimism from pessimism and risk taking from calculation and the shift from one side to another is a matter of epiphany not ratiocination. As Frank Cottrell Boyce reflected about the Games' Opening Ceremony, 'everyone tuned in because they were sure it was going to be rubbish, but then it started and it was great'.[13] Cynicism about the financial muddles and organizational scandals of the Olympic Games' planning could not spoil the artistic triumph that Boyce and his collaborators had achieved: the affirmation of artistic pleasure could silence the negativity of political critique. In the case of Shakespeare, too, the old division between a '"mainstream", implicitly conservative, institutionalised Shakespearean canon' and politically informed, adaptive innovation seems less creatively productive than a primary attention to audience pleasure.[14]

As Dromgoole's later analysis showed, there was no longer any need to insist upon explicit 'adaptation', in the sense of changing the plays' narratives or structures of feeling. It was more that the Shakespeare who belonged to the audience had gone soft round the edges. The boundaries of the texts are no longer defended, and though lazy, outdated protests about the authenticity of this or that manifestation of Shakespeare are still occasionally heard (and brilliantly mocked in Tom Bird's account of the *Daily Mail* non-review of the Q Brothers' rap *Othello*),[15] the adaptive potential of Shakespeare's plays had turned his work into a resource for others' imaginative creativity in ways that did not need to cede any authority to the form of the early texts. In the process, the 'meaning of Shakespeare' shifted from designating hermeneutic metaanalysis or exegesis to a celebratory reference to the emotional force of the narrative and its potential for audience engagement.

Throughout the Cultural Olympiad's Shakespeare festivals, the artistic emphasis was on 'hearing stories and celebrating stories'. This was 'Shakespeare without his language', not only in the use of the international companies' primary languages in performance but in the sense that Shakespeare had meaning that somehow went beyond the words of the script. Indeed the text could be sometimes presented as an impediment to meaning. In his account of Deafinitely Theatre's production of *Love's Labour's Lost*, Stephen Purcell writes that '[director Paula] Garfield argued that previous attempts to do Shakespeare in BSL [British Sign Language] had failed because interpreters had "got too bogged down in trying to translate each old English word"'. Her team had decided that 'the content and the meaning was the main thing'.[16] 'Meaning', in this context, clearly referred to 'communicable emotion': the potential for the performance to address the audience in ways that would secure their assent to the production's structure of feeling and leave no space for scepticism or critique.

The radical scepticism about the social and intellectual accessibility of Shakespeare that had characterized the late-twentieth-century academy[17] could now be challenged both conceptually by empirical research of the kind addressed in Rose Elfman and Tracy Irish's contributions and by the concerted efforts of cultural practitioners who articulated new discourses about Shakespeare and his audience. In the Royal Shakespeare Company's global educational initiative, for example, the young people of the International Youth Ensemble, divided by geography and language, were found nevertheless to make common cause with one another. With the help of the new pedagogy developed by legendary practitioners such as Rex Gibson and Cicely Berry,[18] Irish describes how the participants apparently seized not only on 'Shakespeare', but in some cases Shakespeare texts to find that 'there were always words – but not always the same words – that expressed their own feelings and thoughts despite differences of culture and geography' (p. 68). The Shakespeare plays that seem so forbidding when encountered in the arena of accreditation and examination had been transformed into 'a rich meeting ground for intercultural understanding' (pp. 72–3).

The process by which intercultural understanding was effected is itself interesting. Irish describes how Aileen Gonsalves, who directed the IYE's group performance, 'stripped' the text 'down to "breath – how we use breath to create language and through language we create ideas, hopes, stories, culture"' (p. 74). The intellectual distinctions between the universal human physical process of breathing, the social phenomenon of 'language', and the cultural materials of 'ideas', 'hopes' and 'stories' disappeared in the creative synergy that was imagined between them. The method was of a piece with the imaginative aspiration that had inspired Peter Brook and Ted Hughes to create 'Orghast at Persepolis' in 1971, a form of theatrical communion expressed in a synthetic language, or Antonin Artaud to seek a model for new theatricality in Bali, or Eugenio Barba to gather together his community of multi-skilled international performers in diverse geographical spaces.[19] By 2012, moreover, these experiments were no longer a marginal practice available only to an artistic elite. Their techniques and assumptions had been normalized by the postwar development of theatre studies as a topic for mass higher education so that they could be enacted by international teenagers in a publicly funded education conference at the Tate Modern in London.

A similar sense of a magical, extraordinary event was articulated by Tom Bird in his interview for this volume in his account of the success of the Globe's outreach work: 'it was so extraordinary to be sitting there watching *The Tempest* with 3,000 people from Tower Hamlets because you realise this never happens' (p. 57).[20] For the creative practitioners of the Cultural Olympiad, Shakespeare had become one creative resource among many for a huge community of the willing who demonstrated their commitment to ideals of social community and international communication. Shakespeare took his place in a canon of literary and artistic work whose detailed content and form was less relevant than its capacity to generate thrilling experiences for audiences. As Frank Cottrell Boyce put it in his interview: 'I want them to be thrilled and have a great time and only afterwards think, oh wow, that was William Blake, or that was Milton' (p. 46). The audience is imagined to be part of the same shared creative embrace as the creators. The expensive education,[21] the organizational structures and accumulation of artistic resources that allowed Boyce and his colleagues to develop the depth and range of the performance seemed irrelevant to the immediacy of the encounter. Instead, Boyce's over-flowing creative generosity celebrated the power of the romantic literary and artistic canon to 'trigger all these meanings that go into people's heads' (p. 47) while Irish and her colleagues approached the acknowledged challenges of cultural difference without any fear of failure or calculation of effect.

The success of the creative events lay in effecting an imagined symbiosis between the rich canon of English art and literature, including Shakespeare, and audiences wherever they might be. The creators of the artistic events did not need to pay attention to the material processes that made them possible. Boyce is quite frank that 'we were completely protected from issues about budget or ideology or anything like that' and he wryly acknowledges the earnest ignorance of the politicians who tried to claim a stake in the work (p. 48). In her own interview Irish notes the facilitating role of the funding that the Royal Shakespeare Company received:

> On a very practical level, the funding from LOCOG allowed us to reach out more widely than normal. This meant I could visit other countries to talk, listen and lead workshops, to share their spaces and find out what Shakespeare means for their young people, and it meant we could invite some of those young people and their teachers to come and share our spaces. It meant we could fund students to take the Arts Award, and run a highly subsidised conference to explore what it might all add up to. (p. 69)

However, the money was merely an enabling device that did not compromise the participation of the young people or the findings of the research. Every audience engagement was unique, every encounter with Shakespeare provided different aspirations of breath, culture and stories. As Dromgoole put it, performances 'are what they are'; neither exceptional nor representative.[22] Their emotional 'meaning' is an effect of the synchrony of place and time between that audience and that event. Questions about the text that informs the performance, the history that provides its narrative, or the political and economic structures that enable the audience and event to come together at all are part of a discourse of academic knowledge or cultural policy and have no bearing on the view of the success or failure of the event itself.

As Boyce wrote in an inspired commentary a year after the Olympics:

[T]he important thing about the opening ceremony – the thing that people were responding to – was that it wasn't a vision. It's not what it said that counted, it was what it *was* [...] a new community – a kind of temporary Utopia. While in the rest of the nation, bankers and celebrities and footballers and G4S[23] were being paid massive amounts of money for being rubbish, here were people being brilliant. Not for money, but for the hell of it, for London, for the joy of being excellent.[24]

The appeal of this anti-establishment, anti-materialist discourse lies in its ability to lift the pleasure of the moment out of the realm of calculation and evoke the sense of play that silences dissent and invites collusion in a community of the 'brilliant' in a shared opposition to the other people who are 'rubbish'. All the practitioners were aware that their performances had involved money, but the world of committees and grant applications and political wrangling over public-spending priorities existed in a different sphere from the world of festival. The magical, brilliant realm of performance cannot acknowledge the conditions that make it possible for fear of breaking the spell that assures its audience's momentary consent.

After the event, back through the looking glass to the world of critique and evaluation, consent was sometimes withdrawn. As Colette Gordon shows in this volume, the blogposts and commentary that followed both the Opening Ceremony and the commentary on it in the following year indicated that 'certain sections of British audiences' were indeed 'less than comfortable with a £27 million spectacle featuring a dancing unpaid NHS force and an army of suited speculators guiding the nation onward' (p. 194). However the cacophony of commentary seldom came from those who, however momentarily, had been included in the community of the 'brilliant'. Dissent came from the other strand of English intellectual life that was alert to the historical and political facts that the riches of the industrial revolution were and continue to be unevenly distributed; that the *Empire Windrush* did not bring its passengers to a universal welcome; and that the government priority given to Olympic funding was in competition with possibly more immediate and pressing social needs. Moreover, as both Gordon and Hansen and Smialkowska's chapters for this volume have shown, the distribution of the LOCOG funds themselves did little to mask either the entrenched regional and international inequalities that could be identified in the selection of participants and performers. In spite of its extraordinary ambition and scale, the Cultural Olympiad could not fulfil a utopian promise of egalitarian access to culture because of a fundamental disconnection between its emotional narrative and the material world. Like all public initiatives, including democracy itself, it raised the expectation of equality but it could not create the conditions for securing it. Twenty-seven million pounds (if that indeed was the sum spent[25]) is a big sum of money, but it is only meaningful when set against other big sums – the daily or annual costs of the NHS, or the international aid budget of a major corporation. The choice of comparators itself introduces technical statistical complexities and attempts to do so reveal only the most fundamental disconnection of all: the one between numbers and words.[26]

The disconnection between the materialist and romantic views was less because of the events' manifest content – this or that interpretation of history or Shakespeare – than it was to do with the difference between a world managed by stories and a world managed by economic and bureaucratic structures. The view from the economic perspective on Shakespeare's universality would note the huge supply-side over-production of Shakespeare (and other arts) worldwide. It would also note the infrastructure of ministries of culture and their representatives (whom Tom Bird and Dromgoole invited to the Globe Festival planning meeting) or organizations such as the British Council or London International Festival of Theatre (LIFT), which constitute the global network of arts events that manage, distribute and fund supply.[27] Those processes attract an audience of mobile, comparatively affluent young people, equally at home in any number of global capitals and often forming the most privileged sections of diasporic communities in major cities.[28] As Tom Bird found, the diversity of such diasporic populations complicates the pricing and support required to manage a Shakespeare festival, and as Colette Gordon explains, this global churn of audiences, participants and productions makes national distinctions impossible to maintain, since national populations are cross-cut by differences of access to funding and contacts and training opportunities as much in the arts or education as in sport. The existence of these economic and bureaucratic structures is not the antithesis of 'brilliant' arts events. Rather it constitutes their enabling condition, providing the variety of performance that, as Bird found, was 'happening anyway' (p. 55), reducing the costs of producing new shows from scratch, ensuring the preparedness of shows that had been touring for months if not years, allowing companies to include the single gig at the Cultural Olympiad in a circuit that ensured some return on the significant investment required.

The long distribution chain that connects 'Shakespeare' to individual performances in a time and a space creates a huge diversity of forms whose connection to any essential 'Shakespeare' becomes more and more attenuated with every performance. Its direction from the textual Shakespeare to the performed Shakespeare is changing and may disappear completely as the emotional pleasure and the connection between audience and event becomes stronger and all that remains of Shakespeare in any particular event is a familiar story, a resonant passage or a buried reference known only to the specialist: as Boyce puts it, 'Oh wow, that was Shakespeare'. Nevertheless as Boyce also reminds us, the plays and poems of Shakespeare are always available as a resource. Their textual form continues to exist outside the competition among companies and organizations both charitable and profit-seeking throughout the world who may try to make a case that *their* Shakespeare product is the most authentic, representative and real. Like the songs of Buddy Holly, or the Benin Bronzes or the Himalayas, the plays of Shakespeare are not commodities but non-rival goods that with varying degrees of creativity and work and financial resource can be remade in order to create new events. What they cannot do, except very occasionally and for a tiny proportion of the world's population, is to change the fundamental social relations in which the stories are told, transforming an audience into a lasting community, much less a nation.

Notes

1 Terry Eagleton, 'Afterword', in *The Shakespeare Myth*, ed. Graham Holderness (Manchester: Manchester University Press, 1988), p. 184.

2 Alan Sinfield, *Faultlines Cultural Materialism and the Politics of Dissident Reading* (Oxford: Oxford University Press, 1992), p. 22.

3 Dominic Dromgoole, 'Shakespeare's Globe – the next stage', *Guardian*, 11 January 2014, http://www.theguardian.com/stage/2014/jan/11/shakespeare-globe-new-stage-dromgoole [accessed 14 January 2014].

4 Ibid.

5 Peter Kirwan and Charlotte Mathieson in this volume have noted the recurring reference to the *Henry V* prologue that seems to be a core message of the Globe's communication strategy as well as a standard point of reference for performance studies (p. 244).

6 Dominic Dromgoole, 'Shakespeare's Globe – the next stage'.

7 Cary DiPietro, *Shakespeare and Modernism* (Cambridge, Cambridge University Press, 2006) and Richard Halpern, *Shakespeare among the Moderns* (Ithaca: Cornell University Press, 1997) provide persuasive accounts of the importance of modernism in reimagining Shakespeare for the twentieth century.

8   Hugh Grady, 'Modernity, modernism and postmodernity in the twentieth century's Shakespeare', in *Shakespeare and Modern Theatre: the performance of modernity*, ed. Paul Yachin and Kathleen McLuskie with Christopher Holmes (London: Routledge, 2001), p. 26.

9   Kate Rumbold described this process as it took place in the first decade of the new century in Kate McLuskie and Kate Rumbold, *Cultural Value in Twentieth Century England: the case of Shakespeare* (Manchester: Manchester University Press, 2014), Chapter 6. Recent public statements have begun to shift the funding base for this support. See Arts Council England, 'Our mission and strategic framework', second edition, 2013, http://www.artscouncil.org.uk/what-we-do/mission/ [accessed 5 February 2014].

10 The distinction between advocacy and analysis in cultural policy is addressed in McLuskie and Rumbold, *Cultural Value*, Chapter 1.

11 Laura Marcus, 'Feminist Aesthetics and the new realism', in *New Feminist Discourses*, ed. Isobel Armstrong (London: Routledge, 1992), pp. 11–25 (p. 18).

12 Seamus Perry, 'Half Fox', *The London Review of Books*, 29 August 2013, pp. 13–16.

13 Frank Cottrell Boyce, 'We created the hope of a better Britain. But what remains of the Olympic magic?', *Observer*, 13 July 2013, http://www.theguardian.com/commentisfree/2013/jul/13/olympic-opening-ceremony-britain-cottrell-boyce [accessed 14 January 2014].

14 A description that Pascale Aebischer used to establish the opposite of the innovative, adaptive and creative productions of Jacobean drama that she was describing in the introduction to *Performing Early Modern Drama Today*, Pascale Aebischer and Kathryn Prince (eds) (Cambridge: Cambridge University Press, 2012), p. 2

15 See his interview in this volume.

16 Stephen Purcell, '*Love's Labour's Lost*', in *A Year of Shakespeare: Re-living the World Shakespeare Festival*, Paul Edmondson, Paul Prescott and Erin Sullivan (eds) (London: Bloomsbury, 2014), p. 113.

17 As described, *inter alia*, in John Guillory, *Cultural Capital: The Problem of Literary Canon Formation* (Chicago: University of Chicago Press, 1993).

18 See http://www.teachingshakespeare.ac.uk/ [accessed 14 January 2014]. This site indicates the investment in technology and academic partnership that supports the global ambitions of the RSC's learning methodology.

19 A. C. H. Smith, *Orghast at Persepolis: an account of the experiment in theatre directed by Peter Brook and written by Ted Hughes* (London: Eyre Methuen, 1972); Ian Watson, *Negotiating Cultures: Eugenio Barba and the intercultural debate* (Manchester: Manchester University Press, 2002).

20 The exceptional character of deprived people's attendance at theatre is part of the mythology of the access debate. Though the East End borough of Tower Hamlets includes some of the most deprived people in the UK, it also houses a lively and diverse arts scene. See www.towerhamletsarts.org.uk [accessed 14 January 2014]. It is bordered by Stratford and the Olympic Park, and – across the Thames – the borough of Southwark, home to Shakespeare's Globe. Both government and local authorities are committed to extending marginal groups' access to theatre. See http://www.artscouncil.org.uk/what-we-do/ [accessed 14 January 2014].

21 Education is expensive whether the costs are borne by the state or by the individuals who benefit from it.

22 Compare with Colette Gordon's account of 'stadial history [...] in which representativeness and comprehensiveness were beside the point', p. 193.

23 The private security firm whose mismanagement of the Olympic contract became a national scandal.

24 Boyce, 'We created the hope of a better Britain'.

25 Identifying the details of budget is complicated by the range of partnership and funding sources that were put together for the event as well as the categorizations of the event itself. See the Arts Council's 'Reflections on the Cultural Olympiad and London 2012 Festival', http://www.artscouncil.org.uk/media/uploads/pdf/

Reflections_on_the_Cultural_Olympiad_and_London_2012_Festival_pdf.pdf [accessed 14 January 2014].

26 See the World Bank's 'Measuring the Real Size of the World Economy' (2013), https://openknowledge.worldbank.org/bitstream/handle/10986/13329/9780821397282.pdf?sequence=1 [accessed 14 January 2014].

27 LIFT co-produced a number of 2012 events.

28 Affluent as compared with the working poor of their own societies.

INDEX

Abraham, Eric 199
Abuk, Joseph 214
Adams, Robert 276
adaptation 120–1, 142–5, 164, 187, 300, 323–4, 328
Adébáyọ̀, Ọlásúnkanmi 143
Adébáyọ̀, Ọláwálé 143
Adorno, Theodor 28
Afghanistan 20, 25, 58, 137, 243, 263
Africa xv, 19, 70, 109, 122, 191–217, 243–4, 276
African National Congress (ANC), 209–11
Alabí, Joshua Adémọ́lá 143
Albania 84, 89–91, 139
Albert (Prince) 8–9
Alliance Française 205
Alli-Hakeem, Olúwatóyin 142
Almond, Gabriel A. 296–7
amateurs, amateurism, volunteerism 10, 108–9, 115–22, 124, 194, 208
American National Theatre and Academy 257
Amin, Idi 207–8
Amnesty International 40–1
Anglo-Soviet Friendship Society 263
anniversaries xvi, 229–31, 234, 236, 260
Annalia Dubrensia 5–6

Anouilh, Jean 267, 270
apartheid 208–13, 258
Arab Spring 213–14
Argentina 240
Arnold, Thomas 8
Arpana theatre company 56
Art for the People movement 261–2
Artaud, Antonin 330
Artistes, Producteurs, Associés 109
Arts Theatre Company 260–1
Arya, Sagar 150
Ashtar Theatre 58–60, 140
Asia 243
Asian Shakespeare Intercultural Archive [A|S|I|A] (a-s-i-a-web.org) 304
audiences xv, 58, 71, 76, 82, 90, 112, 133–57, 163–88, 195–200, 202, 204–5, 242, 244, 246, 255, 261–2, 266–7, 269–70, 274–7, 291, 300–3, 312, 324–5, 328–34
demographics 57–8, 134, 138, 142, 145, 148–9, 156–7, 158n., 164–88, 198, 301–2, 312, 330, 334, 337n.
Australia/Australasia 77, 243, 263–4, 268–9

authenticity 9, 74, 163, 165, 180, 186, 192, 197–8, 203, 207, 211, 213–14, 216–17, 238, 326, 333
authority and expertise 122–3, 138, 157, 163–88, 203, 229, 242, 263–4, 275, 303, 324, 328

Baker, Victoria 120
Balkans xv, 84–96, 263
Balme, Christopher 183
Bangladesh 180
Bánkolé, Kẹ̀hindé 143
Barba, Eugenio 330
bardolatry 233–4, 323
Barnum, P. T. 227
Barrault, Jean-Louis 256–8, 262, 268, 272
Baucom, Ian 229
Beckham, David 235, 247
Becque, Henri 268
Belarus Free Theatre 266
Belgium 261
Bell, Steve 308–9
Ben-Ami, Yuval 140
Benin Bronzes 335
Bennett, Susan 178, 230, 239
Bernard, Jean-Jacques 270
Berners-Lee, Tim 24–5
Berry, Cicely 329
Bharucha, Rustom 179
Big Ben 80, 235
Bikelas, Demetrius 254
Billington, Michael 154–5, 300
Bird, Tom 12, 53–64, 142, 285, 311, 328, 330, 333–4
Birmingham 109, 208, 279n.

Bitter Pill Theatre Company (also Bitter Pill and The Theatre Company) 181, 200–3, 205
Bjørnson, Bjørnstjerne 270
Blackman, Malorie 154
Blake, William 29, 45–6, 327, 330
Blondell, John 91
Bloom, Godfrey 308
Bokassa, Jean-Bédel 208
Bolivia 83
Bolshoi Ballet 254
Bosnia 84–7
Boulez, Pierre 257
Boyce, Frank Cottrell 2, 22, 29, 43–52, 327, 330–2, 334
Boyd, Michael 67–8, 110, 290, 299–300
Boyle, Danny 2, 5, 22, 43–52, 80, 82–3, 87–8, 95, 193, 195, 231, 256–7, 276
Branagh, Kenneth 2, 23, 80, 193–4, 231
brands and branding 6, 14–15, 21–2, 108, 285–6, 288–9, 293–5, 298, 314n., 316–17n.
Braun, Kazimirz 265
Brazil 66, 164, 306–7
Brecht, Bertolt 151
Brenton, Howard 59
Bridgend 109
Brighton 109
Bristol 269
British Broadcasting Corporation (BBC) 3, 24, 50, 113, 235, 243, 264, 270–4, 307
 radio 270–4

shipping forecast 46–7
television 273–4, 276,
    see also television (in general)
British Council 10, 29, 65–6, 72, 205, 214, 221n., 237, 240, 254, 261–2, 333
British Museum 67, 192, 209–10, 245
Brogan, Frank 108
Brook, Peter 255, 279n., 329
Broomhill Opera 199
Browne, E. Martin 268
Brunel, Isambard Kingdom 2, 8, 23, 48, 80, 193, 195, 231, 234–5
Buckley, Thea 139
Burnett, Mark Thornton 104

Cameri Theatre 58
Cameron, David 25–6, 288, 308
Cameroon 203
Canada 276
Capitalism 8–9, 211, 289, 325–7
Carey, John 123
Carr, Alison 120
Carter, Thomas F. 15
casting 116–19, 200, 203–4, 208, 241, 244, 268, 311
CCTV *see* surveillance
celebration *see* festivity and festivals
Chekhov, Anton 55, 262, 267, 269–70
Chikura, Denton 197–8, 203, 241
China 22, 60, 72, 240, 247

Churchill, Winston 33n., 46, 80, 234, 281n., 292
Clements, John 268
Clunes, Alec 261
Coe, Sebastian 283–4
Cole, Teju 213
Coleridge, Samuel Taylor 28
Coliseum (Roman) 47
Colley, Martin 5
Collins, Shane 14
Comédie-Française 261, 266, 268–9, 271
Comerford, Philip 89
Conkie, Rob 165
Conrad, Peter 272
Copley, Peter 261
Council for the Encouragement of Music and the Arts (CEMA) 268
Cowie, Andrew 124
Craig, Edward Gordon 265
Cripps, Stafford 255
Critics' Circle 303, 306
Cromwell, Oliver 33n.
Cronin, Jeremy 191, 212–13
Crouch, Tim 3, 70, 152–4
Cuba 164
Cullingford, Lucy 73
cultural capital xvi, 111, 123, 125, 203, 228, 245, 283–313, 329, 337n.
cultural materialism 323–6
Cuming Museum 236
Czech Republic/Czechoslovakia 66, 73, 259–62, 265, 271

Daldry, Stephen 49, 297
Dalton, Hugh 259
Darlington 112

Deafinitely Theatre 327
de Coubertin, Pierre 1, 7–16, 20, 26, 81, 292
de Gaulle, Charles 257
de Grazia, Margreta 234
de Madriaga, Salvador 271–2
Dekker, Thomas 246
Devlin, William 273
Dhaka Theatre 139, 181
Diamond Jubilee (2012), 229–31
Diaspora 166, 176–7, 180, 182–3, 197–8, 213, 267, 334
DiCaprio, Leonardo 24
Dickens 2012 festival 228, 232, 236–40, 242, 244–6
Dickens, Charles xvi, 10, 227–48
digital communication, digital culture 3, 24–5, 57, 66, 70–1, 76, 94, 142, 152–4, 229, 236, 239–40, 242, 266, 304–5
diversity 25, 135–6, 157, 183, 231, 274, 298, 307–12, 325, 334 *see also* multiculturalism
Dobson, Michael 108, 115, 290–1
Dodd, William 234
Doran, Gregory 70, 115, 206–8, 213–14, 244
Dornford-May, Mark 199–200, 206
Dover, Robert 4–5
Dowden, Richard 206–8
dreamthinkspeak 109, 151

Dromgoole, Dominic 12–13, 53, 324–5, 328, 331, 333
Duggan, Mark 26
Durham, William 5

Eagleton, Terry 323, 326
Eco, Umberto 9
Edinburgh 109
Edinburgh International and Fringe Festivals 121, 201, 256–7, 262, 267, 275
education 8, 10–11, 22, 26, 29, 31n., 55, 65–77, 152–4, 210, 215, 271, 292, 307, 329–30, 334, 337n.
  'Stand up for Shakespeare' programme 67
  testing 69
  UK National Curriculum 10, 33–4n., 75, 195, 326
Edwards, Huw 24, 49
Elfman, Rose 139–41
Elgar, Edward 47
Eliot, T. S. 249n., 268, 325, 327
Entertainments National Service Association (ENSA) 260
Enthoven, Dick 199
Equiano, Olaudah 18–19, 21, 33n.
Euripides 267–8
Europe 65, 81, 106, 164, 198, 202–4, 206–8, 243–4, 254, 257, 260–2, 265–7, 271–3
'eurythmy' 13, 27

'fair play' 7, 13, 20–1
Fákúnlé, Ọlárótimí 142
Farage, Nigel 308–10
Fatah party 139
Fawdington, Amy 110
Fearon, Ray 207
feminism 16, 324
Festival of Britain (1951) 232–4, 281n.
festivity and festivals xv, xvi, 13–17, 21, 29, 39–40, 51, 71, 95, 142–3, 145, 151, 164–6, 168, 180, 192, 197, 199, 201, 205, 235, 260, 265, 267, 269, 272, 284, 292, 299, 302, 308 *see also* named festivals
Filipi, Adonis 89
film 3, 44, 71, 82, 153–4, 155–6, 173, 194, 237–8, 256–7, 268–9, 270–1, 273–4, 314n.
  Atanarjuat 155
  Chariots of Fire 24
  David Copperfield (1913) 237
  Hamlet (1948) 256, 258, 267–8
  Hellzapoppin' 267
  Othello (1952) 257
  People Next Door (The) 257
  Shakespeare from Kabul 243
  Splendor in the Grass 155
  Spring in Park Lane 271
  Star Wars 51
Finland 263–4
football 46–7, 50–1, 274 *see also* sport and exercise
Fraine, Laura 111
France 118, 256–8, 261–2

Fricker, Karen 163–4
Friedmann, John 216–17
funding and funding bodies (UK)
  Arts Council England 3, 14, 55, 123–4, 142, 263, 266, 268–9, 326
  disability support 133–4
  military 34
  sport 321n.

G4S (security company) 33n., 332
Gaddafi, Muammar 207
Gandhi, Mahatma 258
García, Beatriz 293–5
Gardner, Lyn 123–4
Gardner, Maureen 254
Garfield, Paul 328
Gavin, Kim 80
Geneva Convention 20–1
Germany 203, 258–9, 261
Gesher Theatre 58
Ghana 208
Gibson, Rex 329
Gide, André 272
Gielgud, John 273
Gilbert, Helen 173
Gilliam, Laurence 273
Girginov, Vassil 287
global and intercultural studies 304–5, 307, 312, 319n.
Global Shakespeares (globalshakespeare.mit.edu) 304
globalism and internationalism 12, 80, 95, 101–26, 150, 184, 191–217, 228–9, 236–40, 243–5, 257–73, 301–5, 326

globalization 101, 104–8, 121, 124, 164, 216–17
Globe to Globe series (1997–2001, 2013–14, World *Hamlet*) 164, 189–90n., 205, 305–6
Globe to Globe Festival (2012) (G2G) xiv, xv, 3, 8, 12, 15, 53–64, 79–96, 109, 135, 137–51, 156–7, 163–88, 191–3, 196–205, 211–17, 240–5, 253, 258, 263–4, 266–7, 272, 285, 298–306, 333
  digital streaming, live broadcasting *see* digital communication, digital culture
  finance 54–5, 57, 64, 197, 204–5, 291, 315n., 332
  media coverage 58–9, 63, 196, 214–16, 295–6, 301–3, 318n.
  productions
    1 Henry VI (Serbian) 79–96
    2 Henry VI (Albanian) 79–96, 139
    3 Henry VI (Macedonian) 79–96
    All's Well That Ends Well (Gujarati) 56, 305
    As You Like It (Georgian) 305
    The Comedy of Errors (Dari Persian) 58, 137, 243
    Coriolanus (Japanese) 303
    Cymbeline (Juba Arabic) 62, 193, 204–5, 214–16
    Henry V (English) 61, 80, 146–8, 305
    Julius Caesar (Italian) 300, 303
    King John (Armenian) 139, 266
    King Lear (Belarusian) 138, 266, 305
    Love's Labour's Lost (British Sign Language) 328
    Macbeth (Polish) 58
    Measure for Measure (Russian) 138
    The Merchant of Venice (Hebrew) 58–60, 258, 264
    The Merry Wives of Windsor (Swahili) 61, 138, 181, 190n., 192, 200–3, 205
    A Midsummer Night's Dream (Korean) 266
    Othello (English/Hip Hop) 62–3, 328
    Pericles (Greek) 54, 63–4, 137, 190n., 266
    Richard II (Arabic) 58–60, 139–40, 258
    Richard III (Mandarin) 60, 300
    The Taming of the Shrew (Urdu) 15–16, 139, 180, 190n.
    The Tempest (Bangla) 57, 139, 181–2, 190n., 330
    Timon of Athens (German) 138, 303
    Titus Andronicus (Cantonese) 55, 138

Troilus and Cressida (Maori) 61, 266
Twelfth Night (Hindi) 56, 61–2, 139, 179–80
The Two Gentlemen of Verona (Shona) 193, 197–200, 205, 240–2
Venus and Adonis (multiple languages) 192, 198–9, 205, 211–12, 305
The Winter's Tale (Yoruba) 141–6, 148, 192–3, 204–5, 300–2
protests 59–60
publicity and marketing 56–7, 85, 179, 190n., 192, 197, 211, 216, 298
surtitles/scene summaries 63–4, 142, 171, 174
Goebbels, Joseph 255
Goffman, Erving 17
Gold, John 298
Gold, Margaret 298
Goldman, Daniel 200
Goldoni, Carlo 269–70
Goldstein, Daniel M. 83
Gonsalves, Aileen 73–4, 329
Goring, Maurius 271
Gorko, Petar 94
Gove, Michael 33n., 75
Gozzi, Carlo 267
Great Exhibition (London 1851) 8–9, 232
Greece 84, 92–3
Greeves, Shane 18
Guinness, Alec 268, 271
Guitry, Sacha 267
Guthrie, Tyrone 263–5, 268, 271–2, 274–6

Habima (National Theatre of Israel) 58–60, 264
Hackney Empire theatre 198
Hague (The) 85
Hahn, Matthew 210
Hall, Tony 14
Hamas party 140
Handel, George Frideric 259
Handelman, Don 83
Handy, Scott 156
Harare International Festival of Arts in Zimbabwe 201–2
Hardwicke, Cedric 268
Harrison, Stephen 246
Harry Potter 292
Hawkins, Jack 261, 271
Hayes, Graeme 27
Hazlewood, Charles 199
Heilmann, Ann 232
Hensher, Philip 247
heritage/*héritage* 68, 93, 167, 177, 182, 203, 211–12, 227–9, 237, 243, 245, 287–9, 297–8
Herlie, Eileen 267
Hindi Theatre Company 61
Hitler, Adolf 81, 95
Hobson, Harold 270
Hockney, David 46
Hogg, Edward 152
Holderness, Graham 323
Honegger, Arthur 257
Hong Kong 55, 69
Honzl, Jindřich 260, 262
Howell, Lord (of Guilford) 308
Huang, Alex 307
Hughes, Ted, 327, 329
Hughes, Thomas: *Tom Brown's Schooldays* 8, 26

Humphreys, Walter 261
Hungary 262
Hunt, Jeremy 2–4, 28, 45, 52
Huq, Konnie 153
Hussein, Saddam 214

Ibsen, Henrik 270, 276
Il-Sung, Kim 214
immigration 25–6, 195, 197–8, 213, 216, 241, 246, 267, 308–12, 325 *see also* diaspora
India 61–2, 73, 77, 149–51, 164, 179–80, 182, 244, 258, 305
Industrial Revolution 2, 45, 80, 192–5, 231–2, 241, 332
Institute of Cultural Capital 135
Instituto Gandarela 306–7
intercultural spectatorship *see* spectatorship
international politics 58–9, 138–41, 148, 207–11, 213–14, 258–65, 271, 307
International Theatre Institute 259–60, 262
Iraq 25, 263, 300
Irish, Tracy 329–31
Isango Ensemble 198–9, 205
Israel 58–9, 255, 258, 264
Italy 259, 267
Iyer, Pico 79, 81

James (King) 246
  The Book of Sports 5
Japan 164, 258–9
Jennings, Humphrey 23, 28
John, Juliet 237, 242

Johnson, Boris 27, 298
Johnson, Samuel 290
Jones, Owen 114
Jonson, Ben 5, 246, 297
Joseph, Paterson 208
Jouvet, Louis 262

Kabila, Laurent 207
Kani, John 208
Karadzic, Radovan 86
Karamichas, John 27
Karan, Amara 150
Kathrada, Ahmad 209–10
Kaye, Danny 267
Kazan, Elia 155
Kendal, Felicity 3
Kennedy, Dennis 163–4
Kenya 181, 200–3
Khan, Iqbal 148–50, 244
Kidnie, Margaret Jane 235
King, Robert 19
Kipling, Rudyard 259
Kirwan, Peter 149, 211, 300
Kissoon, Jeffery 207
Knowles, Ric 163–4, 180, 183
Kotseli, Areti 93

Laffan, Robert 31n.
Lagos Theatre Festival 205
Lan, David 199
languages 163–88, 190n., 273, 284, 299, 328–9
  Arabic 74
  Armenian 54
  Bangla 55, 181
  Belarusian 138
  British Sign Language 305, 328
  Cantonese 54, 138
  Czech 74

English 26, 61–2, 68–9, 75, 112, 163–6, 168, 174, 176, 178–9, 183–4, 215, 241–2, 266, 272, 302–3
Finnish 255
French 272, 305
Georgian 55
German 138, 299–300, 303
Greek 63–4, 254
Gujarati 55
Hindi 55–6, 61, 74, 209
Icelandic 54
Japanese 55
Juba Arabic 204, 214–15
Macedonian 93–4
Mandarin 74
Native American 62–3
Punjabi 55
Russian 138
Serbian 87
Shona 197, 200, 241–2
Spanish 74, 272, 305
Swahili 138, 181, 200–1, 208
Urdu 55, 180
Yoruba 141–8, 182
Zulu 73–4, 190n.
Larlarb, Suttirat 44
Lebanon 58
LeCompte, Elizabeth 155
Lee, Adele 138
Lenin, Vladimir 214
Liew, Jonathan 285
Lincoln, Abraham 235
Lindsay, David 275
Linnemann, Emily 299
Littlewood, Joan 265
Liverpool 269
Liverpool Playhouse 267
Llewellyn, Mark 232

localism and regionalism xv, 101–26, 235–6, 240, 243
London (city of) xvi, 25, 56–7, 88–90, 101, 107, 109, 111, 113–14, 116–18, 183–4, 196–8, 201–2, 216–17, 227–48, 259, 293, 297–8, 332
  7/7 bombings 25
  1991 Meadow Well riots 114
  2011 riots 25–7, 70, 88, 113–14
  CCTV 26, 90
  languages spoken 55, 142, 196–8, 200, 301
  theatre scene 57, 167, 179, 183, 198–202, 204–5, 267–9, 306, 311–12
London International Festival of Theatre (LIFT) 333
London Symphony Orchestra 24
London Theatre Studio 269
London Underground 24
Lorca, Frederico García 262
Lucas, Georgie 139
Luscombe, Christopher 201–2

MacAloon, John 12, 16–17, 21, 27, 285–9
MacColl, Ewan 262
Macedonia 84, 91–5
MacKaye, Percy 1
Mackenzie, Ruth 295
MacOwan, Michael 271
Malefane, Pauline 199
Mandela, Nelson 207–11
Manvell, Roger 271
Marcus, Laura 327

Marlowe, Christopher 268
Marsh, Joss 238
Mary Poppins 2
masques 27–8, 47 *see also* spectacle
Massai, Sonia 139, 202
Mbeki, Thabo 210
McDonald, Ian 7
McKellen, Ian 111
McLuskie, Kathleen 165, 289
Mendes, Sam 3
'merrie England' 5, 9, 297
Middleton, Thomas 246
Milivojevic, Nikita 85–8
Milton, John 46, 195, 330
Mirchevski, Martin 94
Mladic, Ratko 85–6
Mobutu (Sese Seko) 208
Moiseiwitsch, Tonya 276
Molière 258, 262, 267–8
Monty Python 20–1
Morrison, Herbert 232
Moscow Arts Theatre 269
Mountford, Robert 149
Mr Bean 24
Mthembu, Jackson 209
Mugabe, Robert 207–8
Mulcaster, Robert 5
multiculturalism 25–6, 192, 195–6, 211, 231, 298, 307–8, *see also* diversity
Mumbai 56, 61
Münchner Kammerspiele 299–300, 303
Munyevu, Tonderai 197–8, 199–200, 241
Murray, Andy 147
Muscular Christianity 8, 26
Museum of London 236
music 24, 47, 60–1, 89–90, 94, 116, 143, 170, 174, 177, 181–3, 193, 195, 206, 213, 235, 244, 257, 259, 274–5, 296, 300, 302–3
  Arctic Monkeys 24
  Beatles (The) 2, 27, 292
  Buddy Holly 335
  Eurythmics (The) 27
  Underworld 44, 47
Musical Society of Nigeria 204
MyShakespeare 3

narrative 288, 303, 305, 325–6, 328, 331, 333
nation branding 314n.
National Eisteddfod 274, 301
National Health Service (NHS) 2, 28, 194–5, 256, 332–3
National Theatre of Albania 89–91, 139
National Theatre of Armenia 266
National Theatre of Bitola 91–5
National Theatre of China 60
National Theatre of Greece 54
National Theatre of Moravia 265
National Theatre of Poland 264–5
National Theatre of Serbia 85–8
National Theatre (Royal) 67, 152, 221n., 268–70, 303
  Frankenstein 43–4
nationalism, nationhood, national identity xv, 1,

10, 79–96, 102–7, 125,
134, 138–9, 146, 196–7,
239–40, 243, 246,
256–7, 263–4, 267, 327
Albanian 89–91
British 6, 22–3, 26, 50,
61, 80, 83, 106, 125,
146–8, 164, 168, 191–2,
212–13, 228–40, 247,
256–7, 273, 276, 290–1,
297, 307, 325
French 256–7, 287–8
German 81–2
Macedonian 91–5
Palestinian 140, 263
Polish 264–5
Serbian 85–8
South Sudanese 215
Nazi party 81–2, 95, 255, 262
Neagle, Anna 271
Nelson, Trevor 24
neoliberalism 28, 287–8,
314n.
Netherlands (The) 261
Neveux, George 267
Newcastle-Gateshead 12, 57,
102–26, 204, 312
Newcastle Theatre Royal 57,
109, 122, 125–6
New Zealand 118
Nigeria 204–5, 208, 213
non-rival goods 335
Norman, Sarah 200–1, 203
North Korea 306
Northern Sinfonia 119
Northern Stage (The) 110
nostalgia 8, 193, 232, 234–5
Nri, Cyril 207
Nye, Joseph 307
Nyere, Julius 208

Office of Subversive
Architecture 89
Oguntokun, Wole 204–5
Ogutu, Joshua 201–2
O'Hea, Brendan 148
Old Vic 260–1, 263–4, 267–9,
271, 276
Oily Cart 108
Olive, Sarah 138
Oliver, Emily 138
Olivier, Laurence 256, 258,
260–1, 264, 267–71,
273
Olsen and Johnson 267
Olympics (in general) xiv, 9,
27, 79–80
brand 6, 22, 285–6, 288
ceremonies 22, 81–2, 292
charter 135
Cultural Olympiad 9, 12,
81–2, 96n., 255, 292–3
history
Ancient Greek Olympics
4, 7
Cotswold Olimpick games
4–6, 8
Modern Olympics 7, 292
Much Wenlock games 8
International Olympic
Committee (IOC) 6–7,
20, 29, 31n., 254,
285–7, 298
philosophy ('Olympism') xv,
7–10, 12, 90, 286
rings 44–5, 94, 193, 232,
293
spirit 5, 134–57
torch 6, 247, 292–3
Olympics (Beijing 2008) 1, 22,
247

Olympics (Berlin 1936) 1,
81–2, 255, 259, 293
  media coverage 82
  Opening Ceremony 81–2
  salute 81, 95
  torch and cauldron 82, 293
Olympics (Helsinki 1952) 254,
264
Olympics (London 1948) xvi,
11, 81, 239, 253–77
  media coverage 253–4
  Opening Ceremony 259
  torch 259
Olympics (London 2012) 179,
193, 213, 243, 286,
288–9, 293, 301
  bell 194, 295
  branding 108, 245, 293–5
  Cultural Olympiad (and
London 2012 Festival)
xiv, xv, 2–4, 13–15,
21, 29, 64, 65, 68, 80,
134–6, 146, 191–3, 196,
209, 228, 254, 284,
290–8, 325, 333–4
  Closing Ceremony 4, 46,
48–9, 79–80, 234,
291–2, 295–7
  commemorative coins 16–21,
29
  finance 14, 48, 50–1, 54–5,
57, 64, 82, 194, 287–8,
291, 312–13, 327,
331–3
  legacy xvi, 57, 76, 88, 228,
283–312
  London Organizing
Committee of the
Olympic and Paralympic
Games (LOCOG) 25,
53–5, 69, 135, 146,
283, 290–1, 331, 333
  logo 18, 293–5
  media coverage 4, 24, 49–50,
75–6, 88, 133–4, 191–2,
195–6, 247, 277, 285–6,
288, 295–6, 310
  Opening Ceremony 2, 4, 5,
8, 21–9, 43–52, 79–83,
85–8, 90, 94–6, 145,
191–6, 231–2, 235, 241,
247–8, 256, 276–7,
291–2, 295–7, 327,
330–3
  Paralympic Games 133–4,
285, 294–5
  Paralympic Opening
Ceremony 4, 48, 291–2,
295–7
  planning and preparation 14,
88–91, 283–91, 305, 327
  protests 59–60, 89–90, 247
  sponsorship 35n., 39
  torch and cauldron 24,
39–40, 87, 246–7
Olympics (Munich 1972) 255
Olympics (Rio 2016) 306–7
Olympics (Sochi 2014) 7
Oman 66, 72–3
Orkin, Martin 103–4, 106,
110, 123
Orobíyi, Motúnráyọ̀ 142
Osborne, George 133–4
Ovalhouse theatre 201–2, 204
Over the Edge theatre 201, 203
Owusu, Jude 70, 153–4
Oxford English Dictionary 4–5

Pakistan 180, 240
Palestine 58, 139–40, 258, 263

Palmer, Catherine 14
Parker, Jamie 61, 146–8
Parsons, Elinor 299
Pearson, Keith 200
People's Theatre (The) 119–20, 123
Perceval, Luk 299–300, 303
Perry, Seamus 327
Phillips, Louse 287
Piccolo Teatro di Milano 267
Pirandello, Luigi 267
Pohlmeier, Arne 197, 199–200, 203
Poland 262–4
politics and governance (British)
    austerity times (1940s and 2000s) xvi, 27, 110, 124, 194, 253, 255, 258, 268, 274
    'Big Society' 124
    Civil War and Interregnum 5, 83
    Coalition government 25, 124, 133–4
    empire and colonialism 8, 19, 26, 103, 164, 191–2, 194–5, 212–13, 215, 231–2, 291, 307
    global ambitions xvi, 34n., 69, 193, 288, 298, 307–8
    Gulf War 19–21, 25, 33n., 214
    New Labour 287
    postwar rebuilding xvi, 195, 232, 253–77, 326, 330
    Reformation 5
    slave trade and abolition 18–19, 21
    Thatcherism 287
    UK Independence Party (UKIP) 308–10
    Wars of the Roses 79–96
postcolonialism and postcolonial studies 103, 127n,. 148, 191–217, 276, 324
Powell, Peter 271
Prescott, Paul 137, 156, 241, 318n.
Priestley, J. B. 255, 259–60, 262, 269
Purcell, Stephen 244, 328

Q Brothers 62–3, 328
Quarmby, Kevin 150–1

race 24–6, 195, 200, 203–4, 206–7, 213, 216, 276–7, 310–11
Raffles, Gerry 262
Rascal, Dizzie 235
Rattle, Simon 24
Ravenhill, Mark 155
Ravensbourne College of Design and Communication 71
Redgrave, Michael 267
Redgrave, Steve 247
Reed, Henry 271
Renegade Theatre 141–8, 204–5
Richardson, Ralph 260, 268–9
Rider, Paul 148
Rimbaud, Arthur 23
Robben Island 208–11
Robins, Kevin 104–5, 107
Roblè, Emanuel 267
Rogers, Jami 310

Rokison, Abigail 148
Royal African Society 206
Royal Family 229–31, 239
Royal Mint 18–19, 29
Royal Shakespeare Company (RSC) xiv, 3, 10, 29, 57, 65–77, 101, 109–12, 115–16, 119–20, 122, 124–6, 136, 148–57, 192–3, 196, 206–11, 213–14, 263, 274, 276, 291, 299–300, 303–4, 311–12, 326, 331
  Complete Works Festival (2006–7) 299–301, 303–4
Rumbold, Kate 150–1, 289
Russia and former USSR 92, 138, 254, 259, 262–4, 265, 274, 279n.

Sage Gateshead (The) 109, 112–14, 116–20
Saint-Denis, Michel 269, 271
Salacrou, Armand 267
Sanders, Julie 141
Sarte, Jean-Paul 267, 270
Schalkwyk, David 210
Schama, Simon 3
Schiller, Friedrich 262
Schiller, Leon 265
Schlegel, August Wilhelm 254–5, 272
Scofield, Paul 279n.
Seacole, Mary 33n.
Sealey, Jenny 292
Serbia 84–8
Shakespeare's birthplace 227–8, 247
Shakespeare Birthplace Trust (The) (SBT) 40–1

Shakespeare's Globe xiv, 3, 13, 53–64, 79–96, 136–48, 163–88, 191–3, 196–205, 211–17, 240–5, 263, 274, 291, 302, 305–6, 308, 324–5
Shakespeare, William
  as brand 6, 14, 22, 288–9, 295
  as 'national poet' 6, 103, 105, 126n., 197, 228, 256–7, 284, 290–1, 298
  as 'world's playwright' 11, 67, 75, 244, 284, 298, 306
  authorship debate 72
  language, poetry 47–8, 51–2, 65, 67–8, 72–3, 75, 80, 94, 163–6, 176, 183–4, 186, 190n., 194, 207, 241, 272, 301, 328–9
  the man 2, 4–6, 39, 66, 80, 306
Shakespeare, William (plays)
  1 Henry IV 61, 247, 273–4
  2 Henry IV 61, 273–4
  1 Henry VI, 79–96, 273–4
  2 Henry VI, 79–96, 273–4
  3 Henry VI, 4, 79–96, 273–4
  All's Well That Ends Well 54
  Antony and Cleopatra 13, 272
  As You Like It 262, 265–6
  Coriolanus 258, 268
  Hamlet 18, 20, 54, 55, 254, 256–7, 261–2, 265, 267, 269, 271–3, 276
  Henry V, 51, 146–8, 194, 244, 274
  Julius Caesar 3, 17, 208

King John 7
King Lear 54, 73–4, 254, 261–2, 273, 276
Macbeth 73, 254, 272–3
The Merchant of Venice 72, 264, 276
The Merry Wives of Windsor 5, 265
A Midsummer Night's Dream 265, 305
Much Ado about Nothing 265
Othello 206, 254, 261–2, 265, 271, 273, 300, 303
Pericles 19, 54
Richard II 273–4
Richard III 54, 261–2, 264, 268, 273–4
Romeo and Juliet 24, 49, 54, 113, 241, 254, 273, 276
The Taming of the Shrew 264
The Tempest 2, 4, 10, 13, 15, 18–19, 22, 24–5, 26, 27–8, 45–9, 52, 79–80, 193–5, 231, 235, 257, 265, 286, 291–2, 295, 305, 308–9
Troilus and Cressida 4, 54, 275
Twelfth Night 262, 265
The Two Gentlemen of Verona 265
The Winter's Tale 143–4, 265
Shapiro, James 195
Sharma, Madhav 149
Shaw, Deborah 290
Shaw, George Bernard 260–1, 268, 276
Shepherd, Scott 156
Shilling, Jane 155
Sinclair, Ian 1
Sinfield, Alan 324–5
Silvera, Frank 276–7
slavery 18–19, 21, 47
smart phones 304
Smith, Peter J. 139
Smith, Rick 44, 47
Şóbándé, Idiat Abísọ́lá 144
soft power 307–8
Solga, Kim 215
Sophocles 264, 267
South Africa 73, 164–5, 198–200, 203, 206, 208–12, 215, 258
South America 257
South Sudan 72, 204–5, 209, 214–15, 263
South Sudan Theatre Company (SSTC) 62, 204–5, 214–16
Spall, Timothy 80, 235
spectacle xv, 22–3, 27–8, 44–5, 79–96, 164, 180, 193–5, 197, 207, 229–30, 232, 246, 275–6 *see also* masques
spectatorship xv, 15–16, 133–57, 163–88, 197, 276, 302–3
Spencer, Charles 300
Spier Festival 199
sport and exercise 1, 4–5, 7–12, 14–15, 20–1, 31n., 46–7, 50–1, 60, 63–4, 80, 92, 133–4, 136, 146–8, 151–2, 156, 235, 243–4, 246, 254–5, 267, 273, 274–6, 283–4, 292–3, 295, 321n., 334

Starkie, Chris 148
Steevens, George 5–6
Stendhal 262
Stratford-upon-Avon 3, 4, 12, 31n., 39–40, 101, 107, 109–11, 115, 136, 149, 208, 242, 244, 247, 280n.
Strauss, Richard 259
Strindberg, August 270
Sullivan, Erin 10, 139, 231
surveillance 26, 90, 152
Sweden 262, 265
Syria 58

Tangram Theatre Company 200
Tanzania 208
Tate Modern 3, 66–7, 77, 330
Tavener, Simon 155
Taylor, Paul 155
television *see also* British Broadcasting Corporation (BBC) (television)
  Antiques Roadshow 3
  EastEnders 229
  Twenty-twelve 285
  Shakespeare Unlocked 3, 307
Thames (River) 229–30, 236, 243
Theatre Company (The) *see* Bitter Pill Theatre Company
Theatre Wallay 180
The Space (www.TheSpace.org) 3, 94, 142, 266, 305
Thieme, Thomas 300
Thorndike, Sybil 260–1
Thorton, Dora, 209

Three Mills 44
Tildesley, Mark 43–4
Tillyard, E. M. W. 273
Tompkins, Joanne 173
touring (theatre) 55, 109–11, 122, 125–6, 163–9, 182–3, 197–205, 221n., 243, 253–77, 334
tourism 149–51, 164, 197, 227, 236–46, 326
translation 72, 163–7, 202, 254–5, 272, 300
Trinidad 208
TR Warszawa 152
Travers, Tony 288
Tuckett, Will 116, 118
Tunisia 109, 111
Twitter, tweeting 25, 155, 235, 310
Two Gents Productions 197–8, 200, 202–3, 205, 216, 240–3
Tynan, Kenneth 256–7, 268
Tyne, Aale 255

UK Home Office 310–11
Uganda 208
uMabatha: The Zulu Macbeth 165, 189–90n.
United Nations 259
United States of America, 62–3, 73, 91, 116, 155–7, 161–2n., 195, 201, 208, 240, 267–70, 271–2, 275–6, 307–8
universality 7, 9, 12, 22, 28–9, 79, 105, 118, 125, 134–6, 146, 157, 171, 174, 186, 190n., 207–8, 211–12, 256–7, 264–5,

267, 274, 323, 326,
329, 333
utopianism 29, 325–6, 332–3

Vakhtangov Theatre 262
Venkatrathnam, Sonny
209–11
Venning, Harry 295–6
Verba, Sidney 297
Victorians and
neo-Victorianism 8, 18,
231–4, 237, 239, 247,
251n.
Voltaire 272, 290
volunteers, volunteerism *see*
amateurs, amateurism

Wagner, Richard 193, 255
Walbrook, Anton 267
Wales 274, 301
Wallace, Charles William 12
Wanamaker, Sam 9, 279n.
war and warfare 1, 7, 12,
20–1, 80, 83–96, 194,
208–9, 232, 257–8
Watson, Nicola 237–9
Wedgwood, C. V. 271
Welles, Orson 257
West, Mae 267
White, R. S. 104, 106
Whitson, David 18
Williams, Harcourt 268, 270
Williams, Jean 6
Williams, Raymond 14
Williams, Tennessee 267
Wilson, John 119
Wilton's Music Hall 199
Windrush (SS *Empire*) 47, 195,
241, 276–7, 333
Wolf, Matt 180

Wooster Group (The) 154–7
World Fairs 9, 196
World Shakespeare
Bibliography 304
World Shakespeare Festival
(WSF) xiv, xv, 3, 6, 53,
64–77, 101–26, 134–6,
146, 148–57, 196, 228,
235, 240–6, 263, 284,
290–1, 298–304 *see also*
Globe to Globe
digital streaming, live
broadcasting *see* digital
communication, digital
culture
finance 68–9, 291, 315n.,
331–2
media coverage 75, 196,
206, 210–11, 213–14,
216, 295–6
productions and events
2008: Macbeth (TR
Warszawa) 152
I, Cinna (The Poet) (*Julius
Caesar*) (RSC) 3, 68,
70–1, 76, 152–4, 157
In a Pickle (*The Winter's
Tale*) (Oily Cart) 108–9,
112
Julius Caesar (RSC) 70,
109, 193, 196, 206–8,
213–14, 244, 276, 312
King Lear (RSC
International Youth
Ensemble) 67, 73–4, 77,
329–30
*Macbeth: Lëila and Ben
– A Bloody History*
(Artistes, Producteurs,
Associés) 109

Much Ado about Nothing (RSC) 148–50, 157, 196, 244–5, 312
Open Stages project (RSC) 109, 115–22, 124, 204
Quick Bright Things (*A Midsummer Night's Dream*) 120–2
The Rest is Silence (*Hamlet*) (dreamthinkspeak) 109, 151, 157
Rodney and Julie J. (*Romeo and Juliet*) 120–2
Romeo and Juliet in Baghdad (Iraqi Theatre Company) 300
Shakespeare: Staging the World exhibit (RSC/British Museum) 193, 209–11, 245
Timon of Athens (National Theatre) 152–3, 303
Troilus and Cressida (RSC/Wooster Group), 154
West Side Story (The Sage Gateshead) 109, 112–14, 116–20
Worlds Together conference (RSC/Tate) 3, 66–8, 73, 75–7
Y Storm (*The Tempest*) (Theatr Genedlaethol Cymru) 301
publicity and marketing 6, 192, 206, 208, 216, 298
World War, Second 92, 232, 257–9, 264
Worthen, W. B. 164–6, 168–9, 178, 183
Wright, Joseph (of Derby) 44–5
Wulff, Christian 138

Xiaoying, Wang 60

Year of Shakespeare xiv, 137–41, 148, 211, 242, 301
York 10
Young Vic 198–9, 269
Yugoslavia 84, 92, 97n., 262

Zeimoglu, Feridun 300
Zetterling, Mai 267
Zimbabwe 197–8, 200–4, 216, 242
Zola, Émile 270
Zuckmayer, Karl 270
Zuma, Jacob 210

www.ingramcontent.com/pod-product-compliance
Lightning Source LLC
Chambersburg PA
CBHW050134240426
43673CB00043B/1663